ELECTRIC BOATS
ON THE THAMES
1889 – 1914

Edward Hawthorne

ALAN SUTTON PUBLISHING LIMITED

First published in the United Kingdom in 1995 by
Alan Sutton Publishing Ltd · Phoenix Mill · Far Thrupp · Stroud
Gloucestershire

British Library Cataloguing in Publication Data

A catalogue record for this book is available from the British Library.

ISBN 0-7509-1015-1

Title page photograph: BOULTER'S LOCK, MAIDENHEAD. Andrews electric launch *Bream* and another electric boat entering the lock. (*Courtesy of the Francis Frith Collection and Maidenhead Library*.)

Typeset in Bembo 11/13pt.
Typesetting and origination by
Alan Sutton Publishing Limited.
Printed in Great Britain by
Butler & Tanner, Frome, Somerset.

CONTENTS

ACKNOWLEDGEMENTS

My grateful thanks to all who have regaled me with their memories and allowed me to publish material and photographs from their collections. Their names have been acknowledged in the footnotes and picture captions, but there are others who have had a more general influence on the genesis and completion of this history of electric boating, notably, the late Viscount St Davids, founder of the Electric Boat Association, who did so much to revive interest in electric boating; Rear-Admiral Percy Gick, the current President, who has provided much practical advice and encouragement; Kevin Desmond, himself a well-known writer on electric boating and a dynamic force in expanding the EBA, who introduced me to some of the early history; Emrhys Barrell and Roy Devereux, successive editors of the *Electric Boat News*, who have been a constant source of support; George Banham, whose great knowledge of the Maidenhead and Windsor boating scene and loan of the Ray Motor Co. records prompted me to start on this project; Harry Horsham, who gave me access to his collection of photographs; Jim Cowan, who allowed me to reproduce pictures from his copies of the *Lock to Lock Times*; Paul Wagstaffe, who brought his encyclopaedic knowledge of the boating industry to bear upon many questions; Patrick Cavendish for his continued interest and guidance; Rosy Thacker, Librarian of the National Tramway Museum, who so willingly supplied me with copious extracts from technical journals; the staff of Maidenhead and other libraries who helped me to seek out many, and some obscure, sources of information; and Dinnie, my wife, whose own enthusiasm for electric boating was an important element in bringing this book to fruition.

The date given in the caption heading for each illustration is, as far as is known, that of the original picture. The photographs are reproduced by kind permission of those whose names are given after the captions. Additional acknowledgements and notes on some of the illustrations are given in the section 'Illustration Notes' on pages 219–20.

INTRODUCTION

The Thames Valley in the late 1880s was rapidly becoming the summer resort of wealthy Londoners and, thanks to the Great Western Railway, the day-trip playground of the growing middle class. To go boating on the Thames was to slip into another world, where the new was tempered by experience, rich and poor rubbed shoulders in the locks, and every boat had a story to tell. Maidenhead, located close to the royal residence at Windsor Castle and Ascot racecourse, was the gateway to two of the widest and most attractive reaches of the river and soon became one of the busiest boating centres.

Steamers had been in use since 1814, carrying passengers up and down the river, and it was not long before the riverside residents and holiday visitors acquired their own steam launches. However, during the 1880s the technologies of electric motors and lead acid batteries developed to such a point that, brought together by a handful of enterprising engineers and investors, the electric boat became a practical reality capable of competing with the steam launch.

The enthusiasm of the Victorians for enjoying the river and its activities during the last decade of the nineteenth century led to a rapid growth in the demand for privately owned electric launches while the boatyards had few problems in hiring out the electric craft in their fleets by the day or even the season. The Prince of Wales, later King Edward VII, was often to be seen passing through Boulter's Lock during his visits to Windsor and for three years chartered Immisch's flagship, the 65 ft electric passenger boat *Viscountess Bury*, which is still afloat at Ely.

Unfortunately the development of electric boating was slowed down by the outbreak of the First World War and was further threatened by improvements in the internal combustion engine which, despite its greater noise and pollution, held out the promise of higher powers and longer range. Although the social life of the river gradually recovered after the war, the petrol engine continued to reign supreme over both steam and electric propulsion.

Three-quarters of a century later, however, electric boating on the Thames, and indeed worldwide, made a revival. The Victorians had found that electric boats produced less dirt, smoke and smell and today's generation is even more aware of the need to reduce pollution with some countries banning internal combustion-engined craft on their lakes. This has led to a steady growth in the numbers of electrically powered craft as more people experience the near silent pleasure and convenience of electric boating.

This resurgence has brought to light a fund of information and pictures of the Victorian and Edwardian electric boat scene. These have been assembled in this book as a story of an era in which exciting things were accomplished, the memories of which have been etched in the long history of the Thames.

ABBREVIATIONS AND CONVERSION FACTORS

Many of the early press reports quote the power of electric motors installed in boats in horsepower. It is often unclear whether this was input or output power, but throughout this book, horsepower (hp or bhp) is used where it is known or likely that the figure quoted is output power and, similarly, kilowatt (kw) is used for input power.

Conversion Factors:

ABBREVIATION	MEANING	MULTIPLY BY	TO OBTAIN
BOT (usually called Unit, sometimes, confusingly, written BTU)	Board of Trade Unit (i.e. the measure of electricity consumed)	1	kilowatt hour
cu in	cubic inch	16.387	cubic centimetres
ft	feet	0.305	metres
hp	horsepower	0.746	kilowatts
in	inches	0.025	metres
kg	kilogramme	2.205	lbs
knots	nautical mile per hour	1.152	miles per hour
kw	kilowatts	1.341	horsepower
m	metres	3.281	feet
mph	miles per hour	0.869	knots

Other Abbreviations:

Ah	ampere-hours (i.e. capacity of battery)
amps	amperes
BET	British Electric Traction Company
bhp	brake horsepower (i.e. output power of motor)
cwt	hundredweight (=112 lbs)
EMF	electromotive force (i.e. volts)
EPS Co.	Electrical Power Storage Company
LWL	Length at waterline
RMC	Ray Motor Company
rpm	revolutions per minute
s, d (or -/-)	shilling, pence
TVL	Thames Valley Launch Company
wh/kg	watt-hours per kilogramme
wh/l	watt-hours per litre

Chapter 1

DAWN OF AN ERA

One September morning in 1882 a boat was slipped into the Thames amid London's Docklands. To the dockers and seamen, she was just another small ferry boat joining the dozens which plied between the great ships loading and unloading in the busiest port in the world. To the group of engineers and boatbuilders watching the launching, she was an experiment, heralding a new method of propulsion which would do away with the dirt, smoke and inconvenience of the steam engine. On board, she carried a ton of batteries which were to provide the electricity to motors connected to the boat's propeller. Appropriately, this 26 ft long iron-hulled boat capable of carrying twelve passengers was named *Electricity*, and the following day *The Times* reported that she was 'the very first in which the electric propulsion of a boat has been undertaken on a commercial scale'.[1] She heralded eight years of development which laid the foundations for the rapid growth of electric boating on the Middle Thames.

Among the watchers was Anthony Reckenzaun, a brilliant engineer who had arrived in this country, aged twenty-two, from Austria ten years earlier. Trained in marine engineering, he worked first at Ravenhill & Miller and then at Easton & Andrew. In 1878 he became interested in electrical engineering and joined the Fauré Accumulator Company's British branch. He transferred to the Electrical Power Storage Company (EPS Co.) in 1893 and, with his background, it was not surprising that the company decided to build an electric boat.[2]

The layout he evolved used batteries – accumulators as they were called in those days – developed from the Planté system by Sellon and Volckmar of the EPS Co., and two motors manufactured by the Siemens Company.[3] The motors were connected through belt drives to the propeller shaft, reducing the speed from 950 rpm at the motors to 350 rpm at the propeller. On her first trial, on 29 September, she ran up from Millwall to London Bridge and turning came down on the ebb tide to berth again at Millwall 24 minutes later.[4]

The trials of *Electricity* proved that sufficient accumulators could be carried in a realistic layout to provide the energy necessary to obtain acceptable speeds and duration. However, it was clear that the weight and size of the motors and their gearing had to be reduced. The first step was to use only one motor coupled direct to the propeller. This reduced the weight from 812 lb to 658 lb.

The new design was put into practice in 1883 when the second electric boat was launched into the Thames. Again, she was fitted out by the EPS Co. at their works at Millwall, but the hull and superstructure were designed and built by Messrs Yarrow at their yard at Poplar, just a short distance upstream. This launch of galvanized steel was

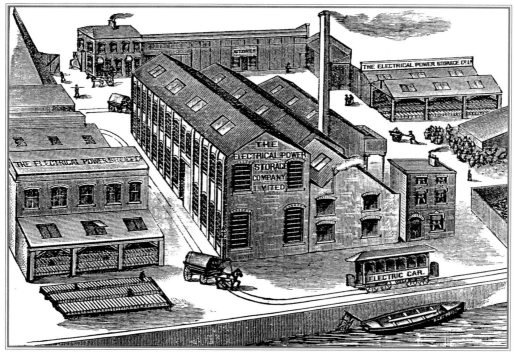

1. **WHERE IT ALL BEGAN: THE ELECTRICAL POWER STORAGE COMPANY'S WORKS,**
1885. The works at Millwall in London's Dockland was the centre of the development of electric boats built
on the Thames. Here, important advances in the technology of accumulators were made by Sellon and
Volckmar. Anthony Reckenzaun joined with them to design and fit out the first electric boat, *Electricity*, to
be launched on the tidal reaches of the Thames. *Electricity* is shown in this drawing moored against the wharf
on which an electric tramcar, no doubt battery driven, is waiting. Also shown are a man wheeling a barrow
carrying a carboy of acid; several stacks of finished batteries or possibly lead bars; and a hansom cab waiting
outside the offices for an important customer. The EPS Company supplied the accumulators for all of the
electric boats built on the Thames until about the middle of the 1890s.

By kind permission of the Marquess of Tavistock and the Trustees of the Bedford Estates.

40 ft length and 6 ft beam and, by placing all the accumulators and machinery under the
floor and seats, she could carry forty passengers. The accumulator cells were connected
in groups so that fresh cells could be brought into use as others discharged, and a running
time of five to six hours could be achieved at normal speeds.

On her first trip the launch made the 6 mile journey down river on a moderate tide
from Temple Pier to Greenwich in thirty-seven minutes. Over a measured mile an
average speed of more than 8 mph was obtained.[5] The reporter from the journal, *The
Electrician*, was clearly impressed: 'For such work as that now done by steam launches on
the Thames, the electrical system is simply perfection. The expense will be, on the
whole, about that of steam, but to those who keep steam launches expense is a secondary
consideration, and it must not be forgotten that a 20 ft electrical launch will afford at

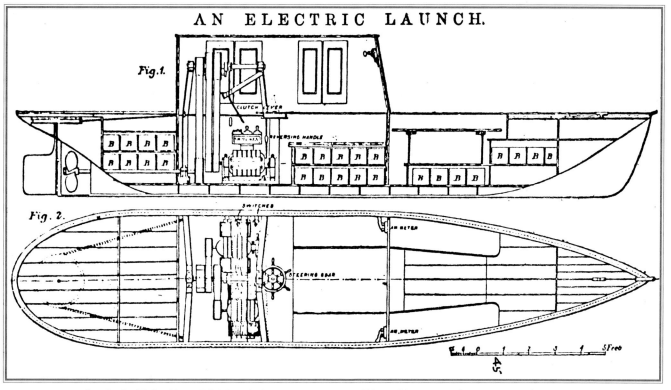

2. LAYOUT OF THE PROPULSION SYSTEM, *ELECTRICITY*, 1882. This system was designed by Anthony Reckenzaun of the EPS Company and launched at Millwall in September 1882. Steel-hulled with a length of 25 ft, she could carry twelve passengers with seats running along each side of the cockpit and was capable of a speed of 9 mph.

Engineering, 6 Oct 1882

least as much accommodation as a 30 ft steam launch. Little difficulty should be encountered in charging the cells, and this is merely a question of detail.'[6]

Following numerous trials on the Thames, Yarrow's launch was exhibited at the Electrical Exhibition in Vienna where she made many trips up and down the Danube.

In 1884 Reckenzaun designed the electrics for the third launch to appear on the Thames. *Australia* was built by Messrs Forrest & Sons to the order of Messrs Stephens, Smith & Co., engineers, for an Australian firm.[7] The hull was of mahogany, 25 ft length and 5 ft 7 in beam. At the end of September that year, a race between *Electricity* and *Australia* was held over a course from Millwall to Charing Cross bridge and back to Greenwich, it being arranged that both machines would be supplied with 3,730 watts of energy.[8] Two stoppages of about ten minutes each were made, one to cool and slacken the stern gland on *Australia*, the other to bale out *Electricity* after shipping water when passing a large steamer. Allowing for the stoppages the total travelling time was 70 minutes. After reaching Greenwich both boats cruised about for another couple of

To Illustrate Mr. A. F. Yarrow's Paper on The Electrical Launch.

3. **YARROW'S ELECTRIC LAUNCH, 1883.** Designed and constructed in galvanized steel by Messrs Yarrow of Poplar at London Docks, this 40 ft launch with a beam of 6 ft and a speed of 8 mph was fitted out by the EPS Co. to the design of Anthony Reckenzaun. The launch was open with seats running down each side of the boat and capable of accommodating forty passengers. He had sufficient confidence in her to send the launch over to the Electrical Exhibition in Vienna where she showed her paces on the Danube.

Trans. Inst. Naval Architects, Vol XXV, 1884

hours. There is no record of which boat won, but apparently *Australia* was very slightly ahead at Charing Cross on the way upstream.

Stephens, Smith & Co. must have been satisfied with *Australia* for they contracted for a second boat, the 36 ft galvanized steel-hulled *Volta*. Launched in August 1884, she incorporated a number of new features, chief of which was the use of two Reckenzaun motors coupled in line to the propeller shaft. Seventy EPS accumulators were connected through a switch by which the motors, either singly or together, could be run in series or parallel. Even more original was that sails could be hoisted when especially long trips had to be undertaken.

In September 1886 *Volta* crossed the Channel, solely under electric power, from Dover to Calais and back in a total time of 8 hours and 5 minutes, stopping for just 42 minutes at Calais. She probably covered an extra 2 or 3 miles on the journey to Calais because the tide carried her off course. The weather, however, was ideal, the sky cloudless and the seas 'as quiescent as by any chance they ever are'.[9] No electric boat has crossed the Channel since.

In December 1885 Mr Reckenzaun attended another launching, this time at Westminster.[10] The Duke of Bedford had been for a trip in *Australia* and decided that a similar launch would make a good tender for his steam yacht *Northumbria*.[11] The new boat was 3 ft longer than *Australia* but her electrical system was much the same. With 29 EPS cells, the launch could run at 6.9 mph for 4½ hours on one charge. A new idea, however, was that when the launch was in the davits the batteries were connected up to the yacht's lights and thereby eliminated the flickering associated with the dynamo previously used for the lighting system.

At this time it was reported that Reckenzaun had several designs in progress.[12] One was for a naval vessel for the Italian government and another for an Indian prince. This latter boat was 'luxuriously arranged with saloon and magnificent furniture' and splendidly illuminated by incandescent lamps. Also the all-important ventilating fans were run from the batteries.

The potential of electric boats was slowly being realized. In May 1887 a new boat, *Countess*, belonging to the Electric Locomotive and Power Co. was launched.[13] Built by Messrs Lester & Perkins at the Royal Albert Docks, she was 90 ft in length, 11 ft 6 in beam and draught of 3 ft. The countess in question was the wife of the Earl of Galloway, chairman of the Elieson Electric Co., which designed and supplied the electrical system. Fitted with a Crompton motor producing 20 hp the *Countess* had a maximum speed of 7 mph.

Unfortunately Elieson adopted unnecessary gearing for the launch, causing the motor speed of 1,000 rpm to be reduced to 100 rpm for an intermediate shaft and then back up again to 200 rpm for the propeller shaft, with the result that a bad vibration was set up.[14] This may have accounted for the fact that little was subsequently heard of the *Countess* and the title of 'largest electric boat in the world' was taken over by the 65 ft *Viscountess Bury*, launched in 1888, which held this record until 1905 when the 93 ft *The Victory* was launched by the Thames Electric Launch Co.[15]

The day before the Boat Race, in April 1888, another new boat, the *Lady Cooper* was launched by the EPS Co.[16] Constructed of steel she was built by Messrs Redpath & Paris

4. *LADY COOPER*, 1888. The *Lady Cooper* was the first ever electric launch to be present at the Boat Race. Built of steel by Redpath & Paris of Limehouse to the designs of Anthony Reckenzaun at the EPS Co. Her speed was claimed to be 11½ mph. Her length is not known, but it was reported that it was intended to fit a 7 ft long cabin.

Electrician, 13 April 1888

of Limehouse to Reckenzaun's design. She was fitted with sixty-six EPS cells of the latest T, or traction, type each fitted with twenty-three plates and having a capacity of 175 ampere-hours (Ah). Most of the cells were placed under the floor and the rest under the seats which ran along each side of the boat. The motor was designed specifically for the boat and was claimed to have had efficiencies between 78 and 85 per cent between half and full speed, which was 500 rpm. She could reach 11½ mph on the tideway and was to be fitted with a 7 ft long cabin. The designers probably had in mind the high speed market, such as police boats, for which use she would have been fitted with a searchlight. She also had an electric gong in place of the ordinary whistle fitted on steamboats.

During these six years from 1882 to 1888 Anthony Reckenzaun, backed up by Sellon and Volckmar of the Electrical Power Storage Co. and supported by a few entrepreneurs and boatbuilders, laid the basis for the growth of electric pleasure boating during the 1890s. They showed that electric propulsion was a practicable proposition and might have real commercial potential particularly for ferry and leisure craft. They adapted land-based electrical technology used in pumping systems, tramways and electric lighting installations to suit the environment of waterborne craft. They realized, for example, that weight and size were more important than in stationary situations; that gearing between motor and propeller was both unsatisfactory and unnecessary; that the weight of accumulators and motors could be used to advantage in improving the boat's stability by fitting the equipment under the floor and seats, thereby overcoming the disadvantage of the high centre of gravity of the heavy boiler of a steam launch; that such designs improved the economics of this size of boat by providing more room for passengers; and that electric boats could cope with the rough conditions of the tidal Thames and, provided the weather was good enough, cross-Channel expeditions.

They demonstrated electric boats ranging in size from 20 to 90 ft; single and twin motor systems; geared and direct drive; currents up to 90 amps and EMF's up to 120 volts; battery capacities up to 370 ampere-hours from cells containing forty plates and having a specific output of 42 wh/kg; motor powers up to 7 hp; and boat speeds up to 11 mph.

The technology was ready for a man of vision to seize the opportunity it presented. That man was Moritz Immisch.

Chapter 2

MORITZ IMMISCH — PIONEER

Born in 1837 in Thuringia, Moritz Immisch graduated from a German university and emigrated to London during the early 1860s. There he rapidly established himself as a well-known watch and clockmaker whose achievements included the award of a prize for an essay on the isochronism of the balance spring.[1] Like others with great skill in instrument making, he became enthused by the opportunities presented by the new discoveries in electricity and in 1880 he formed a partnership with Fritz Hubel, a fellow-countryman, and others to develop and manufacture electric dynamos and motors.[2]

By 1884 Immisch was in business as an Electromotor maker at Perren Street, Ryland Road, Kentish Town, London NW5. That same year, in company with Anthony Reckenzaun, he visited Glynde, near Lewes, to tender for the motors required for a mile long aerial ropeway designed to transport four 'trains' of ten skips carrying clay. Their business finished, they went on to Brighton to see Magnus Volk and his electric railway.[3]

Son of a clockmaker who had emigrated in 1841 from Langenbach in Baden at the age of seventeen and set up in Brighton, Magnus Volk was trained as a scientific instrument maker and, having an inventive turn of mind, he very quickly became involved in a number of electrical developments. One of his ideas was to build an electric railway along the sea-front at Brighton. On 29 June 1883 the Council gave its permission and on 4 August the railway was up and running over a distance of a quarter of a mile.

In 1887 Magnus Volk decided to have a go at building an electrically driven 'horseless' carriage. Making contact with Immisch and Reckenzaun, he modified a three-wheeled dog-cart to take a half-horsepower motor and a sixteen cell battery of 30 ampere-hours capacity. He used such a low-powered motor because, of course, the law still prohibited self-propelled vehicles from exceeding a walking pace.

News of this vehicle spread across the world fairly quickly, even in those days, and Abdul Hamid, the powerful Sultan of Constantinople, was shown a picture of the dog-cart reproduced in the German *Illustrierte Zeitung*. The Sultan promptly ordered one and Magnus, having decided that a four-wheeled vehicle would be much better than the three-wheeled prototype, had it ready by September. The coachbuilder was Mr Pack of the Sussex Coach Works in George Street, Brighton. Built of walnut on an enamelled steel chassis, the fittings were all silver plated and the upholstery was embroidered with the Turkish Imperial crest. Immisch supplied the 20 amp 48 volt 1 hp motor incorporating some new design features which he had patented. The EPS Co. provided twenty-four small accumulator cells.

The trials took place at the skating rink, St Paul's Road, Camden Town, but consisted

5. **MAGNUS VOLK 1851–1937,
PHOTOGRAPHED ON HIS EIGHTY-
THIRD BIRTHDAY**. With Moritz Immisch,
he was responsible for starting up the Immisch
launch business and works at Platt's Eyot,
Hampton, where he was the Manager and
Designer for four years from 1888.

Conrad Volk and Phillimore & Co.

of little more than a few runs round the rink. 'No great speed could be attained on account of the confined space,' but 'the carriage appeared to run very smoothly and to be under perfect control'.[4] The design was criticized by *The Engineer's* reporter as being too like a dog-cart with the shafts removed and not giving 'the appearance of a carriage specially adapted for the new mode of propulsion'. However, the Sultan was obviously impressed for he promptly ordered another carriage and an electric launch as well!

Despite a fair amount of publicity, no other orders were received and Magnus went back to coping with his railway, and discovered he was virtually bankrupt. A discussion with Immisch and his partner, A.F. Snell, resulted in an agreement that Immisch would take over the Sultan's contract thereby freeing Volk to concentrate on putting the railway business back on its feet.

Immisch, meanwhile, had moved to new premises at Malden Works, Prince of Wales' Road, London NW. He was also a Director of the Lamina Accumulator (Elieson's British Patent) Syndicate Ltd and he was a prolific inventor, filing over forty patents between 1881 and 1890, five of them covering designs for propellers and shafts.[5] He was making motors for all kinds of application and won medals at the 1885 Inventions Exhibition and Antwerp International Exposition. His advertisement in the 1889 Electrical Directory ('Blue Book') mentions 'Motors for Locomotives, Tramcars, Launches, Fans, Lifts, Cranes, etc., wound to any tension,' and proudly states, 'Only medal ever awarded for Electrical Haulage, Newcastle, 1887'.[6]

6. **VISCOUNT BURY**. An enthusiastic promoter of railways and tramways, Viscount Bury was a staunch supporter of Moritz Immisch in his battery electric developments for tramcars and boats. He was also a keen promoter of the bicycle, the new form of personal transport for leisure activity.

Norfolk County Council Library and Information Service

Immisch was also one of the early pioneers interested in electric trams. The first tramway, horse-drawn, in the UK was set up in 1860 by an American called, surprisingly, 'Train', but during the next three decades, tramway promoters had to overcome a lot of resistance. Trams remained horse-drawn or steam-driven and it was not until 1881 that the first electric tram was put into operation in Germany. It was only in 1883 that the first UK electric tram began running at Portrush in Northern Ireland. Even so, electric trams were installed in Britain very slowly; in 1896 there were only 80 miles supplied by electricity out of a total tramway system of 1,000 miles.[7]

During 1885 a battery locomotive, built to the design of C.P. Elieson and James Jarman and fitted with an Immisch motor, was put on trial on the North Metropolitan Tramway line in North London. About this time, the Electric Traction Syndicate was set up with Viscount Bury as Chairman to develop battery operated trams.[8]

Viscount Bury, following service in the army, became an MP in 1857 and served as Under-secretary at War for two periods between 1878 and 1886.[9] In 1876 he joined the Society of Telegraph Engineers (later the Institution of Electrical Engineers) and, with Lord Rayleigh, promoted in 1886 a bill to amend the Electric Lighting Act of 1882. He succeeded to the Earldom of Albermarle in 1891.

His interest in the new technology of electricity led him to meet Thomas Edison during a visit to Canada and the USA in the 1870s. They discussed the possibilities of building trains or trams powered by batteries of a type developed by Edison.[10] It was thought that these would eliminate the unpleasant effects of steam trains on routes running through long or frequent tunnels, such as on the Metropolitan line in London or the Swiss railways running through the Alps. On his return to this country, Viscount Bury sought to implement this idea, and during 1884 he formed the Westminster Electric Traction Co. and later was involved in the Electric Traction Syndicate.[11]

The Syndicate's initial project was to convert one of the Brighton and District Tramways horse-cars to battery operation by installing eighty Tatham cells supplying an Immisch motor. This was run experimentally in 1887 for a few months and led to a closer association between Immisch and Viscount Bury, and in January 1888 the Syndicate obtained an option to purchase the Immisch business in 1890. In 1889 the Syndicate built and ran five battery-operated tramcars on the North Metropolitan line between Barking and Canning Town. The trams each travelled 60 miles per day and kept within 2 per cent or so to their scheduled timetable.[12]

This experience further strengthened the partnership between Viscount Bury and Immisch and the option between the two companies was duly exercised by forming them into the General Electric Power and Traction Company.

Meanwhile, the two men turned their attention to the scope for developing battery electric boats. By the year 1888 the principles of an electric propulsion system for boats had already been established by others, especially Reckenzaun and the EPS Co. Immisch, however, was probably the first person to realize the potential of setting up a hire fleet of electric boats operated in conjunction with a chain of charging stations so that the use and range of the boats could be extended.[13]

His first action, therefore, was to purchase, in early 1888, a 'roomy hulk'. This was one of the large house-boats that were becoming popular on the Middle Thames and was 70 ft length by 14 ft beam. William Sargeant, a well-established boatbuilder at Strand-on-the-Green in London, adapted the hulk to take a 20 horse-power Fowler under-type steam engine coupled up to one of Immisch's dynamos. The hulk made its first appearance, albeit without the dynamo, when it was moored off Mortlake and used as a corporate entertainment boat for Immisch's friends and customers to watch Cambridge win the 1888 Boat Race.

While the party-goers were enjoying themselves, they were visited by the small electric launch *Lady Cooper*, which had made her trial trip only the day before.[14] This caused considerable interest and, when the race was over, some of Immisch's guests embarked in the *Lady Cooper* and had a 'very merry and somewhat adventurous journey' back to Temple Pier. Several scratch races were held with steam launches and *Lady Cooper* was adjudged to be capable of holding her own with any craft of similar size.[15]

At the same time Immisch commissioned William Sargeant to design an electric launch to be built by Maynards of Chiswick. By the end of June the launch was completed and, after being christened *Malden* by Mrs Immisch, a party of guests was taken for a trip up river for dinner at Eel Pie Island, returning afterwards to the charging station, which was the 'hulk' with the dynamo fitted and moored just below Kew.[16]

The *Malden* was used principally as an experimental craft and apparently yielded much useful data. For example, on one occasion she travelled 56 miles downstream at 10 mph on only a single charge. With a length of 30 ft 6 in and 4 ft 10 in beam, she was fitted with a 6 in Immisch motor and forty-eight accumulators. The propeller, 2 ft diameter and running at 550 rpm, was directly coupled to the motor and was made by Thornycroft.[17]

The year 1888 proved to be an exciting one. In July the 'roomy hulk' was towed up to Henley accompanied by *Malden* and a small electric skiff that was used as a tender for the charging station. Moored opposite the steward's barge by the winning post, the charging dynamo was used after dark to provide a display of arc and incandescent lighting.[18]

Earlier in the year Immisch had decided to build the largest passenger electric launch in the world. He again commissioned W. Sargeant of Chiswick to design and build the boat. She was 65 ft length, 10 ft beam, 12½ tons displacement and could carry eighty passengers. The two hundred EPS Co. accumulator cells supplied current to two 7½ hp Immisch motors directly coupled to twin Thornycroft three-bladed propellers. She was launched during Christmas week and suitably named the *Viscountess Bury*.[19] She was still carrying passengers until 1991 and is now owned by the Viscountess Bury Trust which plans to restore her to electric drive.

Others were impressed by Sargeant's designs and construction and the *Viscountess Bury* was followed on the stocks by a similar but smaller launch *Ray Mead* for Mr Bowen, owner of the Ray Mead Hotel at Maidenhead. Launched in April 1889, she had a length of 60 ft, was licensed to carry eighty passengers and was also fitted with Immisch motors.

Maidenhead was already well established as a centre for pleasure boating. The Great Western Railway had brought trippers from London since 1838, the Brigade of Guards Boat Club had been a centre of attraction since 1865, and wealthy Londoners rented summer houses from which they could visit Ascot, Marlow and Henley and picnic with their friends on the river. The enthusiasm for a day on the river and the rapidly improving transport system to most points on the Thames meant that by 1888 there was already a sophisticated public anxious to take advantage of anything new on the boating scene.

Immisch was keen to press ahead with his plans for charging stations and a fleet of launches and his association with Volk provided the method by which these could be turned into reality. Volk needed money, and although the exact arrangements between Volk and Immisch are not known, the upshot of their discussions was that in 1888 Volk contracted, as manager of the proposed Platt's Eyot Works at Hampton, to set up a business to design and install a number of charging stations and to manage a fleet of electric launches.

The plan for the launch business was to have one fixed and five floating charging stations and a fleet of hire launches in operation in time for the 1889 Henley Regatta. It was proposed that Immisch and Co. supplied the electrics, EPS Co. would supply the batteries, and the hulls were to be designed and built by established boatbuilders.

In October 1888 Immisch ordered five electric launches, each about 35 ft in length, from Tagg and Son of Island Works, East Molesey.[20] These were to be launched in the following spring and were to be named *Alpha, Beta, Gamma, Delta* and *Eta*. To a large extent these launches served as the model which other boatbuilders copied.

During the winter Volk concentrated on the job of installing the fixed generating set at

FOR SALE

FOR HIRE.

THE IMMISCH ELECTRIC LAUNCHES
AND CHARGING STATIONS.

BY THE OPENING OF THE BOATING SEASON, ARRANGEMENTS WILL BE COMPLETED to enable the river-loving public to avail themselves of this innovation in boating that provides a more comfortable Launch than the old-fashioned steamer.

Gives the whole of the Boat to The Passengers.

NO SMOKE.
NO NOISE.

NO FIRE.
NO SMELL.

PERFECTLY SIMPLE AND UNDER ENTIRE CONTROL.

No Machinery to be kept in Order.   No Engineer required for constant attention.

These Launches contain sufficient Power for a good Day's Run, and can be Re-charged during the Night, if required. CHARGING STATIONS are conveniently situated at

RICHMOND.
STAINES.

PLATT'S EYOT, HAMPTON (Principal Station),
HENLEY,

MAIDENHEAD,
READING.

Messrs. IMMISCH & Co.'s Launches can be hired by the day or week, a day's notice being sufficient to ensure a Launch being sent to any landing-place on the river. Terms can be learnt at any of the principal hotels or boat-builders. Charging Stations for supplying Electric Light for Fêtes or Regattas, can also be hired

For Terms, Prices, or Estimates, apply to

M. IMMISCH & Co., Malden Works, Prince of Wales' Road, Kentish Town, N.W.

7. **IMMISCH'S FIRST SEASON: 1889.** Announcing the first appearance of Immisch Electric Launches on the River Thames, this advertisement appeared on the front page of the *Maidenhead Advertiser* of 12 June, 1889. It was inserted every week from 12 June to 25 September during that year's season. Note that there are five charging stations between Richmond and Reading.

Maidenhead Advertiser, *12 June 1889*

the Headquarters which Immisch had set up at Platt's Eyot, Hampton, and fitting other sets into 'hulks' which he had purchased. Living in Brighton and having to travel to Hampton every week was hard work, so Volk and his wife Anna, with their five sons and one daughter, moved in the spring of 1889 into a house in Shepperton, which was close to the boatyard at Platt's Eyot.

Volk was working to a tight programme, and on 12 June 1889 an advertisement appeared in the *Maidenhead Advertiser* announcing that charging stations were now available at Richmond, Platt's Eyot, Staines, Maidenhead, Henley and Reading. The distance between these stations varied from 9 to 15 miles but, of course, the great advantage of the floating stations was that they could be towed to wherever the demand arose. For example, on one occasion the stations at Richmond and Staines were moved to Wallingford and Oxford. However, the main idea was that they should be located at places where there would be proper supervision and maintenance and room for a number of launches to moor up together. The charging sets probably comprised a semi-portable steam engine coupled to a dynamo, charging a number of boats at a time at 30 amps in five or six hours. Thus, with all hands to the pump, the charging stations and the launches were ready in time for Henley Regatta.

The electric boats made an impression, the *Lock to Lock Times* reporting 'Immisch's electric boat has been showing her paces on and off for some days past, much to the wonder of the Henleyites, among whom the popular belief is that it is a real steam launch built to go upside down, with the funnel pointing downwards through the water.'[21]

Meanwhile, Immisch's other two boats, the *Malden* and the *Viscountess Bury* were being hired out. The *Maidenhead Advertiser* in its issue of 26 June 1889 reported that 'on Saturday last, a very large party of ladies and gentlemen from London numbering 181 enjoyed a very pleasant river trip from Maidenhead to beyond Marlow stopping at the latter place for a short time. The party made Ray Mead Hotel their headquarters and had lunch before starting on their delightful voyage and tea on their return, both meals being had on the lawn. The launches chartered were Mr Bowen's *Ray Mead* (electric), Messrs Immisch's *Viscountess Bury* (very large electric), Mr Bill's *Mayflower* and Mr Bond's *Gainsborough*. A string band was engaged.' The *Mayflower* and *Gainsborough* were driven by steam.

The electric boats created much interest and the odd problem. The *Viscountess Bury* 'is not yet certified by the Board of Trade,' wrote the reporter on the *Daily News*.[22] 'Her owner duly applied for a certificate, and received the usual form to be filled up, giving full particulars of her engines and boilers, and the names of those who made them, what pressure they were designed for, and so forth. The only reply that could be given was that there were no engines and no boilers on board, and though some little time has elapsed since this answer was transmitted nothing further has been heard of the matter. Who can say what putting together of heads and grave deliberation this knotty point may not have given rise to in Whitehall? How to certify a vessel the boilers of which might possibly blow up in spite of the best precautions would be easy; but to certify when there are no boilers at all may, no doubt, form a very moot point for the Circumlocution Office.' During the 1980s the Water Authorities also took time to catch up with the revival of electric boats, but they have done better than the old Board of Trade. In 1989 they reduced the licence fee for electric boats.

A highlight of the 1889 season was the visit of the Prince of Wales to Platt's Eyot, where he had a ride in *Viscountess Bury* and several of the smaller launches. He also inspected an electric torpedo boat under construction and spent some time talking with Magnus Volk.[23] Subsequently, the prince took the *Viscountess Bury* on charter for three years.

Marlow Regatta that year was a great occasion with 'houseboats and launches moored from just beyond the bridge to three-quarters of the way along the course at a point opposite Bisham Church. They included the charmingly furnished electric launch the *Golden Grasshopper* doubtless connected with the fine houseboat of that name. The awnings and hangings were of a light material whilst the cushions were plum coloured. Those aboard and all connected with her wore brooches and pins of artificial

8. **IMMISCH PROSPECTUS, 1890**. The cover of the four-page prospectus published by Immisch in the *Lock to Lock Times* of 8 July 1890. This shows the *Viscountess Bury* after the refit at the end of her first season. *Lock to Lock Times*, 8 July 1890.

J. Cowan

The most striking features of the Immisch electric launches are their silent running, absence of boiler and visible machinery, and the attendant heat and smell, dirt and smoke. The whole of the boat is available for the passengers, the motor being placed underneath the flooring. The passenger accommodation is about 50 per cent. greater than that of steam launches of similar dimensions.

These advantages are so obvious that it has been a matter of surprise that scarcely any electric launches have been hitherto seen on the river. This was no doubt caused by the want, until the present time, of the necessary stations for renewing the electrical charge.

The Company, principally with a view of opening up a field for their well-known electric motors, have overcome these difficulties by arranging a number of charging stations along the river where launches can be re-charged at any time and kept in readiness for use. A day's notice will usually ensure an electric launch being sent to any landing-place on the river between London and Oxford. Launches can be left at any of the electric charging stations, which are situated as follows:

RICHMOND,

PLATT'S EYOT, HAMPTON
(Headquarters and Principal Station)

CHERTSEY,	**HENLEY,**
STAINES,	**READING,**
WINDSOR,	**SHILLINGFORD** (near WALLINGFORD),
MAIDENHEAD,	AND **OXFORD.**

This extensive system of floating and fixed stations will ensure a launch being re-charged anywhere between London and Oxford without unnecessary delay ; and again, when these launches are hired for longer periods than a day, they can be re-charged during the night ready for next day's run.

For regattas, fêtes, or parties, several self-propelling stations will be available ; these can be moved to any part of the river, either for re-charging electric launches or for furnishing electric light.

The Company have constructed a large number of electric launches, including one for H.M. the Sultan of Turkey, and one for the Spanish Royal Navy, and have several others nearly finished, the hulls of which have been built by some of the best boat builders on the river. The *Viscountess Bury*, of which an illustration is given on front page, is not only the largest of the fleet, but is also the largest electric pleasure launch in the world, and is most luxuriously furnished and equipped, accommodating from 60 to 70 people. Dimensions, 65 feet long by 10 feet beam. Twenty-four people can dine at the same time in the saloon. There are separate lavatories for ladies and gentlemen. The dimensions of the other electric launches vary from 30 to 40 feet in length : they will hold from 10 to 30 people each.

All these boats carry sufficient electrical power for a whole day's run, and can travel at the maximum speed permitted by the bye-laws of the Thames Conservancy

The Company either undertake to supply electric launches complete, or to furnish any electrical equipment that may be required by owners who are having hulls constructed to their orders, and they also offer for sale or hire any vessel of their existing fleet.

9. **PROSPECTUS FOR IMMISCH LAUNCHES**. Pages 2 and 3 of the prospectus published in the *Lock to Lock Times* of 8 July 1890. The launch built for the Sultan of Turkey was presumably the one which was ordered at the same time as the second dog-cart in 1889. The four electric launches running at the Edinburgh Exhibition may have been from the first batch of launches built by Tagg & Son for Immisch during the winter of 1888.

J. Cowan

grasshoppers and the launch and its party were the centre of attraction.' There was also a 'display of launches. Immisch's *Viscountess Bury* and Mr Bowen's *Ray Mead*, both electric launches, attracted no little attention, each being well decorated.'[24]

Up to June 1889 Immisch had apparently invested £10,000 in charging stations, all floating, and sited or planned to be sited at Richmond, Hampton, Staines, Maidenhead, Henley, Reading and Wallingford as well as two self-propelled stations ready to move to other sites as required.[25] Not all of these can have been installed during 1889, however, for in January 1890 *The Electrical Review* reported that Immisch had only five charging stations, four floating and one stationary, the latter at Platt's Eyot, Hampton.[26]

By the end of 1889 there were about fourteen hire and private electric launches on the Thames, compared with only three or four at Henley in 1888, and by the spring of 1890 another eight were on order. In addition, launches were being ordered for use on other waterways. There was therefore some justification for the electric boat supporters' enthusiasm and even for the firmly expressed view of Professor G. Forbes that 'there is hardly the slightest doubt that in the course of a very few years the steam launch as a pleasure boat on the River Thames will be entirely abolished'.[27] He also suggested that 'negotiations should be opened by somebody who has the energy to do so with the Thames Conservancy and also with the mill owners – which exist at nearly all the weirs – so as to establish charging stations with water-power and thus to establish what would undoubtedly be a most perfect method of launching in any part of the world.'

Professor Forbes chartered Immisch's *Delta* for some weeks, during which he made some performance tests. She was 33 ft length, 6 ft beam and fitted with forty-four cells. He lived at Bray and towed her upstream every night to the charging station at Maidenhead. On one test he found that the input power was 1,794 watts and the thrust equivalent to 1,074 watts giving an overall motor and propulsion efficiency of 60 per cent.[28] Another test had been made on the *Eta*, which was taken from Hampton up to Oxford and back. Not only did *Eta* take the then record for distance but also for endurance, since she ran the 60 miles from Goring to Oxford and back on one charge.[29]

For Moritz Immisch, 1889 was a busy year. His company more than doubled its output of electrical plant for lighting and power transmission compared with the year before. It supplied pumping and hauling plant to collieries in Normanton, Pontypool, West Calder and Bohemia. For seven months Immisch tramcars on the Barking–Canning Town route were run first with horses and then entirely on battery electric systems. The fleet of seven electric launches and five charging stations on the Thames were in great demand and showed a profit.[30]

However, Magnus Volk was beginning to get restive. Although the 1889 season had been a success financially for the launch business and 1890 was to see an expansion in the number of charging stations and launches, he was not really interested in the day-to-day running of the fleet. Besides, things were happening at Brighton in which he wished to get involved again and his family were not looking forward to another long winter in the damp atmosphere of Shepperton.

Immisch & Co. was also absorbed into the General Electric Power & Traction Co.[31] and the effects of this on Volk's contract were uncertain. So, early in 1890 Volk moved his family once again, this time to Wandsworth. Here he was still able to look after the

CHIEF ELECTRIC LAUNCH CHARGING STATION, HAMPTON-ON-THAMES.

ELECTRIC LAUNCH, "EPSILON."
Length 42 feet ; will accommodate 25 passengers.

10. **IMMISCH PROSPECTUS, 1890**. The back cover of the four-page prospectus published in the *Lock to Lock Times* of 8 July 1890. The top picture shows the Immisch HQ at Platt's Eyot. The launch *Epsilon* was one of the second batch ordered from Tagg & Son to be built during the winter of 1889 in order to bring the Immisch fleet up to twelve launches for the 1890 season.

J. Cowan

launch business, but he could more easily make plans for his return to Brighton. There was still plenty to do to prepare for the 1890 season. Immisch's fleet of seven launches was to be augmented by the addition of another five, which were similar to his existing small launches. Thirty to forty feet in length, each was powered by a single motor driving a 17½ in propeller. It is reported that each boat was fitted with thirty to forty storage cells giving an average current of 27 amperes. Presumably the motors were either 36 or 72 volts, depending on whether the batteries were in series or parallel, and they would have had a rating of 1 or 2 kilowatts.[32]

The *Viscountess Bury* was modified. A certain amount of 'deadwood' was fitted under the stern to improve the steering performance. The saloon was lengthened and refurbished to accommodate sixty or seventy people and to improve their comfort. It was provided inside with electric glow-lamps, and electric side-lights (navigation lights) were fitted on the outside. The twin motors and propellers were replaced by a single 7 kw motor of 164 volts driving a 19 in propeller. The batteries comprised 164 cells and the motor drew 45 amperes. She was steered from the bow end of the upper deck and, 'as a rule, runs at about seven miles an hour'.[33]

The one land charging station was at Platt's Eyot and there were plans to equip three more land stations. The rest of the charging stations were floating. Of the two largest, one was already moored above Boulter's Lock at Maidenhead, the other (the *Watt*) was to be moored at Henley and the rest would be at places like Reading, Windsor and Staines.

The weather in 1890 seems to have been good. The *Maidenhead Advertiser* of 21 May reported, 'The fine weather on Sunday brought out a large number of river-loving folk. The down trains were loaded, the hotel proprietors did a brisk business and the boatbuilders' establishments were besieged. Every launch that was safe and sound was out including the fine electric launch *Ray Mead* which was an object of admiration.' Again, on the last Sunday in June over 100 launches, including a good sprinkling of electric boats, most bedecked from bow to stern with flowers, passed through Boulter's Lock, not to mention over 600 smaller craft.[34] Even Cookham Regatta, held at the end of July, attracted very nearly 10,000 people on land and water.[35]

But there was a sting in the tail of the year. Frost was recorded on 25 November and this persisted until the New Year accompanied by dense fogs, low cloud and snowstorms. The bad weather seems to have continued until Easter of 1891, judging by the complaints that Easter had somehow got mixed up with Christmas. 'Easter may be cold or dull or dusty or moist but it ought not to be tempest-rent and snowy and generally repellent.'[36] The awful weather continued right until the end of May, with only 300 craft going through Boulter's on Whit Sunday compared with a thousand in 1890.

The sun came out at last on 31 May 1891 and some 250 craft passed through Boulter's including 'one or two of Mr Bowen's pretty little electric launches and two or three of Immisch's electric launches'.[37] During the previous decade there had been a steady increase on the Upper Thames in the number of steam launches. By June 1890 this had reached the huge total of 278 and more were expected to be registered before Henley Regatta.[38] Electric launches were beginning to appear more often and in July 1891 it was reported that 'the number of electric launches on the Upper Thames increases rapidly. On Sunday, nine were charged at Immisch's station above Boulter's Lock.'[39]

The General Electric Power and Traction Company's (Ltd.)
(IMMISCH)

Electric Pleasure Launches
AND
Electric Charging Stations
ON THE THAMES.
SEASON 1891.

THE GENERAL ELECTRIC POWER AND TRACTION COMPANY (Limited),

HAVE NOW ESTABLISHED

ELECTRIC CHARGING STATIONS

on the River, situated as follows: Platt's Eyot, HAMPTON (Head-Quarters and Principal Station), Staines, Windsor, Maidenhead, Henley, Reading, Oxford, and are prepared to sell, charge, or let on hire

ELECTRIC PLEASURE LAUNCHES.

For Regattas, Fêtes, or Parties, Self-Propelling Charging Stations will be available, and can be moved to any part of the river, either for re-charging Launches or for supplying Electric Light.

One day's notice will ensure a Launch being sent to any landing place on the river between London and Oxford.

All Particulars, Estimates, &c., can be obtained on application to

THE GENERAL ELECTRIC POWER AND TRACTION COMPANY (Ltd.),

PLATT'S EYOT, HAMPTON, OR 35, NEW BROAD STREET, LONDON, E.C.

Telegraphic Addresses :—" VARIFORM," London ; " IMMISCH," Hampton.

LOCAL AGENTS, MESSRS. SALTER BROTHERS, FOLLY BRIDGE, OXFORD.

11. **IMMISCH ADVERTISEMENT, 1891.** This advertisement appeared in the 1891 Salter's Guide. Most of Immisch's boats built during the first few years of his business were named after the letters of the Greek alphabet. There is no record of whom this one, *MAY*, was named after. Windsor and Oxford had been added to the list of charging stations since this advertisement.

J. Cowan

12. **ELECTRIC LAUNCHES AT EDINBURGH, 1890**. At the International Exhibition of Electrical Engineering, General Inventions and Industries, four electric launches gave rides to the public on the Union Canal. The boats were designed by Messrs Morton & Williamson, built by T.B. Seath & Co. of Glasgow, and the electrical system was supplied by Immisch & Co.

Central Library, Edinburgh

It was not only on the Thames that electric boats were to be seen. The International Exhibition of Electrical Engineering, General Inventions and Industries was held in Edinburgh during the summer of 1890. The Exhibition spanned the canal over which a 30 ft wide bridge was built and a landing stage sited in the centre of the grounds from which visitors could board one of the four electric launches carrying forty passengers each and be taken to the Canal Basin on the Lothian road. Designed by Messrs Morton and Williamson and built by T.B. Seath & Co. of Glasgow, the launches were fitted with 3½ hp 800 rpm Immisch motors connected to forty-eight Electric Construction Corporation accumulators. A new feature was the use of Immisch's patented design of a ball thrust bearing constructed in combination with a plain bearing, which reduced the propeller shaft losses and cut down noise and vibration. The reversing and speed gear was controlled by an Immisch patent switch, fixed alongside the steering wheel and it was said that one man could easily control the launch. The charging plant comprised a 25 hp steam engine driving an Immisch dynamo rated to supply 120 amps at 140 volts and capable of charging the four launches simultaneously.[40]

Back on the Thames the social round continued as before and electric boats were much in evidence during the year. The large hireboats were kept busy with Immisch's *Viscountess Bury* taking members of the Hygienic Congress on the river in August.[41] Bowen's *Ray Mead* was out frequently, on one occasion with a 'large contingent of the theatrical profession' on a trip from Boulter's to Henley organized by Mr Maurice Abrahams.[42]

Despite the Prince of Wales' interest in Immisch's electric boats, he and his party were still to be seen at Bray boarding Tagg's steam launches *Princess Beatrice* and *Princess Victoria* to go up river for tea with the Duke of Westminster at Cliveden.[43]

A new event was an auction held by Messrs Beningfield & Son at the Thames Hotel in Maidenhead. They sold off several steam launches and houseboats and about fifty new and second-hand skiffs, punts, gigs, canadian and other canoes, and dinghies. Electric boats were still too novel to turn up at auction.[44]

But new electric boats were still being launched; the private electric launch *Gambol* was seen passing through Boulter's in September,[45] and the boating fraternity finished the season in considerably better spirits than could have been guessed during the bad weather in the spring.[46] Immisch's launches shared in the good business, but while the future looked good 1892 was to mark a change in management at Platt's Eyot.

Chapter 3

IMMISCH ELECTRIC LAUNCH COMPANY

Magnus Volk had been discharged from bankruptcy in August 1891 and could once again raise capital for his Brighton railway. In February 1892 his contract with Immisch was finished and, keen to get back to the work he loved, he severed his links with Immisch and electric launches and moved back to Brighton to begin work on his unique 'Daddy-long-legs' railway running along the sea-bed on the front at Rottingdean.[1]

After Magnus Volk's departure in February 1892, Immisch set out to find a suitable replacement. One person with the necessary knowledge and experience was Mr Rowland Edwards. He had worked for the electrical firm Woodhouse and Rawson United Ltd and currently was Assistant Manager at their Electric Launch Works.

In 1890 Woodhouse & Rawson had taken over Mr W. Sargeant's boatbuilding business at Strand Works, Chiswick, retaining him as Manager. Sargeant had built Immisch's first charging station, the large electric launch the *Viscountess Bury* and other Immisch boats, so Edwards would have been well acquainted with the electric boat business and Immisch in particular. Immisch headhunted Edwards and installed him as Manager of the Launch Department of the General Electric Power and Traction Co., which was the name of the holding company for Immisch's interests.

On his appointment Rowland Edwards took over a fleet of fourteen or so electric hireboats and eight charging points[2] which were located at:

CAVERSHAM
HENLEY   Above the bridge.
BOULTER'S LOCK   Above the lock island.
WINDSOR BRIDGE   Above the bridge (Berks. side).
BELL WEIR LOCK   Half-a-mile below the lock (Bucks. side); i.e. near the London Stone, about half-way between the lock and Staines Bridge.

PLATT'S EYOT   On the Eyot at Hampton.
RICHMOND   Above the bridge.
STRAND-ON-THE-GREEN   At the Electric Boat Works.

The 1892 season started off with the bad news that the subscribers of the Great Marlow Regatta had decided to cancel the event because of increasing difficulty in getting enough subscriptions and entries.[3] However, the weather during that spring was good, and on a lovely day in April, watched by enormous crowds, Oxford won the Boat Race.[4] The better weather encouraged the owners of riverside residences to put up their rents for the season despite the fact that the rental market was slow to pick up.[5] All this must

13. **IMMISCH** *DELTA,* **FROM IMMISCH BROCHURE OF 1904**. One of the first five electric hire launches operated by the Immisch Launch Co. she was built in 1889 by Tagg & Son of East Molesey. Originally licensed to carry twenty-two passengers but in 1904 this was reduced to eight. Length 33 ft, beam 6 ft, draught (fwd) 15 in (aft) 18 in. Motor: Average 23 amps at 78 volts giving 1.8 kw, battery: forty-four cells weighing 2,520 lb.

Capt. F.J. Turk, MVO

have rekindled the enthusiasm of the Marlow people because they organized another meeting in May and decided to hold a regatta after all. However, this one was to be called the Marlow Regatta – by which name it is still known.[6]

By this time other boat hirers and builders were taking more interest in electric boats. Mr K. Bowen, the owner of the Ray Mead Hotel at Maidenhead and of the large electric hireboat *Ray Mead* had an electric launch built for the Duke of Sutherland who owned The Willows, a large house on the river at Windsor.

During the summer the weather continued fine, so much so that the river level was the lowest for many years and on average was some 9 inches below normal height. The lack of rain was the main cause but the water companies were taken to task for extracting too much water![7]

On 5 June the highest number of boats ever recorded passed through Boulter's: altogether 1,400 including 70 steam and electric launches. The very large steamboat *Queen of the Thames* had such a large party on board that the steersman had some

14. **IMMISCH *ETA*, FROM IMMISCH BROCHURE OF 1904**. Another of the first five electric hire launches operated by the Immisch Launch Co. *Eta* was built in 1889 by Tagg & Son of East Molesey. Larger than the *Delta*, this launch was originally licensed to carry thirty-four passengers. In 1904 it was registered as a sixteen passenger boat.

Capt. F.J. Turk, MVO

difficulty in seeing to steer the monster and collided with both Cookham and Bourne End bridges. Among the smaller electric boats afloat were *Iola*, *Quita*, *Jim*, *Multum in Parvo*, *Pluvia*, *Alert*, and the Immisch launches *Lady Lena* and *Alpha*.[8]

The *Ray Mead* was well booked, making a couple of trips during one week to Reading at £10 per head. 'Mr Bowen finds his electric business pays well, I guess,' hazarded Triffler in the *Maidenhead Advertiser*.[9]

Easter 1893 was during the first weekend in April and presaged fine weather for the rest of the year. Again a new record was set at Boulter's Lock, where it was said that Turner, the lockkeeper, had not had such a busy time at Easter for many years. It was the year in which Mr William Astor, the future Lord Astor, bought Cliveden for a rumoured £300,000, giving the Duke of Westminster a profit of £75,000. The Ray Mead Hotel also changed hands, Mr K. Bowen selling out to Mr Stopes but retaining his electric launch hire business alongside.[10]

A number of new electric boats made their appearance, most of them powered by

Immisch's motors and systems. In April *Jim*, Mr Waggs' electric launch passed by Boulter's looking very trim and comfortable. Mr Bowen's pretty little electric launch the *Champion* made a trip with Mr and Mrs Seebohm on board. During the year the boats in evidence included *Mu*, *Gamma*, *Loch Leven*, *Loch Lomond*, *Theta*, *Lady Leven*, all of which were Immisch's, while *Gambol*, *Psyche*, *Dabchick* and *Tadpole* were either Bowen's or private. Mrs Annie Smith of the Fishery Estate, Bray, had bought *Convolvulus*, a very pretty little boat and much admired. Also noted was Mr H. Gold's large electric launch *Loosestrife*.[11] Immisch was also present at Henley Regatta mooring his charging station, the *Viscountess Bury*, and several of his smaller boats to the bank opposite the Steward's barge at the end of the course.[12]

That same year the World's Fair and Exhibition of Trade and Industry was held at Chicago. Britain's industrial representation included one of Mr Bowen's electric launches; not that his was the only electric boat on show. The American Electric Launch & Navigation Co. supplied fifty-five 34 ft electric launches to the exhibition and carried over a million passengers some 200,000 miles.

Meanwhile, discontent with the management of the Thames simmered on and the Thames Public Rights Association was set up in March 1893 to 'protect the interests of all residents along the Upper Thames and to place the Thames Conservancy Board on a more popular basis, more in touch and sympathy with modern wants and ideas'.[13]

Immisch's losses on his trams probably came to a head during 1894. Although electrification had been developing quickly in America, the British companies had still been making good profits on their horse-drawn systems and were reluctant to incur the heavy capital investment needed for overhead wire or third rail systems.[14] However, they were prepared to allow experiments on battery operated trams to be carried out over part of their systems.

Although Immisch's experimental service was reputed to run successfully, the idea of battery operated trams was superseded by the more efficient overhead wire arrangement and Immisch's experiments came to nothing, no doubt having absorbed large sums of money in the process.

Consequently, an extraordinary meeting of the General Electric Power & Traction Co. finally resolved in November that year to put the company into voluntary liquidation and close down the motor manufacturing works at Malden. However, the launch business was considered to be viable and there was a white knight in the wings in the shape of Emile Garcke. The Immisch Electric Launch Co. was therefore set up on 9 May 1894 in preparation for taking over the Launch Department after the liquidation of the holding company. The purchase money was £8,965, payable in fully paid £1 Ordinary shares, and £1,000 was raised by the issue of two thousand 8 per cent Cumulative Preference shares, 10s paid. The Directors were E. Garcke (Chairman), M. Immisch and F. Pears.[15]

Emile Garcke was the founder and Managing Director of the British Electric Traction Co. (BET) and was recognized in the City as the leading personality in electrical development. Born in Germany in 1856, he settled in England, becoming naturalized in 1880. In 1883 he was appointed Secretary of the Brush Electrical Engineering Co. He rapidly became Manager and then Managing Director. During the 1880s he started up the Electric and General Investment Co. of which Mr George Herring, a wealthy

15. **IMMISCH LAUNCHES AT HENLEY REGATTA, 1893**. The launches with striped awnings are three of Immisch's electric launches, the one in the foreground being the 33 ft *Delta*, built in 1889 and carrying up to twenty-two passengers. The three launches are moored against the *Viscountess Bury* which is herself moored against a two-storey staging or houseboat.

J. Cowan

rentier, became Managing Director. This company helped to finance the founding of BET and no doubt was the channel used to raise money for the Immisch Electric Launch Co. Garcke lived at Ditton House and, having founded Garcke's Electrical Directory[16] and the Electrical Press in Maidenhead, he would have witnessed the growth of electric boating on the Thames. In Garcke, Immisch had a powerful ally.

F. Pears was also a great asset. One of the famous brothers of Pears soap fame, he lived at Hampton and was a great enthusiast for trams, although his scheme for creating the Brentford and Isleworth Tramways Co. never got going. His brother Andrew, who lived up river, had been an enthusiastic user of electric launches, having had two large launches built by William Sargeant in 1889 and 1891.

During the 1890s the Prince of Wales frequently travelled in Immisch's launches and this undoubtedly provided good publicity. For example, in 1898 he visited the Grenfells at Taplow Court for the weekend and was twice out on the *Lambda*, which was described as a 'cabined boat nicely upholstered in brown repp with red curtains and awning and florally worked cushions in blue and white'.[17] The British Electric Traction

Co.'s history mentions that the company 'always did a stylish business, Eastern Princes and Rajahs providing a number of orders for the launches,' and notes that in 1890 the King and Queen of Sweden journeyed from Richmond to Hampton Court in one of Immisch's boats.[18]

BET acquired the Immisch Electric Launch Co. in 1897, stating that 'although its profits were on a modest scale, the illustrious type of passenger made up for the slender cash returns'. Mr F. Pears was replaced by J.S. Raworth, a Director of BET. There were nine shareholders and the assets of buildings, plant and launches had risen to £10,612.[19]

Fairly soon after its formation, Immisch's launch business had opened a depot at Riverside, just below Boulter's Lock at Maidenhead, and by 1898 it had depots at Platt's Eyot, Bray, Maidenhead, and at Henley during the regatta week. It seems to have had land-based charging stations at these depots and had charging arrangements at other boatyards up the river. From its first years the company had three steam floating charging stations, named *Volt*, *Ohm* and *Ampere*. Unfortunately, after a few years the boiler of the *Volt* burst and the barge sank. The charging stations were often used to supply electricity for other uses, such as operating the yards' machinery and, at Platt's Eyot, where electricity was supplied across the river to the Hurst Park racecourse.

By 1900 the company had built the hiring, housing and repair business up to an income of £3,559 and a dividend of 2 per cent was paid on the Ordinary shares. During 1901 the company invested in campshedding and a large new shed at Platt's Eyot and a

16. TITLE PAGE OF IMMISCH BROCHURE, 1904. When the Immisch Electric Launch Co. was reconstituted as the Immisch Launch & Boat Co. in 1904, a new brochure was produced.

Capt. F.J. Turk, MVO

Oxford to Richmond.

fishing waters of Hedsor; the two on the right are backwaters made by Formosa Island, the largest island on the Upper Thames, and said to be about fifty acres in extent. The only Hotel on the banks of the river here is the justly popular "FERRY" HOTEL.

Cookham Lock. Cookham Lock is the most beautifully situated on the river, just under the woods of Hedsor and Cliveden. A little below the erry is the spring and cottage, and farther yet is a magnificent view of Cliveden, formerly the seat of the Duke of Westminster, subsequently the property of Mr. W. W. Astor, who in the spring of 1900 presented it to his son as a wedding present.

Boulter's Lock. On the right bank, below Boulter's Lock, is the "NEW THAMES" HOTEL. Below that, on the hill above, embedded in trees, is Taplow Court. On the right bank, and above the road bridge, **THE IMMISCH COMPANY** have premises, at which Launches, Boats, and Punts can be hired. On the left bank, near Maidenhead Bridge, is "SKINDLES" HOTEL, probably the best known Hotel on the river.

MAIDENHEAD. Below Maidenhead Bridge is the Great Western Railway Bridge, supposed to be the largest single span brick bridge in the world, with a singular echo lurking in its enormous span, and on the right bank is the pretty dwelling known as Orkney Cottage. A mile from Maidenhead is the pleasant village of Bray, where there is one of the **IMMISCH COMPANY'S**

(9)

17. **IMMISCH BROCHURE, PAGE 9, 1904**, showing a section on chief places of interest.

Capt. F.J. Turk, MVO

TERMS – Net Cash at Time of Hiring.

RATES OF HIRE

(INCLUDING SERVICE OF CAPTAIN AND ALL LOCK DUES).

LAUNCH.	PASSENGERS. Convenient Carrying Capacity.	RATES PER DAY. Sundays during June and July.	Saturdays during June and July.	Other Saturdays and Sundays.	Other days.
		Guineas.	Guineas.	Guineas.	Guineas.
C ROSALIND	50	12	10	9	7
C VISC'TESS BURY	40	12	10	9	7
C FLOSSHILDE	25	10	8	7	6
C ETA	16	7	6	5	5
C LAMMDA	16	7	6	5	5
C EPSILON	11	6	6	4	4
C EMERALD ISLE	10	6	6	4	4
C LADY LENA	10	6	5	4	4
C EKSEI	10	6	5	4	4
C IOTA	10	6	5	4	4
A VIOLA (Steam)	10	6	5	4	4
A SPY (Petrol)	8	5	4	3	3
A ALPHA	8	5	4	3	3
A GAMMA	8	5	4	3	3
A DELTA	8	5	4	3	3
A THETA	8	5	4	3	3
A KAPPA	8	5	4	3	3
A ALOHA	8	5	4	3	3
A TAU	8	4	3	3	2
A SIGMA	6	4	3	3	2
A PHI	6	4	3	3	2
A MU	6	4	3	3	2
A NU	6	4	3	3	2
A ZETA	4	4	3	3	2
A RHO	4	4	3	3	2
A B. E. T. (Petro	6	3	2	2	1½
PORTIA (Petrol)	4	3	1½	1½	1½

C—Cabin Launch. *A*—Awning provided.

The above rates of hire apply to Hampton, Windsor, and Maidenhead, but arrangements can be made on special terms for Launches elsewhere. The Company reserves to themselves the right to increase these rates during Henley Week, and on any special occasions.

Quotations given for continuous lets.

(32)

18. **IMMISCH BROCHURE, PAGE 32, 1904**, showing the Immisch fleet. *Spy, B.E.T.*, and *Portia* were petrol-engined launches, *Viola* was steam. All the others were electric.

Capt. F.J. Turk, MVO

new launch of the *Mu* type was purchased. In 1902 the launch and boat business of H. Rose at Riverside, Maidenhead, was acquired.

In May 1903 the prospects for electric boats looked good. 'Looker-on' in the *Maidenhead Advertiser* was writing that 'our genial lockkeeper will shortly be regulating flotillas of diversified craft through Boulter's Lock, and new spick and span electric launches adorned with flowers and attractive awnings will soon be in larger numbers than ever gliding noiselessly up and down our reaches'.[20] Little did he, or most others, realize the impact that the internal combustion engine was going to have within a few years on the Maidenhead boatyards and hotels.

However, it was nature which dashed everybody's hopes for another successful season. The weather in 1903 was atrocious. In June rain fell for sixty hours in the Maidenhead area, the river rose rapidly and the floods were devastating. There were eight columns in the *Maidenhead Advertiser* describing the floods up the Thames valley, with most riverside fields and gardens submerged and water flooding through dozens of houses.[21] On Ascot Sunday there would normally have been 1,200 small craft and 300 launches passing through Boulter's Lock. On this Sunday in 1903 the gates were not opened once. One boat hirer estimated his losses for the week, including Ascot Sunday, to be £700 and others quoted losses between £300 and £500.

The total rainfall in the Maidenhead area that year was 17.5 inches above the annual average. The wettest month was October with a rainfall of 7.5 inches, June was a close second with 6.42 inches and even July had 5 inches.[22] Small wonder that visitors came into residence late and left early. But the real storm cloud for the electric boat business was the rapid growth in motor boats. In July 1904 a commentator in the *Gentlewoman* expressed the view that 'small motor boats are making huge strides in popularity and big motors will grow bigger and bigger'.[23]

In 1901 Immisch's receipts were reduced to £2,915.[24] The dividend was cut to 1½ per cent and to zero between 1902 and 1904. Receipts in 1903 were not much better at £3,184, and in 1904 they had fallen to £2,568. Although the value of launches and plant in 1904 was put at £18,862, in November the company was reformed as the Immisch Launch and Boat Co. Ltd with an issued capital of £9,975. The new Directors were C.L. Robertson (Chairman), S. Sudworth and H.S. Day. The Secretary was W.S. Wreathall who later was appointed a Director. S.E. Garcke (Emile Garcke's son) was appointed as Technical Secretary and he also was later appointed to the Board. At this time the company owned a fleet of twenty-six electric launches on the Thames and the freehold of part of Platt's Eyot, where E.P. Mancey was Manager. There was also the depot at Maidenhead where all kinds of pleasure craft were built, housed or let for hire. Significantly, the company stated that it intended to develop the petrol launch branch of the business and that it had become the sole agent in the Thames district for the Scout motor.[25]

The brochure distributed during this period shows that Immisch still had its Headquarters at Platt's Eyot at Hampton and depots at Bray, on Ray Mead Road above the bridge at Maidenhead, and at Henley during regatta week, but its other charging stations, ashore or afloat, are not mentioned.[26] It lists twenty-three electric launches, the ten-passenger steam launch *Viola* and three petrol launches, *Spy*, *B.E.T.* and *Portia*, seating eight, six and four passengers respectively.[27] It also contained a short guide to the

19. IMMISCH HEADQUARTERS AT PLATT'S EYOT, FROM THE 1904 BROCHURE. The boat could be the *Zeta*, listed in the brochure as carrying four passengers.

Capt. F.J. Turk, MVO

chief places of interest between Oxford and Richmond, including detailed maps, and a list of recommended riverside hotels. It noted that the Queens at Reading had a 'large covered yard for motors' and the Crown at Marlow had a 'Motor House'. However, the Crown & Thistle at Abingdon only kept 'posting and livery stables', while the White Hart at Sonning maintained 'a garage, stabling and motor cars on hire'.

The change to petrol engines was heralded by a notice in the brochure stating that 'The Company is now building Standard Electric and Petrol Launches of the very latest design . . . the prices for Petrol Launches range from £115 in the case of an 18 ft boat fitted with a 3 hp Motor, but a cheaper boat can be built if required. . . . With regard to Electric Launches, the Company have a large fleet, any of which they are prepared to dispose of on reasonable terms or, if required, a new Electric Launch of any size can be built at very short notice.'

Recognition of the inevitable came in 1905, when the BET house magazine announced that 'owing to the nature of the electric launch business having considerably changed during the past few years, due largely to the competition of motor cars and lately of motor boats, the future policy of the company will be to change the existing electric into a petrol launch selling and electric business. Although the petrol launch is not yet as noiseless as the electric it has many advantages compared with it in the matter of speed and economy in working.'[28] The final seal was placed upon the new policy when the Immisch Launch and Boat Co. had a stand at the Motor Show at Olympia in November 1905. It exhibited an

THE IMMISCH ELECTRIC LAUNCH Co., Ltd.,

BUILDERS OF ALL KINDS OF CRAFT.   Established 1887.

Pioneers of Electric Launches on the Thames,

RIVERSDALE WORKS, RIVERSIDE, MAIDENHEAD.

Charging Stations—BRAY, near Maidenhead.   Building, Repairing and Housing Sheds, and Premises—PLATT'S EYOTT, HAMPTON-ON-THAME

Launches to carry 4 to 80 Persons.

Illustrated Pamphlet and Price List free on application.

POPULAR CHEAP RATES for Launch Parties—from £2 2s. upwards.

Estimates Free for Season Lets, at greatly reduced prices.

The Immisch Co.'s Launches are the BEST EQUIPPED . . FLEET OF LAUNCHES ON THE THAMES.

Punts, Skiffs and Canoes for Hire by the hour, day, week or month.

All orders punctually attended to.

Bookings by Telegram or Telephone.

Please NOTE the following—

Telegrams:
    "Immisch, Riverside, Maidenhead."
Telephone : 0122, Maidenhead.
Telegrams : "Immisch, Hampton."
Telephone : 17, Molesey.
Telegrams : "Immisch, c/o Garche, London."
Telephone : 6821, 6822, Gerrard.

IMMISCH'S Electric Launch "ETA," leaving Boulter's Lock, with H.M. THE KING on Board.

Patronised by English & Foreign Royalty.   Electric Launches ready at a minute's notice upon application to the Manager, Riverside, Maidenhead

20. **IMMISCH ADVERTISEMENT, 1906.** *Eta* is shown leaving Boulter's Lock with King Edward VII on board.

Mr J. Hazelton

18 ft dinghy, a 28 ft open launch, petrol marine motors of 3, 6 and 12 hp, and the Gaines reversible propeller which was fitted to all their petrol launches.[29]

The demand for new electric launches was falling off rapidly, but the existing fleet was kept going as long as possible. For example, in July 1908 the Immisch launch *Gamma* was hired out by the Maidenhead Depot to The Ray Motor Co., which had operated a number of electric boats at their boatyard just above Boulter's Lock. In May 1913 the Ray Motor Co. was asked to repair a section of a Jacoby White armature and turn up the commutator. Between 1908 and 1913 the Immisch Maidenhead Depot's Manager was J. Williams, and during Ascot week in 1913 he hired out the old electric launches *Delta*, *Eta*, *Lambda*, *Zeta* and *Rosalind*.[30]

Thereafter, construction of petrol commercial craft became a flourishing side of the company until its sale to Thornycroft in 1914.[31] At that time the business at Platt's Eyot

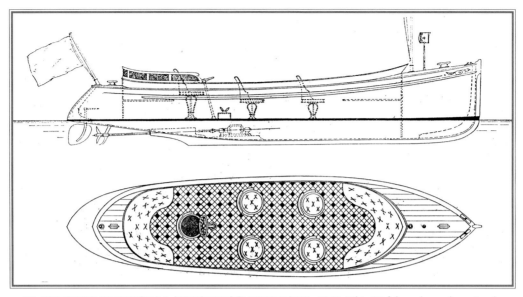

21. **IMMISCH ELECTRIC LAUNCH FOR THE EAST, 1912**. This 20 ft launch was luxuriously fitted out by the Immisch Launch Co. at their Hampton yard for an 'Eastern Potentate' to be used on his private lake. The *Motor Ship and Motor Boat*, 31 Oct 1912.

National Motor Boat Museum, Basildon

included building petrol launches for pleasure and commercial purposes; motor cargo launches (paraffin fuel); agents for Thornycroft motors; and contractors to the Admiralty. The Directors were H.S. Day (Chairman), S.E. Garcke, and W.S. Wreathall (Secretary in previous years). Nevertheless, the company built the occasional electric boat, such as the sumptuously fitted 20 ft launch for an 'Eastern Potentate' for use on his private lake.[32]

In 1913 Thornycroft acquired the Platt's Eyot yard, changed the company's name to Hampton Launch Co. and turned the business over to the construction of petrol-engined boats for the war effort.[33] In addition, on 1 January 1914 the company's fleet and letting business at Maidenhead was acquired by Mr George Bond.

What happened to the remaining electric launches is not clear, but they were presumably stored or used for war service, probably having their electrics stripped out and replaced by petrol engines. Only the *Viscountess Bury* and *Lady Lena* are known to have survived.

Moritz Immisch did not live to see the collapse of the electric boatbuilding business, although he would have been aware that it was imminent. He died suddenly on 20 September 1903, aged sixty-six, and was cremated three days later at Golder's Hill Crematorium in the presence of a large number of mourners, including the employees of the Immisch Launch Co., some of whom had been with him from the early days.[34] A trailblazer, he overcame many obstacles and set a pattern of design and operation which, over the twenty-six years that the business lasted, was followed by most other builders and hirers.

Chapter 4

THAMES VALLEY LAUNCH COMPANY

In 1895 William Rowland Edwards formed the Thames Valley Launch Co. Ltd with a capital of £10,000 of which shares to the value of £2,000 were issued. The headquarters were set up at Riverside Works, Weybridge, close to his home Rosedale.

Edwards already had considerable experience of building and operating electric boats. He had worked for Woodhouse and Rawson United Ltd, electrical manufacturers, and when they took over W. Sargeant's boatbuilding business at Strand-on-the-Green he was appointed Assistant Manager of their Electric Launch Works. In 1892 he became Manager of the Launch Department of Immisch's company, the General Electric Power & Traction Co. However, the businesses had to be restructured in 1894 and the Launch Department was turned into a separate company, the Immisch Electric Launch Co. Ltd. No doubt convinced that electric boats were a growth business, Edwards set up his own company and by 1896 was seeking to expand further upstream and especially to Maidenhead, the centre of the Thames boating scene.

During 1896 Lawrence Statta Carr was looking for a job. He had been apprenticed to James Simpson & Co. of Pimlico in London and had spent the following three and a half years with them as a designer. Subsequently, he took out a patent in conjunction with a Captain Shipton for a component for bicycles and the two of them bought Messrs Calvert & Co. of Yiewsley in Middlesex to manufacture it. Capt. Shipton became Managing Director and Carr was the Manager of the Engineering Department. However, during the spring of 1896 the company ran into difficulties, was unable to raise additional capital, and went into liquidation. Capt. Shipton and Carr were appointed Official Receivers and Managers and they managed to sell the plant and stock to Messrs F.A. Swanzy for £250 plus a 5 per cent royalty on the manufacture of pulleys.

In answer to an advertisement for a Works Manager placed by AEG in *The Engineer* in June 1896, Carr mentioned that he had continued to patent a design for bicycle wheels and two other designs connected with bicycles and motor cars and that a syndicate was being formed to exploit these. Presumably nothing came of this scheme and that year Carr moved to Maidenhead where he did some electrical work, such as fitting lights for Mr Montague in the billiard room of the Ray Mead Hotel. Whether his company, the Ray Motor Co., was formed then or a few years later is not clear but certainly he teamed up with Rowland Edwards to set up and run the Thames Valley Launch Co. depot at Maidenhead. The site chosen was on land owned by Oxford University on Boulter's Lock Island, with frontage on the west side to the lock cut and, on the other, to the old mill stream.

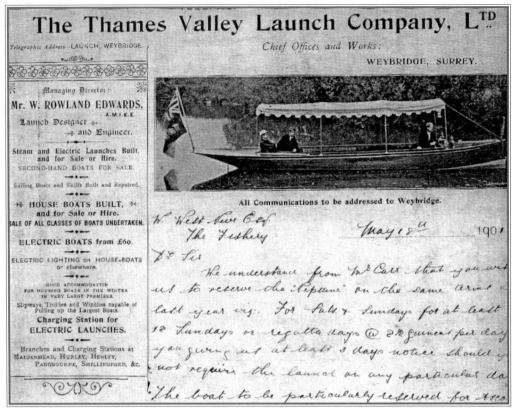

22. **THAMES VALLEY LAUNCH COMPANY LETTER HEADING**. It was probably used from 1896 onwards. The launch is the 30 ft *Trout*.

G. Banham

During the next three years Edwards and Carr expanded the hire business to include nearly forty electric launches ranging in size from 18 to 45 ft in length; not that they were averse to building and hiring out steam and oil-engined boats as well. The introduction to the TVL brochure, published about 1900, stated that 'of all kinds of launches, the Electric Launch undoubtedly holds the premier position. Since their first introduction, an immense amount of time and money has been spent in perfecting them, and at the present time this Company own and build boats that cannot be matched for beauty, simplicity of working parts, and reliability, although they by no means confine themselves to the building of Electric Launches, as they have, in fact, built a great number of Steam and Oil Launches as well. Steam Launches are very enjoyable, especially for large parties and there are a large number of Oil Launches now on the river, but neither will compare with one of this Company's Electric Boats for comfort, cleanliness and freedom from vibration, and to the motion of which no other means of locomotion can compare.'[1]

23. SPECIFICATIONS OF THAMES VALLEY LAUNCH COMPANY'S ELECTRIC LAUNCHES.

Reproduced from the company's brochure by permission of G. Banham

Specifications of Electric, Oil, and Steam Launches.

FOR ELECTRIC LAUNCH (High-class Build)

Length 45 ft.; Beam 7 ft.; Carvel built of Teak or Mahogany; Pitch-pine Keel in one piece; English Oak Stem, Stern-post, and Deadwoods; American Elm Timbers, with additional Oak timbers forward, and under after-deck.

Decks fitted fore and aft of Teak, and Teak covering board, with half-round brass, properly screwed on with brass screws Inside the hull, and outside on the bottom, to be painted with 3 coats of best red lead paint, and bottom to receive 2 extra coats of anti-fouling composition. Topsides to be varnished with 5 coats of best boat varnish, properly laid on.

The **Hull** to be copper-fastened, and to be fitted and finished in a workmanlike manner, and best materials only to be used, all the wood being selected for the job.

Cabin of Teak, 9 ft. long over all, with four windows each side (two on each side to slide open) of bevelled glass in cabin, and one outside panel with bevelled glass, ornamented with carved claws.

Roof (inside) to be enamelled white or cream colour, or fitted with Lincrusta-Walton. Sliding doors, with extra heavy brass furniture, fitted at either end of cabin, and bevelled glass panels at the top half of each door. Four bevelled looking-glasses, one in each corner panel of cabin, properly mounted in carved Spanish Mahogany or Walnut, and securely fitted and fixed to the cabin ends.

All the **Ceiling Beams** to be in ornamented Spanish Mahogany or Walnut, and lockers and seats in cabin to be in Teak or Walnut, with small ornamental cupboards or sideboards at both ends of the seats in Spanish Mahogany or Walnut.

The **Cabin** as a whole to be fitted in first-class style, and with best materials only.

Utrecht Velvet or Plush Cushions fitted to seats in Cabin, and silk curtains and cords on brass rods properly fitted. Velvet Pile Carpets and Mats supplied and fitted.

Specifications of Electric, Oil and Steam Launches.

FOR ELECTRIC LAUNCH (High-class Build)—continued.

All the internal woodwork and outside the Cabin to be in Teak; benches, lockers, and narrow vertical strips for the lining, &c. All to be properly fitted and fixed, and all necessary floors, &c., to be laid and fitted with linoleum. Best American leather cushions outside, properly fitted, and heavy brass rails on Cabin top.

Waterproof awning fitted over forward well, on brass stanchions, and properly stayed and fixed.

Heavy gun-metal cleats, fairleads and flag socket and flag. Two gun-metal boathooks, and two Manilla mooring lines to be supplied. Steering from the front, with extra heavy, polished gun-metal steering wheel, properly connected by chains, rods and pullies to a quadrant on rudder head.

Rudder spindle and rudder properly fitted and fixed in a workmanlike manner.

To be fitted with 60 Accumulators of the best type, capable of an output of 30 Amperes for 10 hours (can be discharged at very high rate if required). All properly fitted and fixed in the boat, and properly connected with all necessary cut-outs, &c., to switch and motor.

One "BEEVOR-EDWARDS" single lever switch for full and half-speed ahead, and the same astern, arranged to place the cells in one set, in series for full speed, and in two sets in parallel for half-speed.

One 6 horse power "BEEVOR-EDWARDS" Motor of best make and materials, with thrust block, steel shaft, gun-metal stern tube and propeller, all properly fixed, and with all necessary fittings.

The whole to be supplied, fitted and finished in first-class style, and delivered on the Thames for the sum of	**£750**
40ft. Boat, fitted and finished as above, 6ft., 9in. Beam; 50 Cells; 8ft. Cabin	**£700**
35ft. Boat do. do. do. do. proportionate throughout	**£650**
30ft. Boat do. do. do. do.	**£600**

Specifications of Electric, Oil and Steam Launches.

FOR ELECTRIC LAUNCH.

25ft. long; Carvel built of Teak or Mahogany, with Teak decks and covering boards, and lined inside with vertical narrow strips of Teak. Pitch-pine Keel in one piece; English Oak stem, stern-post and deadwoods; American Elm timbers, Hull copper-fastened. Arranged for Cells and Motor to go under floor, and with seats aft, forming lockers. Painted and varnished with best materials.

Single Lever Switch, arranged for full and half-speed ahead, and the same astern. Gear of the best type. All arranged and fitted on the "BEEVOR-EDWARDS" principle, which gives the greatest economy in space, together with the highest efficiency, whilst being exceedingly simple to manage. Speed 5½ miles per hour (mean) for about 6 hours at full speed.

Willesden Canvas Awning, fitted on brass stanchions. Three wicker arm-chairs supplied and lounge cushions forward.

Gun-metal fairleads, cleats and tiller handle, properly fitted and fixed. Gun-metal propeller, steel shaft, stern tube, gland, thrust-block, couplings, &c., supplied and fitted. *Utrecht* velvet or plush cushions for seats aft, and silk cushions for chairs, supplied and fitted, and linoleum and mats for floor.

Two gun-metal boathooks and staves, and two mooring lines supplied. A very pretty and handy boat, and will carry 8 comfortably.

The whole to be fitted and finished in a substantial and workmanlike manner, and delivered on the Thames at Weybridge, for the sum of	**£250**
23ft. Boat to same specification	**£230**
20ft. Boat do. do.	**£210**

Built of Pine, with Pine Decks, &c., **10 per cent less.**

24. **COVER PAGE OF THE THAMES VALLEY LAUNCH COMPANY BROCHURE.** Published around 1900, the brochure provides a unique record of pictures and details of the electric launches built by the company for hire or sale.

G. Banham

The boatbuilding side of the business prospered. During the winter months from September 1896, Edwards delivered six launches, including one to the War Department, and a large down-river sailing craft of entirely new design to another customer. In April 1897 he was reported to have delivered a 45 ft launch to the Corporation of Southport to run on the artificial lake at Southport, as well as building a 30 ft cabin boat and a small open boat for the Chester Boat Co. to run on the River Dee.[2] By the end of September 1897 he had delivered fourteen boats, including one for Llangollen and several on the Thames.[3]

Nor was the export market neglected. In 1899 the TVL Co. despatched two boats, the *Water Nymph* and *Venus*, to Colombo in Sri Lanka (or Ceylon as it was named then).[4] The local paper pointed out that 'for forty years a ferry has been running across the lake between the Pettah Station and Slave Island, half the time with canoe, and half

44

with steam launches similar to the ones at present in use, which are now rather obsolete; but to-morrow the poorer people of Colombo will have the advantage of being taken across the water in boats propelled by Electricity, for the modest price of two cents.'

These two boats were each licensed to carry fifty passengers. The 4 hp motor was fitted in the stern and the batteries were located under the seats which ran all round the boat. Charging was carried out overnight at Pettah by a dynamo and the battery capacity was sufficient for the boat to run for sixteen hours, the working period being from six in the morning until nine at night. The boats were identical in construction, having a draught of 2 feet, but on trials the *Water Nymph* turned out to be the faster of the two. Not that that would have worried the passengers very much for the electric boats did the journey in two and a half minutes as compared to ten to fifteen minutes taken by the old steam launches. It was noted that the electric boats could be managed by two men, one to work the machinery and the other to steer.

Edwards took over the Upper Thames Electric Launch Co. at Henley in 1899. This gave him another works to complement the three existing depots on the Thames at Maidenhead, Pangbourne and Shillingford Bridge, and his headquarters at Weybridge. At all of these places launches could be hired, boats repaired and private craft moored and housed over the winter. By 1900 the TVL Company also had charging stations at Hurley and, by arrangement with the Oxford Electric Lighting Co., at Oxford. In 1902 two new stations were set up at Windsor and Reading.

There were, of course, a number of other charging stations owned by other businesses, such as Immisch, so that it was possible to find a charging station roughly every 10 miles between Kingston and Oxford. At the TVL Co.'s charging stations, owners of electric launches built by the company were offered a substantial discount on charging costs, the normal price of 1s 6d per unit being reduced to 8d.[5]

The company's brochure gave an unique picture of the range of electric boats which were being built. Ten of these are shown in Figs 25 to 34. At that time there were twenty-nine electric launches in the hire fleet. Of the saloon launches, three were of 45 ft length, two of which seated twenty-five passengers and one thirty-five passengers, and eight launches of 30 to 40 ft seating twelve passengers. The rest of the electric launches were open boats fitted with awnings, varying in length from 22 to 36 ft and carrying from six to twelve passengers.[6]

Two of the 35 ft designs listed had a clipper bow, but all the other launches were built with straight stems. In addition to those illustrated in this chapter fifteen others were listed as follows:

Neptune and *Inyoni*: 30 ft open boats with awnings; strongly built of teak and suitable for coast work, being Pinnace style, with seating for twelve passengers. Price £275.

Jupiter and *Iverna*: 30 ft twelve-passenger saloon boats in teak or mahogany. Price £350.

Venus and *Adonis*: 36 ft open boats with awnings; built of steel sheathed with wood and seating for twelve passengers. Price £450.

25. *TITAN*, **THE LARGEST LAUNCH IN THE TVL FLEET**. Its capacity was twenty-five to thirty-five passengers.

G. Banham

26. **THE TVL 45 FT TWELVE-PASSENGER LAUNCH** *LADAS*.

G. Banham

27. **TVL 35 FT TWELVE-PASSENGER** *HERCULES*.

G. Banham

28. *CARINA*, **A CLIPPER BOW 35 FT TWELVE-PASSENGER LAUNCH IN THE TVL FLEET**. Another was *Dabchick*.

G. Banham

29. TVL 35 FT *CULLA RANEE*.

G. Banham

Al-Kyris and *Andromeda*: 30 ft open boats with awnings; built of teak. The former painted white and arranged for armchairs for eight passengers, the latter varnished with seats along the sides for twelve passengers. Price £265.
Black Swan: 30 ft eight-passenger open boat with awning. Price £230.
White Swan, *Perseus*, *Fortune Teller*, *Water Nymph*, *Luna* and *Mercury*: 27 ft open boats with awning, each carrying eight passengers (ten for *Mercury*). Price £230.
Combination electric and sailing boats carrying three or four people. Price £165. Some of these boats, such as the two with steel hulls, were probably bought in from other yards.

The TVL launches were built to a high standard in teak or mahogany carvel construction with counter stern; detailed specifications are given on page 43. The early TVL launches had been fitted with the 'Beevor-Edwards' control switch, which was usually designed to give only half and full speed by switching the batteries in parallel or series.[7] It was claimed that there was no sparking on the make-and-break

30. **TVL 30 FT LAUNCH** *TROUT.*

G. Banham

31. **TVL 24 FT EIGHT-PASSENGER OPEN LAUNCH** *OMPHALE.*

G. Banham

32. **TVL 22 FT SIX-PASSENGER LAUNCH** *CASTOR*.

G. Banham

33. **TVL 18 FT SIX-PASSENGER BOAT** *DIANA*.

G. Banham

34. **TVL ELECTRIC SKIFF AND PUNT**.

G. Banham

contacts because they were independent of the main switch. There was therefore less danger of burning out the contacts, which apparently was a frequent source of trouble on other boats. Additional contacts could be provided to give a wider range of motor speeds.

In 1902 Edwards and Beevor introduced a new control device. Developed during the previous three years, it comprised a single lever which was located through the floor of the boat. On the top was a small spring clip or button which when depressed switched the motor on. As the lever was pushed forward through a series of step contacts, the boat moved ahead at speeds from dead slow to full speed and, by pulling the lever back, the same variable speeds were available for moving astern. An additional feature was that the control lever was also used for steering the boat so that a side movement of the lever turned the boat to port or starboard. Returning the lever to the upright position and releasing the spring clip switched off the motor.[8]

Launches were usually hired out with a driver, although some owners of private boats would have their own employee, their 'captain' or 'man', both to look after the boat and drive it. Thus, in 1902 Carr wrote to Mr Moore of Maidenhead to inform him that his

51

'launch is now ready at Weybridge. Please send your Captain to collect it. . . .'[9] Frequently, a launch would be hired out for the whole season (usually from mid-May until mid-September) at a cost varying from £125 to £200 for the saloon launches and from £60 for the small 18 ft open boat *Diana* to £125 for the 36 ft *Venus*. These prices included lock passes, free mooring at any of the company's stations and a discount on the cost of electricity for charging. A driver was extra and, as the brochure put it, 'a man can usually be supplied for from 20/- to 30/- a week'.

Edwards also promoted the short break holiday business and advertised a three-day trip from Oxford to Kingston, stopping overnight at Pangbourne, Maidenhead and Kingston. The advertisement proclaimed that the trip by electric launch was the most delightful way of seeing the Thames. Edwards clearly understood that a pleasant dinner and a decent room greatly enhanced the pleasure of the day's run.[10]

The business at Maidenhead built up quickly. The TVL Co.'s hire launches *Dabchick*, *Al-Kyris* and *Luna* were seen passing through Boulter's Lock in May 1899.[11]

On the private side, in July that year Carr wrote to Mr G.H. Stearn, at Victoria Street, London, explaining that it had been impossible to charge up his launch *Little Nell* because the batteries had been allowed to stay flat for too long.[12] During 1900 Carr appears to have been looking after a total of twenty-seven private and TVL launches. In April that year he was apologizing to Mrs Harmsworth that the *Hercules* was out of commission for three weeks but she could have the 45 ft *Titan* sooner. Alternatively, she could have the 35 ft saloon launch *Carina* immediately and because the cushions for the latter had not been made he told her that she could have covers of her own choice.[13] Small modifications were frequently made to meet customers' wishes; for Mr Neve, for example, he removed the locker from the *Neptune* so that the floor would be level throughout the boat and so give room for more chairs.[14]

Undoubtedly, one of the attractions of many electric boats was that the absence of the boiler and engine of the steam launch meant that the floor was clear of obstructions and more free-standing chairs could be accommodated. For example, the 27 ft open launch *White Swan* was fitted out with six wicker chairs and fixed seating for two more passengers. Similarly, the 30 ft open launch *Neptune* could have as many as eight chairs and carry twelve passengers in comfort.[15]

By the turn of the century Maidenhead had become a major centre for hireboats, and there were at least seven hirers of electric boats.[16] The riverside houses upstream continued to be rented for the season by wealthy Londoners; the theatrical stars tended to congregate in the Bray area; and the upper middle class from London kept their houseboats in Botany Bay just above Boulter's Lock. Parties, regattas, concerts and functions at the Guards and Murray's Clubs were immensely popular. Ascot Sunday was the day when hundreds from all classes visited the riverside at Maidenhead to see and be seen. In 1903 the king travelled up to Bray in his new petrol motor launch[17] and the Prince of Wales visited Boulter's Lock twice in one day in his electric launch *May*.[18]

None of the boatbuilders at Maidenhead advertised in the local weekly paper, the *Maidenhead Advertiser*. They were well known and often could only meet the demand by hiring from each other or from boatyards further upstream. Thus, Carr is recorded as

35. **BACK COVER OF THAMES VALLEY LAUNCH COMPANY BROCHURE, SHOWING
THE COMPANY'S HEADQUARTERS AT WEYBRIDGE.**

G. Banham

having hired steam launches such as the *Royal* from Bond's of Maidenhead for ten
guineas less 10 per cent, or the large steam launch *My Queen* from Bates of Chertsey to
pick up a party at Maidenhead.[19]

The export market remained buoyant, and in 1902 TVL delivered a 32 ft smart-
looking pinnace for use in the Bay of Naples and another to the Natal government.
These were both fitted with a 'Beevor-Edwards' motor and batteries of forty-four
Leitner cells supplied by Accumulator Industries Ltd of Woking designed to run 40 miles
on one charge at 7 mph. This was accomplished on a demonstration run during which
the battery voltage varied from 93 volts at the start to 85 volts fifteen minutes after the
finish of the run.[20]

Despite this appearance of good prospects, the electric boating business was going into
decline, as the Immisch company was discovering. Unlike Immisch however, Edwards
was unable to reorganize quickly enough to meet the rapidly changing scene and the
Thames Valley Launch Co. was wound up in 1904.

Rowland Edwards apparently lost no time in setting up another company because Carr wrote to him on 26 July saying: 'I regret being unable to subscribe to your new Company as I have no money to spare at present if I was satisfied with the prospectus or not.'[21] What the business was going to be is not clear; for example, in November Carr wrote that he was prepared to put up a building to make connectors at 2*d* each if the quantity was large enough, but evidently nothing came of that idea and Edwards probably moved out of the boating business altogether. Carr, however, kept the Boulter's Lock boatyard going under the name of his own business, the Ray Motor Company.

Chapter 5

THE RAY MOTOR COMPANY

During November 1904 Lawrence Carr took over the lease of the TVL premises on Boulter's Lock Island and started to trade there as the Ray Motor Company.[1] He also had the use of premises at Maidenhead Court where one of his activities was to recharge electric motor cars. In a letter to Mrs Lewis-Hall of Woodside, Maidenhead, enclosing his account for charging up the batteries on her electric car and launch, he mentions that he has put down a new slipway and is installing a new and complete plant for charging electric cars and launches. For good measure he also suggests that 'now that the Maidenhead Corporation Mains have been put down past your house I venture to ask you to allow me to send you an estimate and specification for an (Electric Light) installation'; he also mentions that he is now installing the light in four large houses in Maidenhead Court.[2]

By 1904 Carr was already involved in petrol-engined boats. In July he was arranging for repairs to the Monarch oil engine fitted in Mr Diederiehen's *Magarida*, and sold a 22 ft launch fitted with a 3 hp two-cycle motor to Mr Harwood. On the other hand, Mr Palmer of Lacock in Wiltshire was anxious to sell his petrol boat and on 5 July Carr wrote to him saying that 'Mrs Palmer does not like the *Fussy* and will not go out in it, but thinks it best to sell the boat.' On 10 September Carr follows this up with the explanation from Mrs Palmer, 'that it was not only the noise of the engine but the general arrangement of the boat that was not liked'. Selling the boat wasn't easy; an offer of £65 was received but as Carr points out, 'Considering the price you paid for the boat, it is a low offer. I cannot sell the boat with engine as perfect although the patch I put in her cylinder seems to be satisfactory.' Mr Palmer was not prepared to let it go cheap and his next move was to ask Carr to get quotations for a steam engine. Judging by Carr's comments about the difficulties of fitting the engine and boiler, that idea probably came to nothing.[3]

Losing the TVL Co. business probably made life difficult for Carr during the next few years. He seems to have had very few electric boats in his care, only *Black Swan*, *Esperanza*, *Tadpole* and *Frou-Frou* being mentioned in the records. Mr G. Smith from Staines had joined his staff in 1901, and in 1905 F. Andrews was on the pay-roll.

In June 1907 Carr had a core of three men: B.B. Jillings, H. Bushnell and F. Andrews working full-time. Another of the Andrews family, O. Andrews, helped out for eight weeks until the end of July 1907 and C. Goodchild, probably a youngster, worked a 31-hour week until the end of December 1907. During February 1908 Carr took on another two full-time men, A. Beeton and W. Horsham, and these five constituted the main workforce until 1913. A detailed record of the activity at Carr's yard is summarized in the time sheets for the period between June 1907 and September 1909.[4]

36. EXTRACTS FROM TIME SHEET BOOK, 1909. Two pages from the 1909 time sheet ledger for the two weeks 24 April–1 May and 1 May–8 May.

G. Banham

'Full-time' in those days meant an average of 56 hours per week, except that F. Andrews clocked up an average of 68 hours per week over the whole two-year period. The summer months were the heaviest, four of the men working a maximum of about 75 hours, and Andrews a maximum of 86 hours in one week, and an average over twenty-two weeks of 65 and 75 hours per week respectively.

These time sheets show that Goodchild was paid 7*d* per hour. Carr also had to pay

Andrews £1 10s and Beeton 12s for their week away in the Territorial Army camp. During the winter of 1908 Carr himself is recorded as doing maintenance work on the petrol engines for the launch *Mayada* and others.

Perhaps one of the most interesting entries was the time booked by Andrews and Jillings in June 1907 for work for Mr Fitch, the owner of the launch *Frou Frou*. The job was to repair the gas engine and fit up a charging box at Fitch's house at Bray. Mains electricity was not available at that time and many of the residences had installed gas or steam engines driving dynamos to supply electricity for the house lighting.

W.J. Horsham was the son of Horsham the boatbuilder at Bourne End and a skilled woodworker. He emigrated to South Africa and set up a business at East London on the Buffalo River. Unfortunately, the business was destroyed by a flood and he returned to this country with his family, his eldest son then being four years old, and joined Carr. It was said of Bill Horsham that he had such a feel for wood that, whenever there was a piece lying about, he would make or carve something out of it to fit on a boat. He must have been a great asset for he enabled Carr to get into the business of building complete boats.

Horsham's first boat to be built at the Ray Motor Co. was the motor boat *Ray*. During the week of 11 April 1908 he spent ten hours making a model of it, and during the following week he laid off the moulds for the full-size boat. He worked on her

37. **RAY MOTOR COMPANY STAFF IN THE 1910s**. From left to right: Lawrence Carr, the owner, Jack Lee, Bill Horsham, Charlie Saunders, George Ayres.

H. Horsham

spasmodically during the summer, finishing in October and immediately started to build a sailing yawl for Mr Ricardo.

During these two years other work carried out included maintenance, repairs, and storage of the following boats:

Electric launches:
> *Asthore, Frou Frou, Gollywog, Tadpole, Mina, Esperanza*, and *Charlotte*.

Motor launches:
> *Avice, Mayada* (owner Hamilton), *Eve, Natalie, Panther, Swanhilde, Maryland, Pearl, Nedda, Di, Midge, Aileen, Yolande, Handor Penelope, White Witch, Batava, Skirmisher, Louie, Overmodest, Puffin*.

Small craft:
> dinghies belonging to French and Fish; Kendrick's skiff; Horsham's and Ricardo's canoes; Preston's sailing boat; punts belonging to Capt. Metcalfe, Dulake, Hamilton, Cox, Mclaughlin, Barker, Headington, Fuller, Paterson, French, Samuelson, Farrer, Leon, Weston, Eglinton, and Davies.

Houseboats:
> *Ladye, Romani*

The rest of the men's time was taken up in general jobs, which covered not only the work about the yard – cleaning boats, charging and looking after batteries and office work – but a variety of outside jobs.

Since the opening of the yard in 1896, Carr had supplemented the boat work, especially during the winter, by carrying out electrical work for many of the property owners along the river in Maidenhead and Bray. This comprised installing electric lighting, supplied initially from dynamos and subsequently from the mains supply, such as the work for Mr Fitch, the owner of the electric boat *Frou Frou*, who commissioned Carr to look after the dynamo which supplied his house electrical installation and the boat's charging system. Other jobs included installing tantalum lighting in Taplow Mill, repairing Smith's motor cycle timing gear, and spending 39 hours fitting the electric launch *Mina* with decorations for the procession in honour of the Olympic crew being entertained at Kessler's house on Cookham Reach.

In 1909 Carr's records indicate that the same electric boats were still in use and being housed and charged at his little boatyard on Boulter's Lock Island. Major Fenner's *Esperanza*, Mr Fitch's *Frou-Frou*, Mr de Lissa's *Gollywog*, Col. Somerville's large electric launch *Mina*, Mrs Cuthbert's *Tadpole* and Mr Kessler's *Charlotte* were still in commission.[5] Carr also charged up Woodhouse's (owner of the Maidenhead & District Boating Co.) launches, such as *Armada, Corona* and *Santarello* and he repaired the armature in *Dace*, the launch built by Andrews in 1902 and now owned by Woodhouse. Electric boats were still in use but they were being patched up and, apart from the launches from Andrews' yard at Maidenhead and the occasional canoe, no new ones were being built.

The site at Boulter's Lock had been rented from Oxford University, but in 1909 Carr was able to purchase the freehold.[6] Just before Christmas 1910, Carr suffered a serious blow. Late on a Friday night, the Maidenhead Fire Brigade were called out to a fire on

Boulter's Lock Island. The building which Carr used for storing motor boats and contents had caught fire and was blazing fiercely. The riverside road leading to Boulter's Lock was flooded but the steam fire engine managed to get through satisfactorily. However, the cab carrying the Chief Officer and other firemen was slowed up by the water running through its floor and by the time they arrived at the scene the building and all its contents had been destroyed.[7]

One of the boats whose furnishings were lost in the fire was the electric launch *Esperanza*, which Carr looked after between 1905 and 1913. The then owner, Major Fenner of Datchet, had to foot a bill of £125 10s for a new set of curtains, carpets, cushions, etc.[8] It was the mats required for this refit which resulted in the letter from the manager at Hill's Rubber Co. in Reading, raising the suggestion that *Esperanza* was built, not by Bond of Maidenhead, but by Saunders of Goring.[9] Mr Kessler's *Charlotte* had not been affected by the fire presumably because it had been kept up at the boathouse at New York Lodge.

During the winter of 1911/12 Boulter's Lock Island was in a state of upheaval. The Thames Conservators had authorized the rebuilding of the lock and its size was increased to 200 ft in length and 22 ft 4 in in width. The lock was brought into use again on 8 May 1912 in time for the summer season. Lord Desborough, Chairman of the Conservators, who lived at Taplow House was, of course, the first to go through and later on presided at the official opening on 3 July.

Feelings ran high; the *Daily News and Leader* lamented that 'the old romantic associations of Boulter's Lock alas are no more. The happy squash of big boats and little boats, steam launches and family punts used to be the great scene of the day here in summers that are past. . . . Boulter's Lock is now modernized beyond all recognition; a twentieth-century vandal monstrosity, electric wires and humming dynamos, hydraulic lifts . . . and other strange devices. It had to be; increasing river traffic demanded it.'[10]

Despite the upheaval, the scene at Boulter's on Ascot Sunday was as colourful and busy as ever. The lock was jam-packed with boats, although not quite reaching the record set in 1907 when 1,096 craft (158 launches and 938 small boats) went through the lock.[11] Thousands of people walked up the promenade from Maidenhead Bridge, nearly every craft was let out, with Bond's at the bridge hiring punts and launches from other firms up river to meet the demand, but the real sign of the times was that hundreds of motor cars were drawn up on either side of the riverside promenade and a vast number more on the private roads nearby.[12] Cookham also had its influx of visitors, the motor traffic through the village being described as enormous, although ferryman J. Brookes took 2,533 foot-passengers across the river in his ferry on that Sunday.

In 1913 Carr and Horsham were becoming interested in the possibilities of building electric canoes, and Carr worked out the specification for a 25 ft canoe. However, there is no record that the canoe was actually built and the project was shelved until after the war.

During the First World War Carr tendered to build 20 to 27 ft whalers and gigs for the Admiralty but his yard seems to have been used mainly to build dinghies for the Army. Bill Horsham enlisted in the Inland Waterways transport section of the Royal Engineers, and shortly after being called up he wrote to Carr saying that he was still doing navvying,

38. **_ARIS_**. Built in 1920, this was the first of a small fleet of beautiful canoes from the Ray Motor Co.

G. Banham

'fed up from morning to night and no sign of anything different in sight'. He said that they had some fine workshops and the best of everything, 'but I have seen no boats to beat ours'. Carr tried very hard to get Horsham released so that he could come back and work on the Admiralty contracts, but even with his MP's help the War Office would not release him. Nevertheless, despite the difficulties, Carr managed to keep some work going on electric launches because a few, such as _Baladeuse_, _Nita_, _La Cerise_ and _Whip_, were kept in commission by riverside families for the use of troops on leave.

Following the war, Horsham and two others rejoined Carr. The launch business was mainly in looking after private petrol-engined boats. In 1923 Carr converted Mr Scott O'Connor's 30 ft electric launch to use a Wolseley petrol engine. The saddest blow for Carr must have been the job of installing an Empire petrol motor in the _Madeleine_ (previously _Mina_), the 30 ft electric launch which Carr had looked after since 1909.[13] There was little interest in new electric launches or cars but Carr's enthusiasm for electric canoes was revived, and in May 1920 he and Horsham built _Aris_ for Mr Anagnos for £460.[14] They continued to build some beautiful electric canoes, one of which, _Gena_, is still in use today.[15] Furthermore, Horsham's pattern-making skills were put to good use by making cast parts for all kinds of boats, and Carr continued to undertake electrical work for houses in the area.

In 1925 Carr may have supplied the electric canoe _Liddesdale_ to Lord Astor at Cliveden. This canoe was restored recently and is now once again at Cliveden in the ownership of the hotel. During 1926 he was advertising the Ray Motor Co. as Electric and Motor Launch Builders and, according to his price list for an ordinary day, had two petrol-engined launches and three electric canoes for hire as follows:

Motor launches:	passengers	guineas
Gerbera (Saloon)	12	5
Gentiana (Awning)	8	3
Electric canoes:		
Gena	6	3
Genetta	6	3
Genella	6	3

The prices were raised by one and two guineas for a day's hire on Saturday and Sunday. 'Special Days', such as Ascot Sunday and regatta days, were by negotiation.

The business continued to hire out electric canoes and the occasional electric launch and there were still a few privately owned electric canoes, including Lord Astor's and Mr Keevil's, which Carr and Horsham repaired and housed over the winters. Carr even arranged some sales, *Yvonne* being sold to Mr Peyton in 1933 complete with Submersible Co.'s motor and a battery of thirty new cells.

Carr retired in 1934 and passed the business on to his three colleagues, Bill Horsham, Bill Emony and Jack Lee, who continued to run it as the Ray Motor Co. In due course, Emony and Lee were bought out, the former joining H. Wilder & Son, and Bill

39. THE RAY MOTOR COMPANY PARTNERS, 1934. From left to right: Jack Lee, general hand and bookkeeper; Bill Horsham, the boatbuilder; Bill 'Toddler' Emony, mechanic and boat driver. These three were Carr's full-time employees until 1934 when Carr retired and handed the business over to them.

H. Horsham

Horsham became the sole owner of the yard on Boulter's Lock Island.[16] In addition to the hiring and repair side of the business, Horsham continued to make a few boats. The largest was a 42 ft cruiser, believed to have been named *Kate II*. In 1940 she was taken down to Southampton en route for Dunkirk where she was said to have been sunk.[17] Probably the last boat which Bill Horsham built was a 22 ft slipper launch which is understood to be still in use on the Thames.

The Second World War nearly finished off the business. Bill Horsham failed to secure an Admiralty contract for dinghies and so he went to work for Bushnells at Wargrave. Here he was joined by his son Tom, who had been working at Woods Nurseries at Taplow until their closure during the war. After the war, Bill and Tom set about rebuilding the tumbledown sheds on the island at Maidenhead and re-established the yard as Horsham & Son. Bill died in 1952 and Tom continued to run the yard until he sold it to Peter Freebody of Hurley in 1979 on condition that he could occupy part of it for as long as he lived. Unfortunately, he survived only for two years, dying in 1981 at the age of sixty.

Thanks to the efforts of Carr and Horsham, combined with their location at one of the main centres of boating on the Thames during the Edwardian period, the little yard tucked away on Boulter's Lock Island was one of the few which kept alive the experience of electric boating for nearly half a century.

40. **THE BOATYARD ON BOULTER'S LOCK ISLAND**. It was started in 1896 as a depot for the Thames Valley Launch Co. and is now under the ownership of Peter Freebody of Hurley.

E.P. Hawthorne

FOUR PRIVATE LAUNCHES

Carr's invoice and record books provide a picture of the work of his yard. The history of four of the private electric launches that he looked after and for which there exists a photograph follows below. The history of a fifth, *Esperanza*, which is still in use at the present time, is given in Chapter 11.

Tadpole

The *Maidenhead Advertiser* for 17 May 1893 reported that 'Mr Phipps was out in the electric launch *Tadpole* in Bray Reach on Sunday'. It seems that this was not his own boat because a month later, on 7 June, it was reported that Mr and Mrs Phipps were out on Saturday and Sunday in the electric launch *Champion*. This latter launch had been added to the small fleet of electric hireboats run by Mr Bowen of Ray Mead Hotel at Maidenhead.

Tadpole turns up in the Ray Motor Co. correspondence in 1904, when Carr wrote to Mrs Budd-Scott on 29 August at her houseboat *Mirabelle* which was moored at the

41. *TADPOLE*.

G. Banham

Fishery Estate below Maidenhead. 'I shall be glad to house your boat *Tadpole* under cover for the winter, take care of the cells keeping them charged, putting the boat in the water and replacing the cells again in the spring for the sum of eight pounds (£8). As regards charging in the summer I will let you know the price per unit when the time comes, when no doubt I shall be able to offer you as favourable terms as the Thames Valley Co. did. I would be glad to moor the boat for the summer. You will find the Mill head an exceptionally quiet mooring now as there will only be private boats moored there. Trusting I will receive your esteemed order.'

Evidently, Mrs Budd-Scott was happy to take up this offer for during the following summer there is a record for 19 August 1905 that F. Andrews, Carr's boatman, booked five hours to fetch *Tadpole*, clean, charge and take her back to the houseboat. The next reference is an invoice, addressed to Mrs E. Budd Cuthbert and dated 2 July 1909, for £6 10s for the cost of housing *Tadpole* for the winter 1908/09. Then, on 14 September 1910, Carr invoiced for charging up with 28 units at 8d per unit, fitting a new shaft and new brushes, moorings for the summer at £6 10s and insurance of 10s for the year. Mrs Budd Cuthbert was also willing to let Carr hire *Tadpole* out because during the summer of 1911 the launch was hired out two or three times at £4 per day.

On 11 May 1912 Carr had to write to Mrs Budd Cuthbert to say that 'on examining the *Tadpole* to find cause of the excessive leaking last year we find the keel has rotted right through about 2 ft from stem & continues for some distance. The keel will have to be preserved throughout together with each garboard strake. This is absolutely necessary before the boat can float, the cost will be £7 10s and will take about 14 working days.' The work was done and invoiced on 15 October along with other work.

Tadpole is afloat again in the form of a new boat of traditional construction, which owes her design to the preservation of a hull which was too far gone to restore and to records of the earlier launch. Built by Peter Freebody during 1994, she incorporates one of the motors used in electric launches of 1910s vintage (see illustration on page 187).

Charlotte

In 1907 Mr George A. Kessler, the American millionaire, bought Riversdale House at Bourne End and also an electric launch.[18] The house had originally been built in the mid-1890s by Mr Adcock, who with Mr Haden-Tebb organized the first Bourne End regatta in 1897.[19] It had cost £10,000 to build and Mr Kessler spent £30,000 on remodelling and extending it in the 'most lavish manner', renaming it New York Lodge. He installed electric lighting, with 3,000 lamps not only in the house but among the trees and shrubs along the riverside, the whole being powered from a dynamo driven by a 65 hp engine.[20]

The launch complemented the house. Built by J. Bond of Maidenhead, she was described as one of the finest boats of her kind on the river and was beautifully upholstered. Launched in June 1907, she was named after Kessler's wife, Charlotte. Carr at the Ray Motor Co. looked after her, invoicing Mr Kessler in the spring of 1909 for housing *Charlotte* over the winter 1908/09 at a cost of £15 and a further £16 10s 6d for varnishing and painting, writing and gilding name and line, sundry repairs, and cleaning awning and curtains.[21] The subsequent history of *Charlotte* is not recorded but it has been suggested that she may have been bought back by Bond when Kessler returned to

42. *CHARLOTTE*, 1908.

B.B. Wheals and H. Horsham

America in 1914 and then sold on, in 1922, to Sir Dhunjibhoy Bomanji who lived at The Willows, near Windsor, and who renamed her after his wife, Lady Frainy.[22]

Mr Kessler made an impression on Bourne End. In 1908 he entertained the competitors, who took part in the Olympic Games in London, to a banquet and fireworks display. In 1910 he went even further by providing extensive support for Cookham Regatta. He not only provided the prizes and contributed generously to the regatta fund, but persuaded the occupants of the villas and bungalows on the Buckinghamshire bank and boat-owners attending the regatta to illuminate their premises and boats.

The result was that Cookham Reach 'has never presented such a remarkably brilliant kaleidoscopic picture of varied coloured lights reflected in the moving waters and scintillating in every nook and cranny among rushes and shrubs and trees making up a scene which defies description. Hundreds of craft displayed lights of some sort. Those taking part in the illuminated procession were a blaze of colour, the Thames being literally "on fire".'[23] New York Lodge itself was brilliantly illuminated with thousands of bucket and fairy lamps and aigrettes (plumes) on fire, Tasmanian ferns and festoons of light against a background of coloured fires. Kessler and his wife appeared on the balcony of the boathouse with the Maharajah and Prince Gackwar of Baroda and their suite. His own launch *Charlotte* was illuminated all over and decorated with coloured electric lights in the form of the Star of India.

There was better to come. Kessler had commissioned Messrs Paine & Son to put on a fireworks display costing £100. The reporter from the *Maidenhead Advertiser* was quite carried away. 'Never have such rockets illumined the heavens, huge showers of every

43. *PEARL*.

G. Banham

conceivable colour burst over the locality. . . . Bombs caused the ground to shake . . . Musical rockets were applauded, firework reptiles and tremulous beams of light excited wonderment. . . .' The setpieces included a firework gymnast performing on a horizontal bar, a firework motor car in motion, a man on a bucking mule, and the display ended with portraits of Mr and Mrs Kessler and a huge 'Good-night' in changing colours. Altogether a night to remember.

Pearl

Dix, in his book on Thames passenger boats, lists a launch named *Pearl* as being owned by the Thames Electric & Steam Launch Co. in 1894.[24] She was built by Immisch in 1893 and licensed as Class 5 (river services in smooth water) to carry twenty-six passengers not below Richmond.

Pearl appears in the Ray Motor Co. books in the time sheets for September 1907, when Jillings spent 17 hours making some repairs and taking her out for trial runs. During 1909 various jobs were carried out including packing the gland, replacing ballast, repairing a leak, the covering board and the magneto, and charging up the battery.[25]

At this time *Pearl* was owned by Major Charles E. Fenner, who also owned the electric

44. ***MINA*, RENAMED *MADELEINE* IN 1920.**

G. Banham

launch *Esperanza*. On 28 June 1911 Carr invoiced Major Fenner for storing *Pearl* over the winter 1910/11 at a cost of £4 10*s*, and painting and varnishing her.

There are no records linking the earlier reference to *Pearl* with Major Fenner's launch, but the launch design is very similar to the clipper bow launches run by both Immisch and Thames Valley Launch Co. Fenner's launch could well have been converted to petrol after the run down of the electric launch businesses from 1904 onwards.

Mina, renamed *Madeleine* in 1920

The electric launch *Mina* was 30 ft in length[26] and was very similar in design to the *Hercules* type of 35 ft launch illustrated in the Thames Valley Launch Co. brochure.[27] Two 30 ft boats, *Jupiter* and *Iverna,* were also advertised in the brochure but without illustrations, and one of these could well have been bought by a private owner when the TVL Co. closed down. These were cabin boats built of teak or mahogany and in 1902 were for sale at £350. The motor was possibly rated at 2.6 kw input power.

The first mention of *Mina* in the Ray Motor Co. records is an invoice dated 25 June 1909 made out to Col. Somerville. It was for work done during May 1909 for 'Repairs, painting etc. on E.L. *Mina* as per est. £10.5.0 and for supplying 1 Green Canvas Awning for £2.0.0'. This invoice was rendered again on 2 July 1909.[28]

The next reference is an invoice rendered on 26 June 1913 to S. Redlich Esq. for:[29]

Mar	Test *Mina*'s motor etc.	3.6
Mar	Supply & erect 3 new Positive Sections & fresh acid	2.3.6
June	Supply & erect 2 Positive Sections & fresh acid	1.9.0
	Mans time Bray to Parallel Motor Fields	2.0
		£3.18.0

On 28 May 1914 an invoice was sent to Mr Redlich for £3 3s for the care of the *Mina* cells and motor during the winter 1913/14 and fitting the launch out in the spring of 1914.

After the end of the First World War, *Mina* was recommissioned by A.F. Ross Esq. who put her into the Ray Motor Co.'s yard on Boulter's Lock Island, Maidenhead, on 8 June 1919. The timbers seem to have been in good condition for the work only included scraping and varnishing all over with four coats of varnish, cleaning and painting the bottom and bilge with black varnish, replacing various fittings and painting the gold lines and her name in gold and blue, all at a cost of £42 18s. One item on this invoice was for 'Cleaning out 28 Accumulators and supplying new 1200 Sp. Gr. Acid and long charge' for £2 14s 9d. The cells were evidently in poor condition and Mr Carr was instructed to order new positive sections.

Delivery of parts by train, especially for the batteries, was always troublesome, usually because the packing was poor, and the condition of the new positive sections ordered from the Electric Power Storage Co. was no exception. The argument about these dragged on and even in January 1920 there was a letter to Messrs Alkey (London) Ltd saying, 'These sections were received by G.W.Rly. Goods shed platform Maidenhead. They were packed anyhow in a light box tied over with two pieces of string. Some of the sections were grouped in threes, others were separate, they were all more or less damaged some badly bent and cracked.'[30]

Eventually, a new set of 36-11 7KA type positive sections of five plates each were purchased from Chloride Electrical Storage Co. and delivered on 9 May 1920. The total cost, including fitting and forming up was £95 3s 9d.[31] However, by this time Mr Ross had sold the launch to Sir Bernard Oppenheimer of Sefton Park, Stoke Poges, Bucks.

During April 1920 the launch was registered at the Thames Conservancy under the name *Madeleine*. By 15 May she had been painted inside, varnished and enamelled etc. for £20; a Lock Pass obtained for £10; and W. Emony appointed as captain at a wage of £4 per week (plus unemployment and insurance of 4d per week). One tin of brass polish costing 11d was used every month and charging the batteries cost 1s 3d per unit.[32]

Sir Bernard not only used the launch at Henley but also hired a punt for the week (at a cost of £6). His captain, Emony, received £1 10s for his expenses during the week.

With the onset of winter that year, the question of Mr Emony's pay came up and Sir

Bernard sought advice from Carr, who, diplomatically and shrewdly, replied that 'This is rather difficult for us as there is no general rule, it practically depends on the feeling between master and man. . . . We do know this, that in Emony you have secured a man of exceptional ability and we strongly advise you to retain his services.'

Carr then proposed that Emony should do all the work necessary to get the launch ready for the next season 'and it would be more satisfactory for you than to pay him for nothing. We suggest your paying him three pounds per week and to make his money up to Summer standard we could find him a few small jobs at odd times.'[33]

Thus were all parties satisfied and Carr had the availability of another pair of hands around the yard.

Madeleine was all done up 'really smart' by 29 April 1921 but, tragically, Sir Bernard can have made little use of her as he died shortly afterwards. On 20 June Carr wrote: '. . . we have given a week's notice to the Captain of the Electric Launch *Madeleine*. We were extremely sorry to hear the sad news of Sir Bernard. We always found him one of the very best.'[34]

Carr seems to have been left to look after the launch as best he could, but at the end of July Lady Oppenheimer visited the yard and was concerned to find that *Madeleine* had been hired out. Carr put the record straight in a letter to Lady Oppenheimer's agent: 'In case her Ladyship imagines we have let the Launch to anybody who came along, we would like to point out that Mrs Seaton is the only person who has hired the *Madeleine* and that has been on three occasions. . . .' As for finding a purchaser: 'It will be a difficult matter until we get the revival of trade everyone is hoping for.'[35]

There are no records of *Madeleine* being used during 1922, and in February 1923 a Mr Sydney Clarke wrote to Carr instructing him to sell the launch. In his reply Carr mentions that he did not know the name of the builder or the year in which she was built but he noted that the motor was made by Messrs Newton of Taunton. Of the sale to Sir Bernard in 1920, he says: 'We had no idea the price was so much as £500 but of course that was the boom year for launches as well as motor cars and cycles. That good time has passed, in fact all last year we did not have one real enquiry for a launch of the *Madeleine*'s description.'[36]

It must have been a difficult time. In September we find Carr optimistically writing that he has had an enquiry for an electric launch to be sent to India and asking what was the lowest price that Lady Oppenheimer would accept.

Then, silence, until 20 July 1926 when Carr writes to Mr J. George, whose address was 17–29 Hatton Wall, EC1, and who owned Ray Mill Cottage next door to Carr on Boulter's Lock Island: 'Following our conversation with you on Sunday last July 18th. re installation of a Brooks Engine in the launch *Madeleine* you have just purchased, we herewith submit an estimate. . . .'

This estimate, totalling £175, included fitting a 10 hp four-cylinder Brooke 'Empire' engine, reverse gear and self starter. The engine case was to be made in teak and the boat cleaned down, pumice stoned and varnished with two coats of best varnish. The bottom, inside and out, was to be dressed with bitumastic solution and the water line to be painted two coats with green paint and the ribbon with white.[37] Work on fitting the Brooke engine began in October 1926.

Carr continued to look after the *Madeleine* until 1933 and the following extracts from his account books give a glimpse of the history of the launch and her owners between 1926 and 1933:

Oct 26th 1926 to J. George Esq. Installation of Brooke 'Empire' petrol engine etc. as per estimate £175.0.0.

May 11th 1927 to J. George Esq. To Balance Installation, Repairs, Alterations and Renovation Account as per our estimate July 20th 1926 £50.0.0

Nov 20th 1928 to J. George Esq. Invoice for 30 items dating from June 1927 to Sept 1928 such as: Hauling out Ferry Punt; Hauling out Dutch Boat, fitting new stem, painting etc. £6.10.0; March 24th 1928. Man's time fetching *Madeleine* from Walton; Aug 2nd 1928. Man's time driving *Madeleine* 7s 6d; July 1928. Hauling out *Madeleine*, cleaning and varnishing etc. £7.10.0; Sept 21st 1928. Repairs to Pram Dinghy

June 18th 1929 to H. Feapt (?) Esq. for the late Mr J. George. To hauling out, repairing, painting etc. £18.5.0. (378).

Aug 23rd 1929 to Mrs George for moorings and housing of *Madeleine* for summer season. 26 weeks @ 5s per week £6.10.0.

June 12th 1930 to Mrs George for hauling out and storing *Madeleine* in shed for winter season 29/30 £5.5.0.

Aug 11th 1930 to Mrs C.A.B. George for housing M.L. *Madeleine* in shed summer season £4.4.0

June 15th 1931 to Mrs C.A. Briscoe George for painting Ferry Punts £4.10.0; varnishing etc. 2 ft 6 in Punt £3.5.0; to housing *Madeleine* in shed winter season £4.4.0. During February 1927, the Yard also made a Ferry Punt 20 ft by 4 ft wide for Mrs George of 2 Westbourne Street, W.2. In acknowledging the order, Mr Lee wrote 'You may rest assured Mr George will have no cause to grumble.'

Finally, on 23 September 1933 an invoice appears to have been sent to Mr F. Hemsleys at Tudor House, Wycombe Road, Amersham for cleaning down *Madeleine*, varnishing, anti-fouling and launching during March 1933.

Subsequently *Madeleine* turned up in the Abbotsbrook mooring owned by Townsend Bros at Bourne End. By then she was in a very bad state with no engine and leaking badly. She was bought by a couple from Windsor, who poled and paddled her down to the millstream at Clewer just above Windsor. Here the new owner fitted a steam engine and used her throughout the Second World War as an occasional refuge from the bombing in London and even cruised her on occasion up to Lechlade and back. Although it was forbidden to use petrol for rivercraft during the war the owner was allowed to run her because there was no restriction on the use of coal. After the war, he sold her for filming purposes.

Eventually, she finished up in a garden of a house in Ascot where her bow section was cut off and used as a garden seat!

Chapter 6

WILLIAM S. SARGEANT – MASTER BOATBUILDER

William Samuel Sargeant appeared on the electric boating scene as early as 1888, when he was commissioned by Moritz Immisch to convert and fit out a 'roomy hulk' as the first-ever floating charging station. At that time Sargeant was trading as Messrs Sargeant & Co., boatbuilder and electrical engineer, at Strand Works, Strand-on-the-Green, Chiswick.[1]

He was born in 1836 at 20 Jeffreys Street, Kentish Town, London, and his brother, Bernardo Herbert Sargeant, who became a mural painter, was born eighteen years later in 1858.[2] Their father was a builder and William may have been apprenticed as a joiner, because his great grandnephew, Tim Sargeant, inherited a long case clock made by him. Whatever his earlier activities, by 1888 William Sargeant appears to have become established as an electrical engineer and boatbuilder. It is possible that there were already

45. **WILLIAM S. SARGEANT, MASTER BOATBUILDER AND ELECTRICAL ENGINEER, 1836–1918**. Reproduced by kind permission of Tim Sargeant, William Sargeant's great grand-nephew.

T.C. Sargeant

46. *VISCOUNTESS BURY,* **FROM THE 1904 IMMISCH BROCHURE**. Built in 1888 and still in use, this is the earliest and largest electric passenger boat in the world. Designed and built by William Sargeant for the Immisch Electric Launch business in 1888, she was run as an electric passenger boat until 1910. She was then converted to diesel power and taken to Cambridge and Ely where she continued to run as a tripping boat until 1991. She is now owned by the 'Viscountess Bury Trust' which plans to re-convert her to electric.

Capt. F.J. Turk, MVO

links between Sargeant and Immisch which led to Immisch ordering from him the floating charging station and his first two electric boats, *Malden* and the famous 65 ft *Viscountess Bury*, the latter being launched on 8 October 1888.[3] It appears that Sargeant designed the 30½ ft *Malden* but had her built by Maynards, the boatbuilder also at Strand-on-the Green, whereas he is believed to have both designed and built the *Viscountess Bury*.[4]

This experience established Sargeant as a designer and builder of large electric boats, and during 1889 he built the 60 ft long *Ray Mead*, launched in April and very similar in design to the *Viscountess Bury*. This was followed by the launch in June of a 40 ft boat for Mr Andrew Pears, the soap magnate.[5] The importance of reducing losses in the propulsion system of electric boats was evidently already clearly understood, for it is reported that this boat for Andrew Pears was fitted with Sargeant's patent combined motor shaft and thrust block in a self-lubricating arrangement that reduced friction.[6]

The *Ray Mead* was built of Burmese teak, 60 ft length by 11 ft beam and a draught of 2 ft 9 in. She had a Board of Trade license to carry eighty-five passengers. The batteries and Immisch motors were fitted under the floor, with the driving position arranged above the saloon. It was claimed that the launch could run for 20 hours at 7 mph, for 50 to 60 hours at lower speeds, and that the batteries could be fully recharged in 4½ hours. The saloon was 'daintily fitted up with the electric light, and stained glass and brass fittings, and yellow curtains that harmonise very prettily with the rich brown of her timber'.[7]

The *Ray Mead* operated from Maidenhead during its early years. In 1896 she was reported as being owned by Taylor of Ray Mead Hotel and Chertsey and 'doing good work down river this season and a day or two since made a capital trip from Reading to Maidenhead'.[8]

Sargeant probably also built the saloon launch *Loosestrife* for Henry Gold who was a partner in the wine merchants, W. & A. Gilbey. Gold had married Alfred Gilbey's sister Charlotte and went to live close to the Gilbeys at Wooburn by Bourne End. Sometime during the 1880s Henry and Charlotte then rented Formosa Place, owned by Sir George Young. Here they brought up a family of five sons and a daughter who married one of the Gilbey sons. The whole Gold family were enthusiastic supporters of the growing activities on the Thames, Henry being one of the founders of the Upper Thames Sailing Club, and his youngest son Harcourt becoming one of the leading oarsmen of his generation. In its obituary of Henry Gold in 1900, the *Maidenhead Advertiser* wrote that 'Mr Gold was, we believe, the first to introduce an electric launch on this part of the river — his commodious and pretty *Loosestrife*.'[9]

47. ***LOOSESTRIFE, 1890***. The picture shows a half model and carries a plaque 'Presented to the Captain by the Designer'. The Captain was Henry Gold and the Designer, and builder, was almost certainly Sargeant.
Reproduced by kind permission of Mrs Moira Robinson, Henry Gold's granddaughter.

E.P. Hawthorne

In fact, in August 1890 the *Maidenhead Advertiser* carried the report that Mr Gold's attractive electric launch *Loosestrife* and thirteen or fourteen steam launches were among the craft afloat at Marlow Regatta. Also, at the end of August 1890, Mr Gold's electric launch *Loosestrife* was seen at the Maidenhead Watermen's Regatta as was the electric launch *Pilot*.

The Golds were fully involved in the Thames social scene and *Loosestrife* was a popular adjunct to the garden parties and regattas which they held at Formosa House in Cookham. For example, in 1894 the Golds held a party for the people of Cookham, many of whom made their first-ever trip on the river in the launch. In 1896 the lease of Formosa House fell due and the Golds then rented Hedsor House from Lord Boston. When Henry Gold died in 1900, he and his wife Charlotte, who died shortly after, were buried together in the secluded Hedsor Church graveyard with the fine view of the valley of the Thames winding through Bourne End and Cookham.

Following Henry Gold's death, *Loosestrife* was sold to a resident of Bourne End, probably Mr F.C. Frye, who was seen with his party on board at Marlow Regatta in August 1900. Frye owned the house called the Platt beside the boatyards at Bourne End and was an enthusiastic supporter of Bourne End Regatta. In 1904 the *Maidenhead Advertiser* noted that Mr and Mrs Warner, the happy honeymoon couple from Holly Lodge, Cookham, were on the fine electric launch *Loosestrife*.

Undoubtedly, a number of companies would have been eyeing the potential of the market for electrical equipment in boats. One such was Woodhouse & Rawson United, manufacturers of heavy engineering equipment and of 'every description of Electrical Plant and Apparatus'.[10] In 1890 they took over Sargeant's business, keeping him on as Manager at the Strand boatyard.[11]

48. ***GLOW WORM*, 1892.** Built in 1891 by Sargeant for Andrew Pears, she had a hull of bright mahogany with teak fittings. In 1897 she was seen at Henley Regatta, being moored in one of the prime positions between Phyllis Court and the winning post. Length 53 ft, beam 7 ft 2 in, draught 2ft 6 in, displacement 5¾ tons, speed 9 mph.

J. Cowan

49. **THE 35 FT *MYIONU*, 1891**. As advertised in the *Lock to Lock Times*, 27 August 1892.

J. Cowan

50. ***VOLT*, 1891**. From the *Lock to Lock Times*, 13 June 1891.

J. Cowan

51. ***LILY*, 1892**. *Lily* had been on show at the Crystal Palace Electrical Exhibition prior to launching at the beginning of June 1892. She was used at Henley Regatta and afterwards moored by the owner at Goring.

J. Cowan

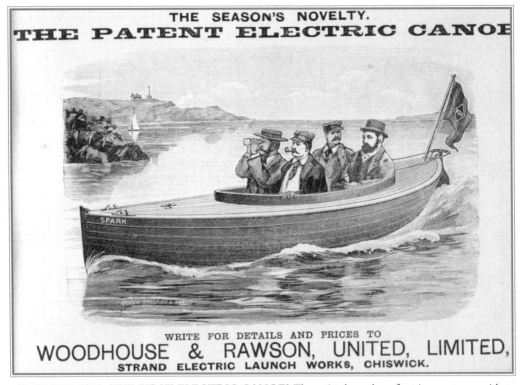

THE SEASON'S NOVELTY.
THE PATENT ELECTRIC CANOE

WRITE FOR DETAILS AND PRICES TO
WOODHOUSE & RAWSON, UNITED, LIMITED,
STRAND ELECTRIC LAUNCH WORKS, CHISWICK.

52. *SPARK*, **1892, THE FIRST ELECTRIC CANOE?** The artist shows her afloat in an estuary with a lighthouse in the distance.

J. Cowan

This move brought more varied business to the Strand yard. In March 1891 a pinnace *Electric* was launched. Intended for the transport of troops between the dockyards at Chatham and Sheerness, she was 48½ ft long overall, 8¾ ft beam, 2¼ ft draught and weighed 4¾ tons; she could carry forty fully-equipped soldiers. Fitted with seventy Epstein cells supplying a motor developing 5½ bhp and driving a 22 in propeller at 750 rpm, the boat was expected to have a maximum speed of 8 knots.[12]

Woodhouse & Rawson, like Immisch, realized the importance of having their own charging stations and quickly set up a land-based charging station at Chertsey under the management of Mr J. Taylor.[13]

Two more electric launches emerged from the Strand yard during 1891.[14] Andrew Pears must have been pleased with his first launch because he now ordered the larger *Glow Worm* capable of carrying forty passengers. With a length of 53 ft, beam of 7 ft 2 in and draught of 2 ft 6 in, she had a displacement of 5¾ tons and a speed of about 9 mph. She was built of bright mahogany with teak fittings and was lit by electricity and – a new feature – carried a searchlight.

The other launch *Myionu* was smaller, having a length of 35 ft, beam of 5 ft 6 in,

53. *FLASH*, 1892, THE SECOND ELECTRIC CANOE? Both *Spark* and *Flash* were built at Sargeant's yard and demonstrated at Henley Regatta in 1892.

J. Cowan

draught of 18 in and a displacement of 3¼ tons. Her maximum speed was also about 9 mph but, unlike *Glow Worm*, the hull was made of mild steel with teak fittings. Her owner, Captain Homfrey of the Horse Guards, probably kept her at Maidenhead.

From 1891 onwards Sargeant built a number of smaller electric launches, such as the *Volt*, the *Lily*, which was shown at the Crystal Palace Electrical Exhibition in 1892, a mahogany launch *Bella*, initially moored at Goring, and the steel-hulled launch *Daffodil*, with saloon and accommodation for ten passengers.[15] It is interesting to note that Sargeant provided different steering positions: in the bow, amidships and tiller steering at the stern. He also produced a rather curious design of 'Patent Electric Canoe' capable of carrying four people. It is reported that two of these canoes, named *Spark* and *Volt*, were on the water at Henley Regatta in 1892 and, if this was true, Sargeant's yard was probably the first on the river to produce an electric canoe. Built of mahogany, they could carry four passengers and had a length of 18 ft, beam of 3 ft 9 in and a draught of 1 ft. The ½ hp Woodhouse & Rawson motor and Epstein accumulators gave them a speed of 6 mph. It is not clear what the 'Patent' referred to but it was said that 'owing to the extreme simplicity of the mechanism and controlling arrangements, there is practically nothing to learn, and customers will find no difficulty in working their own boats'.[16]

54. **GLOW WORM AT HENLEY IN 1900**. *Glow Worm* was still in use in 1900, having been acquired by
T. Shepherd, the owner of the famous Red Lion Hotel and boatyard at Henley-on-Thames.

C.J.B. Miller, The Red Lion Hotel, Henley

In 1897 *Glow Worm* was seen at Henley Regatta, being moored in one of the prime
positions between Phyllis Court and the winning post.[17] She was still in use in 1900, having
been acquired by T. Shepherd who owned the famous Red Lion Hotel and boatyard at
Henley-on-Thames. He advertised outings, daily from Friday to Monday, between Henley
and Pangbourne or Cliveden and back. Leaving Paddington at 10 a.m. in a comfortable first
class compartment, you would arrive at Henley fifty minutes later. A carriage would then
take you to the Red Lion landing stage by the bridge where you would board the *Glow
Worm* or one of three steam launches. You would have lunch on board, and after an
excellent table d'hôte dinner at the Red Lion you would arrive back at Paddington at 10.07
p.m. The cost? One guinea! The *Glow Worm* was licensed to carry sixty passengers but the
hotel pointed out that the comfortable carrying capacity was thirty![18]

Sargeant's business must have been outgrowing the capacity of the Strand yard for during
the winter of 1891 he bought a site at Eel Pie Island, where he set up new sheds and a
large charging station.[19] This comprised a 100 hp steam engine driving two shunt-wound
dynamos. The circuitry was arranged so that voltages between 100 and 300 with currents
up to 200 amps could be fed through twelve circuits. During daytime, when no charging
was being done, the electrical power was used to drive the machinery in the workshops.
This new yard traded under the name of The Thames Electric and Steam Launch Co.
because Sargeant was, of course, still engaged in the building of large steam launches.[20]

55. **THE STRAND WORKS**. This was the original boatyard rented by
William Sargeant at Strand-on-the-Green close to Kew Bridge. Reproduced
from a picture loaned by Brian Hillsdon, historian and librarian, Steam Boat
Association of Great Britain.

Engineering, *23 January 1891*

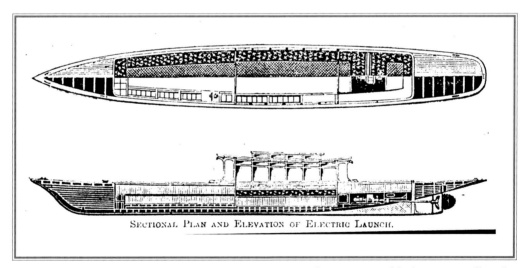

56. **SARGEANT ELECTRIC LAUNCH DESIGN.** General arrangement of the larger types of launch
built by Sargeant, published by the *Electrical Review* to illustrate a report that during 1892 Sargeant was
planning to build a 75 ft electric launch. This would have been the largest electric launch in the world at that
time but there is no record that she was ever built. Compare this with the designs of *Viscountess Bury* and
Glow Worm.

Electrical Review, *4 April 1892*

The last order built at the Strand yard may have been *The Bonnie Southport*, which was supplied to Southport Corporation for use on their artificial lake, and proved very successful during the Easter holidays in 1892. With a length of 38 ft 5 in, beam of 7 ft 6 in and draught of 2 ft 3 in she could carry forty passengers. She was carvel-built with a large counter stern and was fitted with a 5 hp 'W&R' motor. This is the first mention of a Woodhouse & Rawson motor being installed in one of Sargeant's boats.[21]

Sargeant started work at the Eel Pie yard with an order book for at least four electric launches, including the fourth boat to be built for Andrew Pears. Probably named *Pilot*, this was designed especially for speed and somewhat resembled a torpedo boat.[22] Two of the other orders were for the Star and Garter Hotel, Richmond Hill, for use as charter boats. Mr W.T. Crawshay of Caversham Park also ordered a launch *Florentia*, and the *Meteor*, previously named the *Pioneer*, was fitted out for Mr Arthur Ash.[23]

Pride of all was to be a 75 ft long electric launch, which would succeed the *Viscountess Bury* as the largest electric launch in the world. With a beam of 13 ft and a draught of 3 ft 6 in, she would have a displacement of 16½ tons and a speed of 8 knots. The Electrical Power Storage Co.'s accumulators, using ebonite boxes, would supply current at 400 volts to a motor directly connected to the propeller which would run at 600 rpm.

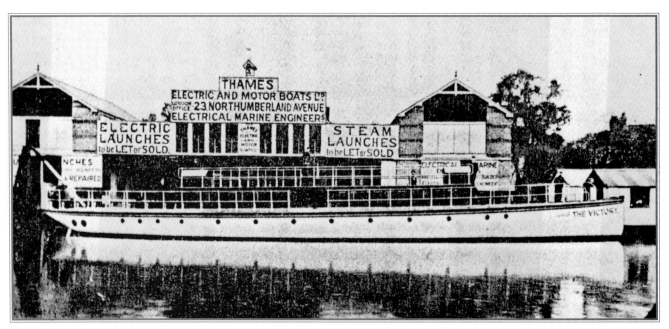

57. *VICTORY*, 1905, THE LARGEST ELECTRIC LAUNCH IN THE WORLD. Sargeant's ambition to build the largest electric launch in the world was achieved with the launch of the 93 ft *Victory*. She exceeded the length of the *Viscountess Bury* by 28 ft. She was bought in 1907 by Joseph Theophilus Mears, who took over the business and boatbuilding works of the Thames Electric and Motor Launch Co. Length 93 ft 2 in and licensed to carry 350 passengers above Westminster Bridge. The original picture is from the W. Caisley Collection and is reproduced from Frank L. Dix, *Royal River Highway*, David & Charles, Newton Abbot, 1985.

Sargeant planned to fit his patented single lever control, which would give the four speeds of half- and full-speed ahead and the same astern. She was intended to run between the new lock at Richmond to Teddington, a distance of 3 miles. Every convenience was to be fitted including 100 volt incandescent lamps and electric navigation lights.[24] However, no further record of this launch has been found and presumably Sargeant had to shelve his plans to build the largest electric passenger launch in the world until he launched the *Victory* in 1906.

The Directors of Woodhouse & Rawson realized that Sargeant was providing them with a platform for developing a global market. During 1892 the editor of the American magazine *Rudder* wrote: 'We call the attention of yachtsmen to the advertisement of the Woodhouse & Rawson Co., the great English electricians, and the original and only successful builders of electric launches. The electric launch is almost unknown in this country, although hundreds of them are electricing upon European waters. The Woodhouse & Rawson Co. will be pleased to correspond with American yachtsmen.' In the same issue Woodhouse & Rawson inserted an advertisement that among others stated: 'The only perfect power-driven pleasure boat. No fire, no smell, no danger. No government licence required.'[25]

At the beginning of 1893 Sargeant reported that business was good. Besides building a number of launches and gigs, he had a 73 ft steam launch on the stocks. This was probably to be used on the Thames but it was to be marketed also for use on the canals of France, Belgium and Holland.[26]

Unfortunately, sometime during 1893 or the early part of 1894, Woodhouse & Rawson were declared bankrupt.

The subsequent story of William Sargeant remains undiscovered. The Thames Electric and Steam Launch Co. does not appear in the receivers' report on Woodhouse & Rawson and was presumably sold off in 1893 or 1894. Dix has reported that during 1894 the company was working from Isleworth with the small twenty-six passenger electric launch *Pearl* and a much larger 120 passenger steamboat *Duke of York*.[27]

In 1896 there is a report that Sargeant, engineer and builder of Chiswick, took a Mr Gudgeon to court to claim the sum of £18 in respect of an electric launch which was exhibited at the Aquarium, Westminster, and afterwards sold for £100. The claim was for expenses in painting and varnishing the boat, and taking it up river to Staines.[28]

In 1905 Sargeant's ambition to build the largest electric launch in the world was achieved with the launch of the *Victory*. With a length of 93 ft 2 in, she outstripped the *Viscountess Bury* by 28 ft and was licensed to carry 350 passengers on the Thames above Westminster Bridge. She was bought in 1907 by Joseph Theophilus Mears, who took over Sargeant's business and boatbuilding works which he then used as a springboard for quickly buying other boats and eventually expanding into the largest passenger fleet on the Thames, keeping *Victory* registered by the Board of Trade until 1913.[29]

During that first decade of the twentieth century Sargeant must have decided that the steam launch, but interestingly not the electric launch, had run its course because by 1907 his business had been renamed the Thames Electric and Motor Launch Co. He himself probably retired at this time although he lived on until 1918, when he died at the age of eighty-two.

Chapter 7

SAM SAUNDERS – DESIGN FOR SPEED

Sam Saunders was well established as a boatbuilder, with a flair for imaginative design and original construction methods, by the time he built his first electric launch in 1895. His activities as a boatbuilder have been chronicled in detail by Wheeler[1] and the subsequent establishment of the world famous flying boat company, Saunders-Roe, has been fully described by Wheeler and Tagg.[2] From an early age Saunders was attracted by the potential of steam power and began to establish his reputation as a builder of high class large and fast steam launches. In the early 1880s he had set up the business of S.E. Saunders, Launch Builder and Engineer at Goring.

As steam engines became more efficient, Saunders sought ways of reducing the hull

58. **THE SPRINGFIELD WORKS AT GORING IN 1900.**

Ray Wheeler

THE THAMES ILLUSTRATED.-Advertisements.

LAUNCH BUILDER AND ENGINEER

ESTABLISHED 1870

S.E.SAUNDERS,

BOAT, PUNT AND CANOE BUILDER,

GORING-on-THAMES,

At the new Springfield Works on the Moulsford Reach is the largest Slipway, Launch Building and Repairing Works on the Upper Thames.

First-class Moorings for Houseboats, Safe from Floods.

Telegraphic Address: "SAUNDERS, GORING, OXON." Station, Goring, G.W.R.

ELECTRIC CHARGING STATION.

IMPORTER OF CANADIAN CANOES.

BOAT BUILDING OF THE HIGHEST CLASS IN ALL ITS BRANCHES.

SAUNDERS' BOAT FITTINGS ARE UNEQUALLED.

STEAM, ELECTRIC, AND OIL LAUNCHES BUILT TO ORDER.

LAUNCH AND BOAT FITTINGS OF ALL DESCRIPTIONS KEPT IN STOCK.

HOUSING, REPAIRING, AND VARNISHING EXECUTED IN BEST POSSIBLE MANNER.

59. **ADVERTISEMENT FROM** *THAMES ILLUSTRATED* **OF 1897**. The electric charging station was used by Immisch's electric launch *Eta* in 1889 and Saunders built his first reported electric launch in 1895.

R.L. Wheeler

weight and, in the early 1890s, he had the idea of using a construction of laminations of wood and canvas sewn together with copper wire, a process which he named 'Consuta'. This reduced the hull weight substantially and enabled him to increase the length to beam ratio, with the result that his launches could achieve higher speeds than those built with conventional materials and designs. This experience of design for high speed was the basis for his subsequent success in boatbuilding.

The experiments on electric launches during the 1880s and Immisch's presence at Henley in 1889 must have turned Saunders' attention to the scope for electric propulsion. He had installed an electrical generating set at the Goring Works to supply lighting and drive some of the new tools, and it was an easy matter to adapt it for charging electric boats. In September of that year the *Electrical Review* reported on a trip made in Immisch's launch *Eta* between Hampton and Oxford. One of the passengers was Mr Saunders of the Miller of Mansfield Hotel in Goring.[3] The party stayed overnight at Maidenhead, where the launch was recharged, and then travelled the 34 miles to Goring where recharging was carried out 'during the small hours of the night at the charging

60. *LORELEI,* **FROM THE SAUNDERS BROCHURE**. Built in 1904 at the Springfield Works, Goring, this was the largest electric launch built by Saunders.

R.L. Wheeler

61. *SOLENT,* **BUILT IN 1903 AT THE WEST COWES WORKS FOR HM CUSTOMS**. Length 27 ft, speed 7½ knots.

R.L. Wheeler

62. **SAUNDERS ELECTRIC LAUNCH** *PH*. This launch was built at the Springfield Works in 1902. Believed renamed *Patricia* in 1908, probably when converted to an Austin 10 petrol engine. Length 30 ft, speed 8 mph.

R.L. Wheeler

station'. Presumably this was at Sam Saunders' works. On the return journey a charge was put into the batteries during a lunch stop at Goring.

In 1894 Saunders moved into Springfield Works, a purpose-built boathouse, where two years later he built the famous 27½ knot *Consuta* launch for the Stewards of Henley Regatta. It was clear that this design would also be excellent as a light low-drag hull suitable for electric power, and in 1895 he built his first recorded electric boat, *Avalon*, which was converted to petrol in 1907. Another of his electric boats, the 40 ft *Magnolia*, is still in use as a 165 hp petrol-engined launch carrying the name *Majestic*.

By the end of the 1890s Saunders realized that he would not be able to go on testing his fast launches on the Thames at Goring and, in 1901, he set up a new works at

63. **BOSSOM'S ELECTRIC LAUNCH** *ROATH'S PRIDE*. The original hull of *PH* was too far gone to be restored and was used by Bossom's Boatyard, Oxford, in 1972 as the plug for a GRP mould. Two GRP hulls were made from this mould – *Patricia* and *Roath's Pride*. The former was fitted with a 3 kw motor at 72 volts and propeller speed of 900 rpm. The latter had a 1.4 kw motor at 38 volts. Length 31 ft 9 in, beam 6 ft 6 in, draught 1 ft 9 in. In 1983 Rear Admiral Percy Gick, President of the Electric Boat Association, took *Patricia* across the Solent to the Isle of Wight for Cowes week and gave HRH The Duke of Edinburgh a trip from the royal yacht *Britannia* to his ocean racer.

Tom Ballance, Bossom's Boatyard

Cowes. He continued to build a few electric launches at both Goring and Cowes but they were very much a sideline, and in any case the petrol engine was now supplanting electric drives. Finally, in 1911 the Springfield Works was sold to the Thames Launch Co. of Hobbs of Henley. After the Second World War, the works fell into disuse, the buildings were pulled down and the site has reverted to nature.

The electrical systems used in Saunders' launches were described in a brochure produced in about 1905. For the large launches a heavy type of battery was used because high speed was not required for very long and they were less expensive than the smaller type of cells used in the faster 30–35 ft launches. In these boats the cells were fitted into nesting boxes, their connections being to Saunders' own design and burnt 'lead to lead' in order to improve the electrical path without the possibility of corrosion. The connections between boxes were through screwed fittings, insulated with tape.

The motors were described in the brochure as being of Saunders' own design and were built to run at a wide range of speeds, without the use of any external resistances and at constant volts. They had two commutators of hard copper and large dimensions, to ensure cool running, and were fitted with carbon brushes. The armatures were slot-wound to ensure long life and protection from mechanical damage. The motors were double-wound so that in effect two series motors were formed.

The controller was also to Saunders' own specification. The battery cells were always kept in series and the controller varied the relationship of one motor to the other, as well as the armatures and field windings, so that a number of speeds (in the 50 ft launch *Lorelei*, 5 speeds) could be obtained both in forward and reverse. Launches of 32 ft length using this electrical system could run at 8 mph for 3 to 3½ hours, at 6½ mph for 5 to 6 hours, and at 5 mph for about 8 hours.

Saunders was one of the main importers of Canadian canoes, which were brought over in large numbers from the builders, the Peterborough Company of Ontario.[4] There is no record that Saunders fitted any out with an electrical system although it would be surprising if he did not at least produce an experimental boat since electric canoes are both elegant and fast.

Table 1 – Saunders Electric Launches

The electric launches known to have been built by the Saunders Patent Launch Syndicate and by Sam Saunders at the Springfield Works in Goring and the Saunders Works at East Cowes have been chronicled in the histories of the Saunders' enterprises by Wheeler and Wheeler and Tagg as follows:

Avalon	1895	Length 42 ft, speed 7 mph. Tunnel stern. In 1907 converted by Messrs Hart, Harden of Hampton Wick for the owner, Mr Hudson E. Kearley to a 24 hp four cylinder Napier petrol engine. Running at 900 rpm, the new motor increased the launch's speed to just over 14 mph.[5]
Arethusa	1899	Length 40 ft, speed 12 mph.
Empress Electra	1901	Length 40 ft.
Magnolia	1902	Length 40 ft, beam 6 ft, speed 10 mph. Built at Cowes in 1902. Converted to petrol and now named *Majestic*, she is currently fitted with 165 hp General Motors engine which gives her a speed of 18 mph. In use as umpire boat at Henley Regatta.
P.H.	1902	Length 30 ft, speed 8 mph. This is believed to have been renamed *Patricia* in 1908. In 1972 the hull was used as a plug for a GRP mould manufactured by Bossoms Boatyard of Oxford.[6] The new hull has a length of 31 ft 9 in, beam 6½ ft, waterline length 30 ft 2 in, draught 1 ft 9 in. New boats made from this mould were *Patricia* and *Roath's Pride*, both fitted with 3 kw electric motors.
Springfield	1902	Length 32 ft, speed 8 mph.
Lorelei	1903	Length 50 ft, beam 7 ft, speed 10 mph, 7½ kw. Controller of Johnson-Lundell type giving five forward and astern speeds.
Solent	1903	Length 27 ft, speed 8½ mph. Used by HM Customs.
Pinnace	1904	Built for the royal yacht *Victoria and Albert*.

Chapter 8

NED ANDREWS – SKILLED FISHERMAN AND BOATBUILDER

Ned Andrews, born in 1846, was the third generation of Andrews professional fishermen. In 1821 his grandfather E. Andrews set up the first boathiring business to operate in Maidenhead but the family treated it simply as part of the service to their clients. Their main livelihood came from fishing and his father, who died in 1863, was 'the finest rod and line fisher, in all styles, ever known on the Thames'.[1] Even in 1886, Taunt noted in his map of the Thames that there were eleven fishermen in Maidenhead, including Ed. Andrews, M. Andrews and C. Andrews and that excellent fishing was available, Taunt extolling the chubb, the capital swims for gudgeon and barbel, and the quantity of jack, perch, trout and other fish.[2]

However, earning a living out of fishing during the 1860s became increasingly difficult. Although Ned knew every inch of the Thames in his area, he found that he couldn't support a family on the eight or ten shillings, less the provision of punt, bait and tackle, that he could earn in a day. The growth in the number of steam launches made decent fishing increasingly difficult and the lengthening of the closed season cut the fishing season down to three months.

In 1872 therefore, Ned decided to revive the boatletting business which had been allowed to run down and to capitalize on his experience of racing punts. He had started punting when only eight years old and became so clever with handling the punt pole that, aged only twenty, he became Professional Punting Champion of the Thames. Tagg of Hampton challenged him for the title in 1877, with stakes of £20 a-side. The race took place over the Championship course at Bray, and Ned won by several lengths. The following year, however, Ned was beaten by Abel Beasley of Oxford and although he continued to win a number of prizes during the next decade, he was again beaten by Abel in 1886, although this time by a narrower margin of only a length and a half.

Ned's boatyard was located on the Buckinghamshire bank alongside the Brigade of Guards Club just above Maidenhead Bridge. As Londoners began to take advantage of the new Great Western Railway trains to Taplow and Maidenhead, he saw the opportunities in hiring boats to the wider public, and by 1890 he 'owned about a hundred handsome and completely equipped boats, punts and canoes of all descriptions'.[3]

During the following year Ned moved across the river and built a new and larger boathouse on Ray Mead Road above Maidenhead Bridge. The larger facilities enabled him to start building steam launches such as *Ned*, *Nell*, *Bertha* and *Nip-Nip*. He also acquired large workshops close by in Oldfield Lane, and in due course built a showroom with living

64. **THE ANDREWS SHOWROOMS, RAY MEAD ROAD, MAIDENHEAD**. The showrooms were on the left–hand side of the road going upstream from Maidenhead Bridge opposite the boathouses. This photograph was taken when the river had flooded over the road; a more or less annual occurrence at the turn of the century.

S. Arthur

65. **ANDREWS 30 FT SALOON LAUNCH** *BARBEL*. Ned Andrews' boathouse in Ray Mead Road, Maidenhead, is in the background.

S. Arthur

66. **ANDREWS 30 FT SALOON LAUNCH *BREAM***. It is said that *Barbel* and *Bream* were identical. *Bream* was converted to petrol by Golding Bros who used her as a tripping boat at Windsor between 1937 and 1950, when she was broken up on the Brocas.

S. Arthur

accommodation over on the other side of Ray Mead Road to the main boathouses. Tragically, Ned suffered a serious loss when his eldest son, also a fine fisherman and punter, died in 1890; his younger son, however, quickly grew into the business while his two daughters looked after the making and upholstering of the punt and boat cushions.

In 1889, when Immisch set up his depot just a little further up the river by Boulter's Lock, Ned, as a fisherman, would almost certainly have been attracted by the quietness

67. **THE 30 FT OPEN LAUNCH *PIKE***. Launched in 1899, *Pike* was run by Andrews until 1937 when Goldings of Windsor bought her. Andrews probably converted her to petrol and Goldings refitted her with another petrol engine.

S. Arthur

and cleanliness of the electric boats, although it was only towards the end of the decade that he actually built his first electric boat. It is reported that in 1898 he launched two electric boats named *Bleak*, described as a splendid little launch, and *Gudgeon*.[4]

When he made his decision, he moved quickly and by 1904 he had a fleet of a dozen or so electric launches, all named after fish except for the flagship which was, of course, named *The Angler*.

THE ANDREWS ELECTRIC BOAT FLEET IN 1904

Name	Probable date launched (or reported afloat)	Length ft
Angler	1902	45
Barbel		
Bleak	June 1898	
Bream	(1899)	30
Carp	(1903)	
Chubb	(1892)	
Dace	1899	
Eel	1903	41½
Gudgeon	1898	
Minnow		
Pike	June 1899	30
Roach	(1903)	
Tench		30

68. **OPEN DAY BOAT *CHUBB*.** Built about 1898, *Chubb* was bought by Golding Bros of Windsor in 1937 and renamed *Chums*.

S. Arthur

In 1910 disaster struck. There was a severe fire in one of his boathouses. The following extracts from a detailed report in the *Maidenhead Advertiser* give a graphic picture of the seriousness of the fire.[5]

A disastrous fire occurred by the riverside on Friday evening last. The total damage being estimated at upwards of £3,000, the great portion being happily covered by insurance. The scene of the conflict so illuminated the sky that it could be seen for many miles. It was one of the extensive boat and launch houses of Messrs E. Andrews and Sons situated on the east of Ray Park Avenue and between this thoroughfare and Ray Mead Road and the Thames. The structure, substantially erected with 14 inch concrete walls and heavy steel girders supporting the roof was used for purposes of boat, punt and launch storage and was about 60 ft by 40 ft. The contents of the boathouse where the fire originated were wholly destroyed.

Seven electric launches were so completely destroyed that only the twisted propellers attached to pieces of charred woodwork remained. Of these launches, four were new and three of them were shortly to be despatched on order to Glasgow. The

69. **THE ANGLER IN 1968**. *The Angler*, built in 1902, was run as a tripping launch by Andrews & Son until 1938 when Golding Bros of Windsor bought her and operated her out of Windsor until 1968. She was then bought by David Roberts and this photo shows her being moved into her new home. In 1992 she passed to Brian Bidston whose boatbuilder, David Graham of Wargrave, is completing the restoration.

David Graham

70. **EEL, RENAMED *WOODLAND LILY*.** Seen here in 1992 at Henley, *Eel* was built in 1903 by
E. Andrews and Son of Maidenhead, and has been in use ever since, first as a tripping boat and since 1966 as
a private launch. Converted to petrol in the 1920s, she was fitted out with steam by Lawrence Weaver in
1966 and renamed *Woodland Lily*. Length 41 ft 6 in, LWL 37 ft, beam 7 ft, draught 2 ft 9 in, speed 7 knots.

E.P. Hawthorne

71. **OPEN LAUNCH *DACE* c. 1912.** *Dace* was bought by Major Bateman of Bourne End in 1899. Carr
at the Ray Motor Co. on Boulter's Lock Island repaired the armature of her motor in August 1913 when she
was in use as a hireboat by Woodhouse of the Maidenhead & District Boating Co. at Maidenhead. Kneeling
on the bank is Bill Horsham's stepson Fred, who later became the Thames Punting Champion.

G. Banham

names of the launches lost were the *Flapper, Crayfish, Rudd* and *Mimi*. The other three were unnamed. The launches were from 28 ft to 29 ft in length. Practically the whole were fitted and furnished. Half a ton of horsehair went up in flames. In the engineers' shop, the electric motors were rendered useless. It may be mentioned that two of the electric launches destroyed were on view at an exhibition at Olympia two or three years ago.

This report is particularly interesting because it indicates that Andrews was still building electric launches as late as 1910 whereas most other boatbuilders had given up electrics and moved over to petrol engines.

Despite the bottom dropping out of the electric boat business, Andrews kept as many of the launches going as possible, converting them to petrol at various times prior to the First World War. The business continued to use some of them as hireboats until the late 1930s when four, *Pike, Bream, Chubb* and *The Angler,* were sold off to Golding Bros of Windsor. Goldings retained their names except for *Chubb* which they changed to *Chums*. *Eel* was sold to Arthur Jacobs of Windsor and *Tench* was sold to a private owner.

When Goldings bought the *Bream*, they removed the saloon and fanlight and used her as an open launch similar to the *Pike*. Both of these launches were laid up between 1939 and 1945 and *Bream* was then sold to Mr Harrison who ran a factory on the Slough Trading Estate. Harrison fitted her out with the saloon which Goldings had removed from *The Angler* and stored under the arches of the railway line into Windsor. *Pike* was sold on to a Thames lighterman who poled her all the way down from Windsor to the Tideway.

Eel, Tench and *The Angler* have survived until the present day (see Chapter 11). *Eel*, renamed *Woodland Lily* in 1966, is fully restored; the other two launches are undergoing restoration and will be back on Thames waters in due course.

The illustrations of these boats are reproduced from pictures supplied by George Banham and Sammy Arthur, both of whom had first-hand knowledge of the Andrews tripping boats still in use during the 1950s. The pictures and additional information for the boats being restored have been supplied by the owners and their builders undertaking the restorations.

Chapter 9

BOND'S OF MAIDENHEAD

Bond's of Maidenhead was one of the earliest boatyards on the River Thames. One report states that the business was started by Jonathan Bond, a drover, who bought the ferry at Maidenhead where the towpath crossed the river.[1] Although the bridge carrying the Great West Road across the river at Maidenhead had been built in 1772, the ferry continued to serve the barge traffic for another century, perhaps because its tolls may have been less than those of the bridge.

The building of the famous Brunel Bridge by the Great Western Railway in 1838 opened up the rail link between London and the West Country and was one of the causes of the gradual demise of the river barge traffic over the next thirty years. During the 1840s Jonathan Bond's business comprised a boathouse, ferry rights and a horse-drawn barge which he used for passenger trips.[2] However, the railway actually brought new opportunities as Londoners discovered the pleasures of getting out of the city. Leaving the train at Taplow, they walked to the river where they found the Orkney Arms pub (now Skindles Hotel), and took a trip on Bond's wherry. As the number of visitors increased, Bond realized that by hiring out skiffs, other people would do the hard work.

From such beginnings Bond built up a business which by 1890 was growing rapidly. Jonathan died of diabetes in 1892 and the business passed on to his son, also named Jonathan, who carried on the expansion. 'In a couple of hours, Mr Bond let out 150 boats,' reported the *Maidenhead Advertiser* on 21 June 1893. Most of these, of course, would have been skiffs and punts but Bond's steam launch *Gambol* was also out. The company soon gained a widespread reputation for building steam launches and by 1895 Bond is reported to have had a fleet of elegant electric and steam launches. There were at least ten of the latter, ranging from the 73 ft *Emperor* to the 30 ft *Gaily*.[3] He also had some hundreds of rowing boats, punts and canoes and five well-equipped boathouses, two of which were adjacent to the Riviera Hotel, two upstream of Maidenhead bridge and the fifth on the Bray side of the bridge.

He also rented what the *Financial Times* of 1891 described as 'next to the site of the Bank of England or the Mansion House the most desirable freehold to own in this country . . .'.[4] A small strip of river frontage, 140 ft long and 28 ft deep, close by Maidenhead Bridge, was let by auction to Bond for a rental of £215 per year. The land was owned by the Maidenhead Corporation and the *Financial Times* reckoned that at 3½ per cent it was worth over £6,000, equivalent to £50,000 per acre. It is said that at the auction an outsider, bidding against Jonathan, congratulated him on having obtained it cheap. 'Cheap,' replied Jonathan, 'You call £215 per year, cheap!' The other stuttered, '£215 per year. I thought it was freehold!'[5]

72. BOND'S BOATHOUSES AT MAIDENHEAD, 1904.

G. Banham

The first electric boats, *Viscountess Bury* and *Ray Mead*, owned by Immisch and Kerbey Bowen respectively, appeared on the river at Maidenhead in 1889. In June it was reported that they were hired by such a large party (totalling 181 guests) from London that two other launches were also required, Mr Bill's *Mayflower* and Bond's *Gainsborough*, both of which were steam.[6]

In 1897, the year of Queen Victoria's Diamond Jubilee, the Maidenhead boatbuilders and hirers were preparing for a busy season. Bond's 73 ft steam launch *Emperor* was taken up the Kennet & Avon Canal for a fortnight and he commemorated the Jubilee by starting work on a large launch to be named *Empress of India*, capable of accommodating 250 passengers. Bond was advertising himself as 'Designer & Constructor of Steam launches' and his advertisement mentioned the 66 ft *Formosus*, and the 50 ft *Sportsman*, *Gainsborough*, *Gambol*, *Gaily* and *Wave*.[7] However, speaking at the Maidenhead and Bray Waterman's annual dinner in September, Bond stressed that the season had not been prosperous for them and blamed, among other things, the Jubilee and the new-found enthusiasm of the ladies for cycling.[8] Bad weather and an early onset of fog and drenching rain in September didn't help either. Nevertheless, Jonathan continued to build the larger steam launches, such as the 83 ft *Empress of India* in 1898 and the 73 ft *Her Majesty* in 1902, thereby establishing his business as one of the foremost builders of steamboats in the area.

Bond's part in the electric boat scene is not well documented. It is probable that in 1898 he built the *Esperanza*,[9] although there is a letter in Carr's records from the Manager of Hill's Rubber Co. in Reading which seems to suggest that Saunders of Goring may have built her in 1896. However, Wheeler has found no trace of such a boat in the Saunders' history.[10]

73. BOND'S ELECTRIC LAUNCHES IN 1904.

Salter's Guide, 1904

By 1900 there were five electric launch companies operating in Maidenhead: Immisch, Thames Valley, Andrews, Bowen and Woodhouse. Bond must have realized that he had to offer electric boats too, and so in 1904 his letter heading styled him as an 'Electric and Steam Launch Builder'. However, he may have concentrated on buying in electric boats for hire as his advertisement in Salter's Guide for the same year listed seven electric launches for hire: *Tagus* 45 ft, *Kerlew* 40 ft, *Primate* 40 ft, *Colonial* 32 ft, *Gull* 27 ft, *Seapie* 27 ft, *Oldfield* 24 ft.[11] Other launches which were in the fleet at various times until the 1930s included *Flosshilde* 55 ft, *St Patrick* 50 ft, *Emerald Isle* 45 ft, *Brown Duck* 35 ft, *Alpha* 32 ft, *Heron* 30 ft, *Marconi* 30 ft, *Rabbit* 28 ft, and *Rowena* 20 ft.[12] Two six-seater launches with awnings, the *Cherie* and *Toni*, were also advertised.

When Jonathan Bond died, his elder son, well liked by the boatmen, should have inherited the business but tragically he had been drowned earlier in the Bray Reach. The business passed to George Bond, who had seen service during the Boer War where he rose to the rank of Major in the Royal Army Service Corps, Inland Waterways Section.

In 1914 George Bond acquired the Immisch Maidenhead business and presumably added some of the Immisch boats to his fleet. When the boating trade came back to normal after 1918, the era of the electric launch had passed but Bond maintained a few electric launches for hire during the inter-war period. His advertisement in Salter's Guide for 1936 shows a picture of an electric launch and states 'Motor and Electric

Phone 16.

BOND'S
Launch and Boat Builders and Proprietors,

MAIDENHEAD BRIDGE
(Adjoining Skindles Hotel)

ELECTRIC
CANOES
A
SPECIALITY.

PUNTS,
BOATS,
DINGHEYS
FOR HIRE.

Motor and Electric Launches for Hire at Moderate Prices.
One of the largest and smartest Fleets on the Upper Thames.

74. **BOND'S ADVERTISEMENT, 1936**. Bond hired out electric launches until 1937 and electric canoes until 1955.

Salter's Guide, 1936

75. **MAJOR GEORGE BOND, 1969**. Aged ninety-four and confined to a wheelchair, George Bond surveys the 52 ft electric launch *Esperanza* being refitted by Lawrence Weaver. Built in 1898 as an electric launch, Bond owned her between 1920 and 1940 and fitted her out with a petrol engine. Lawrence Weaver bought her in 1968 and converted her to steam in 1968. Courtesy D. Roberts collection.

Slough Evening Mail, 3 June 1969

Launches for Hire at Moderate Prices', but in fact all the electric launches had been converted to petrol by the end of that year.

It is also not clear to what extent Bond was involved in building and hiring electric canoes before 1914. It is believed, for example, that he built *Beazie* and *Juliana* in 1908 and 1910 respectively. He also hired out electric canoes to the Guards Club in Maidenhead. However, he was certainly involved during the heyday of electric canoes, which was experienced for a few years in the early 1920s, and he was one of the few boatbuilders who continued to hire out electric canoes until at least 1955.[13] Furthermore, he was responsible for what was probably the last electric canoe launched on the Thames until the 1980s. She was the 28½ ft *Victoria*, built in 1936 and fitted with a 4 kw 80 volt electric motor. She had a top speed of 7½ mph and a possible cruising range of 37 miles.[14]

When petrol rationing was imposed during the Second World War, Bond's converted one of their 25 ft slipper launches, the *Petrel*, to electric by fitting a 2½ kw motor and eighty Britannia nickel iron cells. This gave her a speed of 5 mph and an endurance of about 4½ hours. She was once used to convey a bride and groom from Maidenhead to the reception at Bray, the guests following in the electric launch *Flosshilde*.

Chapter 10

MORE THAMES ELECTRIC BOATBUILDERS

Pleasure boating on the Thames was big business. During the hearing in 1889 on the application for a licence for the Quarry House, now known as the Bounty, at Bourne End, it was stated that at the busiest part of the season, 17,000 boats passed through Boulter's Lock, 14,000 through Cookham Lock and 12,000 through Marlow Lock. In June 1890 it was reported that there were 278 steam launches registered for use on the Thames. Ten years later there were just over 10,000 pleasure boats of all kinds registered.

The number of lock tickets sold in 1898 was 257,307. Indeed, the situation had reached a point where the number of boats passing through the locks had increased to such an extent that people got tired of waiting their turn. For example, on Ascot Sunday 1899, because of the pressure of boats, only 1,000 boats negotiated Boulter's Lock, and it was said that the river downstream of the lock 'presented the appearance throughout the afternoon and evening of Henley Regatta course in miniature, the scene being most brilliant and animated and those on the bank had ample opportunity to admire and criticise the latest fashions in costumes and millinery'.[1] In the middle of all this, the Prince of Wales arrived aboard Immisch's electric launch *Eta* and the way was quickly cleared for him to pass straight through.

The popularity of the river continued to grow; on Ascot Sunday in 1901 new records were set when 240 steam and electric launches negotiated Boulter's Lock.[2] One of these was the electric launch *Midget* with Prince Soltykoff, a familiar face at Newmarket, aboard. Such was the demand for boats that a well-known boathirer kept back an electric launch and made £15 for it for the day instead of the usual £5 or so.

Another great boost to the hiring business came from the demand for boats to attend the regattas. These events were more frequent than today and they became an important date in the social calendar, organized by well-known houseowners along the river and attended by the summer residents and hundreds of visitors who came down by train for the day. Electric launches were much in evidence at these regattas, being moored along the bank and splendidly decorated with flowers and flags. The day's racing was usually followed by a Venetian fête and fireworks in the evening and, of course, electric boats were always well lit and decorated. At the Bourne End Regatta in 1901, for example, the boat winning the prize for the best illuminations was the Abney House Venetian gondola with Mr Leech's electric launch *San Toy* coming second.[3]

These boats were built and serviced by a variety of boatyards, many of which may well have had an electric boat in their stock. Certainly, those boatbuilders who were already active in designing and making steamboats would have had no hesitation in offering to build an electric launch. The gathering pace of interest in electric boats is evident when

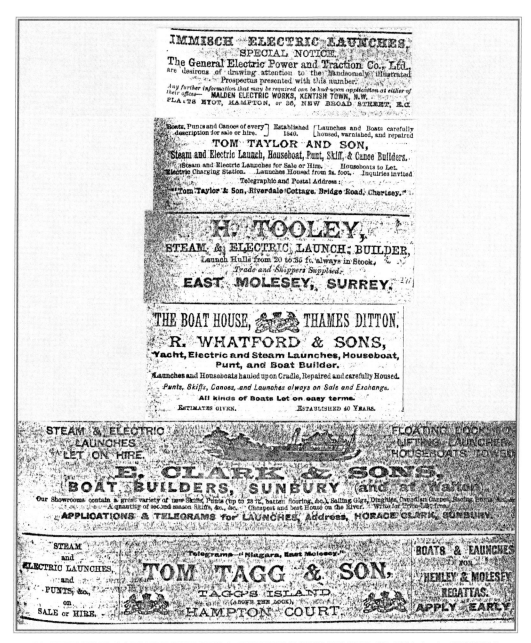

76. **ELECTRIC LAUNCH BUILDERS: WHERE IMMISCH LED IN 1890 (*top*), OTHERS FOLLOWED IN 1892**. These advertisements appeared in various issues of the *Lock to Lock Times* between 1890 and 1892.

J. Cowan

considering that whereas Immisch's was the only electric boat advertisement in the *Lock to Lock Times* during 1890 there were five in the 1892 issues. The number of yards building or hiring electric boats increased steadily until the turn of the century. However, after the electric boat market started to decline in 1904, only a very few yards continued to keep alive the tradition of building electric launches and canoes.

There were, of course, a number of boatbuilders other than those recorded in previous chapters and information on more of the Thames boatbuilders is given below. Appendix 2 lists all the UK electric boatbuilders who have been identified so far between 1882 and 1914. Outside the Thames area, only eight are listed but undoubtedly there would be more yards capable of building electric boats, most of which would probably have been designed as commercial or working boats.

One such business outside the Thames region was Frederick H. Smith & Co. of Liverpool, naval architects and engineers. They were responsible for building a 31 ft launch in 1906 to replace the petrol boat used during the previous eleven years on Lake Vyrnwy by the Water Committee of Liverpool Corporation. She was designed to tow barges laden with stone and other materials, for the transportation of workmen and for use in inspection work.

A long turtle-back deck forward enabled the boat to be used in heavy weather. Charging current was fed through a charging board fitted with reducing resistances and a seven-way switch from a 235 volt mains cable. This was connected to the hydro-electric plant using the compensation water flowing into the River Vyrnwy and supplying power to light the church, hotel and offices nearby. The boat had a length of 31 ft, beam 6 ft 8 in, draught 2 ft 3 in, and could carry twenty-five passengers. There were eighty-eight Fauré-King accumulators from the Electrical Power Storage Co. and these supplied a motor of 6 bhp at 150 volts, and this gave a speed of 7.8 mph and a range of 45 miles. The electrical equipment was supplied and fitted by the Motor Engineering Corporation.[4]

A.H. EAST

In July 1892 East lit up his premises at Caversham Lock, Reading, with a powerful and very brilliant light and at the same time set up an electric charging station.[5] During that year, he brought electric launches into his hire fleet, and in 1895 he was advertising that he built electric launches.[6]

KERBEY BOWEN & CO.

Kerbey Bowen is listed in 1891 as running the Ray Mead family hotel close to Boulter's Lock at Maidenhead.[7] He also ran the Ray Mead Boat Works alongside the hotel and the Folly Bridge Works at Oxford. He was a competent and expert electrical engineer and laid a mains cable across the river to light Sir Roger Palmer's riverside house, Glenisland, opposite the hotel. He was one of the first to realize the potential for electric boating and his advertisement stated that electric launches, pleasure and fishing boats could be hired by the day or year and picnics supplied. In fact, his was the second order secured by

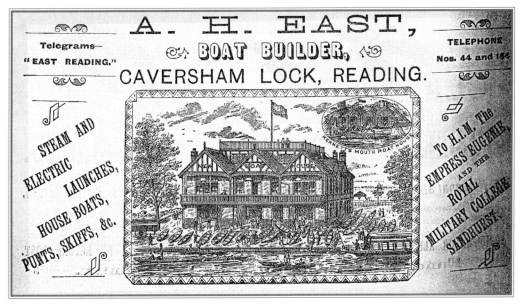

77. EAST, THE READING ELECTRIC BOATBUILDER AND HIRER, 1895.

Kelly's Directory, Maidenhead Library

William Sargeant at Strand-on-the-Green boatyard and the *Ray Mead* was launched during the last week in April 1889.[8]

Just 5 ft shorter than the *Viscountess Bury*, she had a length of 60 ft, a beam of 11 ft and was licensed to carry eighty-five passengers. Immisch and Co. supplied the motors, the batteries were fitted under the cabin and it was claimed that she could run for twenty hours on the stream at 7 mph and fifty to sixty hours at lower speeds. Built of Burmese teak, 'her beautifully equipped saloon is sufficiently large to lunch thirty people and is fitted up with stained glass domes, and lighted by electricity, the old gold silk curtains showing off the richness of the teak and satinwood panels to perfection'.[9]

The author of the above quotation may well have indulged in some wishful thinking when he mentions that apart from running a weekly service to Oxford and back, Kerbey Bowen would arrange trips to the Lower Thames where he had a charging station at

78. BURGOINE OF KINGSTON, 1892. Burgoine is reported to have built *Lady Lena* in 1890 for Immisch's electric launch company.

J. Cowan

79. KERBEY BOWEN'S *RAY MEAD*, **THE SECOND LARGEST ELECTRIC LAUNCH ON THE THAMES**. She was launched in 1889 and hired out from the Ray Mead Hotel at Boulter's Lock, Maidenhead (From a painting by J.W. Redworth; courtesy Phillips, Son & Neale, and James Cowan.).

William Rose

Chelsea. He reported that it was also proposed that a launch would run from Ryde to Bembridge and round the Forts, and ten charging stations would be opened on the Broads and the east coast and between Southampton, Cowes and Plymouth on the south coast. 'It is evident, then, that Mr Bowen is doing everything requisite to perfect the service, and makes a trip like a voyage in Fairyland, free from the danger, noise, dirt, smell and smoke of the ordinary steam launch.' Undoubtedly, Kerbey Bowen had a very enthusiastic supporter.

In 1891 it was reported that Mr Bowen would have an electric launch at the Royal Naval Exhibition at Chelsea,[10] and in June that year it was noted that 'one or two of Mr Bowen's pretty little electric launches passed through Boulter's Lock'.[11] In subsequent years, Bowen built electric launches for the Duke of Sutherland and a few other private owners.

The *Ray Mead* was much in demand; for example, she made two trips to Reading and back during one week in June 1891, and during the next few years the *Ray Mead* was mentioned several times in the *Maidenhead Advertiser* with comments such as 'the fine electric launch *Ray Mead* which was an object of admiration'.[12] Frequent excursions were made to Henley and back and she continued to be run by the hotel until 1896, when she was acquired and operated by Tom Taylor & Son of Staines as a tripping launch carrying eighty-two passengers.[13]

In April 1893 Bowen sold the Ray Mead Hotel to Mr Stopes. However, he retained the electric launch business alongside and in May 1893 was helping the British export effort by sending one of his launches to the World's Columbian Exposition in Chicago.[14] This may not have done much for Britain's export figures but the exhibition served to establish America's foremost electric boatbuilder, the Electric Launch and Navigation

Co., later known as the Electric Launch Co. (ELCO). ELCO built fifty-five 36 ft electric launches which, during the six and a half months of the exhibition, carried over a million passengers a total distance of 200,000 miles.[15]

Bowen continued to add to his fleet, one of his new smaller launches *Champion* being seen on the Bray reach in May 1893. In 1896 it is recorded that the firm had a charging station and yard on Marsh Lock Island, Henley-on-Thames, advertised building of electric and steam launches, and ran open and cabin launch trips locally and three-day trips between Windsor and Oxford.[16] Presumably, the Marsh Lock station had been established earlier in the decade, perhaps to provide an opportune charging point for the *Ray Mead* during its longer excursions to Henley or during Henley Regatta week.

HOBBS & SONS LTD

S.E. Hobbs owned the Ship public house at the bottom of Wharf Lane in Henley-on-Thames.[17] During the 1880s he bought the commercial wharf on the riverfront, erected a number of boathouses and set up to build and hire skiffs, punts and canoes. In 1898 he also bought Thames Meadow upstream of Henley Bridge and installed an electric charging station adjacent to the new boathouse. The site was next to the frontage used by Searles who were bought out by Hobbs in 1925.

Hobbs did not build any electric boats until the firm moved to Thames Meadow and even then it is probable that they only started after 1918 by building electric canoes. However, they may well have bought in electric boats for hiring purposes. Unfortunately, there are no records which shed any light on these activities except for an advertisement of electric and motor canoes for hire in a brochure printed sometime before 1928. This brochure also includes a picture of a motor canoe showing the characteristic lines of the Hobbs canoes.

At the turn of the century there were six Hobbs brothers in the business, which expanded very fast in the period between 1908 and 1912 when they bought up East's yard at Shiplake and Saunders' at Goring. East's would have had charging facilities and, of course, Saunders had been famous for his electric launches built on the Consuta principle. In 1925 Hobbs bought Shepherd's boathouse and frontage beside the Red Lion Hotel in Henley, but there is no record whether electric boats were still being operated from that site.[18] They also bought two yards at Pangbourne: Franklins in 1920 and Ashley in the 1930s.

MEAKES & REDKNAP OF MARLOW

Joseph G. Meakes, with the help of his father who was a well-known ironmonger in Marlow, set up as a boatbuilder and hirer on his twenty-first birthday in 1886.[19] The site chosen was on the Berkshire bank of the Thames just upstream from Marlow Bridge. While they were constructing the buildings, which came to be called the Bridge Works and Victoria Boathouse, they operated the hiring business from the lawn and frontage of the Anglers Hotel. On completion, Meakes and his wife moved into the flat above the boathouse where they often found themselves marooned during the winter floods. Within a year or two, Joseph Meakes took in W. Redknap as a partner and the business became known as Meakes & Redknap.[20] Redknap was a Queen's Waterman and the royal coat of arms was displayed on the boathouse, where they soon built up a thriving business building and hiring steam launches, punts, dinghies and canoes.

Little is known about the company's activities in electric boating. There are indications that it built an electric canoe in 1907 and there is also in existence a drawing of the lines of a 32 ft open cockpit electric launch.[21] Designed by Hart & Harden of Kingston-on-Thames, she had a clipper bow, counter stern and split rudder. With a full rounded keel, the bilge was a foot deep, quite sufficient to accommodate the motor. Whether or when Meakes built this or any other electric launch is not known.

In 1912 Meakes suffered a heart attack. He must have recovered well because he continued to live an active life until he was sixty-six years of age. Nevertheless, the experience persuaded him to give up the Victoria Boathouse and move across the river into the boathouse by the bridge on the Buckinghamshire bank and to set up home alongside in Thameslea, the white house still standing just upstream of Tierney Court. George Currall, a marine engineer, had joined Meakes in 1912 and proved to be a tower of strength during Meakes' illness. Unfortunately, being on the army reserve, he was called up in 1914 and served throughout the war in No. 4 Squadron of the Royal Flying Corps. Consequently, Meakes found himself having to take over responsibility again for the Bridge Works and Victoria Boathouse, where all efforts were then concentrated on building anti-submarine boats. When George Currall returned in 1918, he announced that the boating business was not going to make enough money to support both Meakes and himself and he therefore planned to set up a garage and, at the same time, marry Meakes' daughter. The wedding was quite an occasion, the bride setting off from the Victoria Boathouse in a white electric canoe to journey upstream to the service at Bisham Church.

Meakes' friendly neighbour downstream, in the house named Riversleigh, was Captain P.M. Brooke-Hitching, who in 1913 bought the electric launch *Esperanza* from Major Fenner.[22] It is thought that Brooke-Hitching may have taken an interest in the Meakes business, but in 1925 John Hobbs, of the well-known Henley boatbuilders, bought Riversleigh, then owned by a Russian princess, together with the boatyards on both the Berkshire and Buckinghamshire banks. However, he retained the name of J.G. Meakes and ran the business until he retired in the 1970s. A few years later the Victoria Boathouse and works were sold off for development into residential property, the Buckinghamshire boathouse having been disposed of earlier.

S. ROSEWELL

Located at Walton-on-Thames, Rosewell was established in 1850. In 1904 the business was advertised as a Boat, Punt and Canoe Builder and hirer of steam and electric launches.[23]

SALTER BROS

In 1904 Salters of Oxford advertised two electric launches for hire in the tenth edition of their *Guide to the Thames*. One was *Galatea*, a straight stem counter stern saloon launch suitable for eight to ten passengers and hired out on normal days for three guineas a day. The other was the smaller *White Wings* with accommodation for four to six passengers and hired out at two guineas per day. Salters stated that both these launches could make a journey out and home of about 20 miles without recharging.

ROBERT SHAW & SONS

In 1897 Shaw advertised the construction of electric launches.[24] He had owned the yards at The Bridge, Marlow, and next to the Upper Thames Sailing Club at Bourne End since the early 1880s. In 1900 Shaw published a timetable of trains between Paddington and Bourne End which carried an advertisement announcing that the business built electric and steam launches and had an electric charging station at Marlow Bridge.

JAMES TAYLOR

Taylor was famous as a builder of steam launches and an advertisement in 1904 shows King Edward VII aboard the launch *Favourite*. The same advertisement mentions that electric launches were also for sale and hire.

80. **SHAW OF MARLOW AND BOURNE END**.
Postal Directory 1897, Maidenhead Library

T.G. ELECTRIC POWER & TRACTION CO.

Advertised in the *Lock to Lock Times* of 6 June 1891 from the addresses of 35 New Broad Street and Platt's Eyot, Hampton: 'Elegant Electric Launches, 14 in number, available for hire'. The telegraphic address was given as Variform, London, and Immisch, Hampton. This was the name of Immisch's holding company, 'T.G.' standing for 'The General'.

H. TOOLEY

Located at East Molesey, Tooley advertised as a steam and electric launch builder.[25] Launch hulls of 20 to 30 ft were held in stock and trade and shippers were supplied.

UPPER THAMES ELECTRIC LAUNCH CO.

The works and charging station were at Rod Eyot, Henley-on-Thames, where electric launches were built and sold at prices from £150 to £600. The Chief Engineer and Manager in 1896 was Ewingfield Bowles with an address in Victoria Street, London. Electric launches for hire included *Loch Ness, Loch Leven, Loch Awe, Loch Earn* and *Loch Katrine*.[26] This company was taken over by the Thames Valley Launch Co. in 1899 and two of these launches were advertised in the TVL brochure published in 1900.

R.WHATFORD & SONS

Claiming to have been established as a boatbuilder at Thames Ditton for forty years, Whatford advertised in 1892 as a builder of 'Yacht, Electric and Steam Launches'.[27] C. Whatford had a boatyard at East Molesey and another Whatford relative joined the well-established yard of W.T. Abnett also at East Molesey. There are no records of electric boats built by any of the three yards.

H. WOODHOUSE

The gravestones in Bray churchyard bear witness that the Woodhouse family lived in the parish for some four hundred years.[28] In 1870 Henry Woodhouse was running a boatbuilding and hiring business at the George Hotel in Bray. Maidenhead, of course, was the place to hire out boats and so he arranged with William Deacon at the Ray Mead Hotel, opposite Boulter's Lock, to move his hiring business alongside the hotel. The business prospered to such an extent that in 1886 he was able to buy the site on which the present Thames Hotel on Riverside at Maidenhead now stands. Woodhouse married in 1876 and to help the family finances his wife started to take in paying guests; it was no surprise therefore that they built a hotel on the new site to go with their boathiring business.

In 1897 Woodhouse expanded the hotel considerably to provide 'thirty lofty and convenient bedrooms, suites of private apartments, luxuriously furnished coffee rooms, a billiard room with two fine tables and a photographic dark-room'.[29] As a result, the hotel became well patronized, his guests including King Edward VII's brother, Queen Alexandra's brother and the Duke and Duchess of Teck, Siamese Princes and peers galore.[30] He advertised as 'Steam Launch, Boat, Punt and Canoe Builder'.[31] He had also persuaded the General Post Office to install a postal telegraph office in the hotel – his number was Maidenhead 9, and the GPO provided a clerk every day to man the switchboard.[32]

During the 1890s Woodhouse built up a fleet of about twelve launches, all steam. The pride of the fleet was *Queen of the Thames*, converted from a house-boat, which could take 150 passengers and could be hired, in 1890, for two guineas per day.[33] Like other builders and hirers, he would rent boats from other owners. For example, in July 1889 he hired the steam launch *Austral* from Meakes & Redknap of Marlow for a party. Being a hotelier, Woodhouse also supplied the food and service. This was a particularly unfortunate trip because one of the waiters, while carrying some dishes, fell overboard at the Spade Oak Reach, Bourne End, and drowned.[34]

Woodhouse built his first punt in 1870 and became a specialist in racing punts. In 1878 he provided the punts for the famous championship race between Ned Andrews and Abel Beasley. He continued to supply the punts for championship races for a number of years and an example of his excellence was demonstrated one year when there was a difference of only 2½ lb in weight between three punts which were made for a particular race. Punting skills ran in the family, his two daughters, Nellie Louise and Winifred Violet, being taught by Abel Beasley and becoming 'very graceful punt propellers and pretty scullers'.[35]

In June 1899 it was reported that Mr Woodhouse was building a 'very large and convenient boathouse with dressing rooms, etc., erected on his ground above Boulter's Lock. It will be a very fine structure and will stand higher than any other residence in Maidenhead Court.'[36] When it was completed in May 1901, the *Maidenhead Advertiser* was even more eulogistic: 'It is one of the finest buildings of its kind on the Thames and has evoked the admiration of not a few. There is a private residence over the boathouses, approached by an iron spiral staircase with a long balcony in front, commanding a magnificent view of the Thames and Taplow and Cliveden woods. In the centre is a capital clock which will be a boon to all who use this part of the river. A spacious lawn and flower beds at the front lend *éclat* to the whole'.[37]

Woodhouse also had boathouses at Bray and at Staines. A disastrous fire broke out in the Bray boathouse just after midnight on a June evening in 1901. Among others, half-a-dozen of Immisch's men, who were on the launch *Delta*, tried to help douse the flames. There was considerable confusion in getting a message to Captain Wilton of the Maidenhead Fire Brigade, which eventually turned out at 2.30 a.m. by which time the boathouse was a heap of ruins.[38] No electric boats were lost, but one steamer and thirteen or fourteen other boats, punts and canoes, and a large amount of stores were destroyed.

It is not known when Woodhouse acquired his first electric boat but he was

81. INVOICE LETTER HEADINGS OF TWO MAIDENHEAD BUILDERS AND HIRERS, 1906/7.

G. Banham

operating *Armada* in 1898, and in 1904 Carr's records at the Ray Motor Co. show that he was invoicing Woodhouse for charging *Armada*. By 1906 Woodhouse had at least another electric launch, the *Corona*, which he hired out to Carr for the day on 20 June. Woodhouse's bill was rendered in September 1906 and paid at the end of April 1907! Thus it was perhaps not surprising that in 1910 Woodhouse faced bankruptcy proceedings, when he owed £1,431 to eighty-four unsecured creditors.[39] He claimed that he had run into trouble because of bad weather and that trade had fallen off 'on account of motor cars which did me a lot of harm'. The business was bankrupted by the failing of the Law Guarantee Society and the mortgagor foreclosing.

However, earlier in 1910 he had hived off his interests in the boating side of the hotel business into the Maidenhead & District Boating Co. This was formed with a capital of £4,000 but only five hundred £1 shares were issued and these were to members of his family. The Directors were himself, his daughter Winifred and Mr

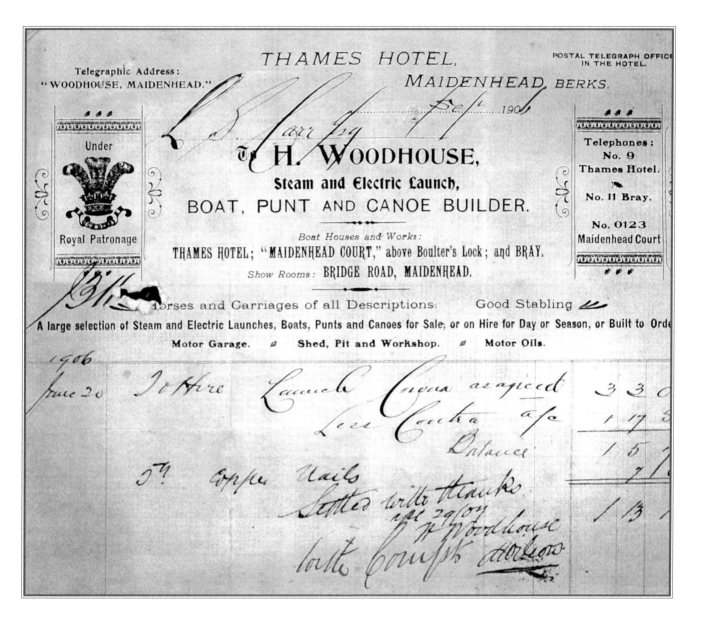

Wilson, the bookkeeper at the hotel. The company acquired all the assets of the boating side of the hotel activities and was therefore able to continue the hiring business.

By 1911 Woodhouse seems to have acquired at least five electric launches and the next mention in Carr's papers is of accounts rendered for *Armada*, *Corona*, *Santarello* and *Fleurette* being charged up on a number of days during the 1911 and 1912 seasons. *Santarello* also had spare brushes fitted to the motor in June 1911, the armature taken out and commutator turned up and new brushes fitted a week later. *Dace* had her motor armature repaired in 1913.[40] In June 1913 Carr provided a quotation for supplying and fitting *Santarello* with thirty special fifteen-plate horizontal traction type sections having a capacity of 157 ampere-hours.

H. WILDER

Like the Andrews family, the Wilders of Maidenhead were well-established fishermen and provided fishing punts for their anglers. They were therefore well placed in the 1880s to build up their hiring business to meet the rapidly growing demand for boating outings, and in 1891 Harry Wilder built a boathouse replete with a dressing-room and other facilities for his customers. In 1904 he was advertising[41] electric launches for hire along with pleasure boats, punts and canoes, and by the time of his death in 1910 he had built up a business with over two hundred boats. Run by his son Henry John, they were established in an elegant boathouse between Maidenhead Bridge and the New Thames Hotel.[42]

The most important electric boat in the Wilder fleet in 1912 was the 35 ft launch *Avondale*. Converted to steam she was restored during the 1970s and is now afloat under the name *Hero* (see Chapter 11).

EXPORTS

The boatbuilders were quick to take advantage of the export market — after all it was the period when most foreign countries looked to Britain for advanced technology and it would not have been surprising for rich foreigners to desire one of the latest types of launch, or for ferry companies to see advantages in this simple type of powered ferry boat.

There were undoubtedly many export orders for which records no longer exist but the following give an idea of the types of orders fulfilled:

The first recorded export was the 25 ft *Australia* built in 1884 by Forrest & Sons for an Australian firm.

A boatyard at Hammersmith was reported in 1890 to be building a flat-bottomed electric launch for Baron de Rothschild to use on the Dutch canals and private waters.[43]

Immisch, of course, was very active in the export business. The British Electric Traction Co., when they took the launch company over in 1897, noted that Eastern princes and rajahs ordered a number of launches.[44] In 1912 the Immisch Launch Co. was still exporting electric boats, sending a 20 ft launch to an Eastern potentate, perhaps Siamese.

In July 1895 T.G. Tagg & Son of East Molesey launched an 8 mph launch destined for the Czar of Russia for use at the Imperial Palace at St Petersburg where it would join the *Princess Beatrice*, a similar electric launch sent out in 1893.[45] She was fitted with sixty Electric Power Storage cells in teak boxes and a 7 in Immisch motor giving

82. THE WATERMEN OF MAIDENHEAD AND BRAY, 1934, photographed during the annual
Watermen's Regatta.

H. Horsham

1. Fred Sammons; 2. ? Wadhams; 3. Jim Hooper; 4. ? Dunkells; 5. ? Heavens; 6. ? Mitchell; 7. Bill Brown
(Capt. of Bond's Steam Launch *Her Majesty*); 8. –?–; 9. ? West; 10. 'Spider' Edwards (Punting Champion);
11. Dick Gumm; 12. Horace Chamberlain; 13. ? Brown; 14. Wilson Edwards ('Spider's twin); 15. Jack Lee;
16. –?–; 17. ? Cooke; 18. Major Bond; 19. Harry Rose; 20. H. Wilder; 21. –?–; 22. Harry Maisey;
23. A. Wadham; 24. Harry Sammons; 25. Bert Joel (Bond's steersman); 26. 'Dad' Saw (Bond's steersman.
Ret'd 1956); 27. Ben Charles; 28. Fred Horsham (Punting Champion); 29. 'Tubby' Fisher.

seven to eight hours duration at full speed. The hull was varnished mahogany with white awnings and brass stanchions and handrails. The seats were teak with morocco leather cushions and india–rubber mats.

In 1902 it was reported that the Thames Valley Launch Co. had launched a 32 ft pinnace intended for use in the Bay of Naples. Fitted with a 'Beevor-Edwards' motor, forty-four Leitner cells manufactured by Accumulator Industries of Woking and Edwards single lever gear, the boat was designed to run 40 miles on one charge at 7 mph. A similar 32 ft pinnace was under construction for the Natal government.[46]

Chapter 11

Boats Originally Electric and Still in Use

The following selection of histories of boats which were built before 1914 mainly covers the saloon launches – perhaps because these were strong or useful enough to survive – and concentrates on the period during which they were electric. A few canoes also have survived, although the heyday of electric canoe building seems to have been during the early 1920s, as described in Chapter 13. The degree of repair and restoration varies from the on-going work required to keep a boat in operation to a virtual rebuild of a boat left abandoned and rotting. All the launches and the canoe *Juliana* were converted to oil, petrol or steam propulsion. The boats recorded are:

Launches
    Viscountess Bury
    Esperanza
    Lady Lena, renamed *Silver Stream* and then reverted to *Lady Lena*
    Angler
    Eel, renamed *Woodland Lily*
    Tench
    Abel, renamed *Humble*
    Avondale, renamed *Hero*
    Magnolia, renamed *Majestic*
    Mary Gordon

Canoes
    Princess Beatrice, also named *Halcyon*
    Beazie, possibly originally named *Aegina*
    Cymba
    Juliana

VISCOUNTESS BURY

The 65½ ft *Viscountess Bury* was named after Sophia, wife of Viscount Bury and daughter of the Honourable Sir Allan McNab, Prime Minister of Canada.[1] Viscount Bury, the eldest son of the Earl of Albermarle, was fifty-six years old at the time of the launching, and as Chairman of the Westminster Electric Traction Co. had joined with Moritz Immisch to form a syndicate in 1888 to develop and build electric trams, trains and boats.[2]

83. **THE ORIGINAL FIGUREHEAD OF THE *VISCOUNTESS BURY*.** It was carved by David Gibb of Limehouse.

A.E. Cripps

Following the launch on 8 October 1888 from the builder's yard, Strand-on-the-Green, Chiswick, this description of the boat appeared in the *Electrical Review*:[3]

This is the largest electrical boat which has yet been seen on the Thames, or probably in the world, if we except that of Mr Elieson.[4] She is intended for public use and will carry upwards of eighty passengers comfortably.

The *Viscountess Bury* has been specially designed and built for a private company by Mr W. Sargeant, electrical launch architect and constructor, Chiswick, Middlesex.[5] She is 65½ feet long with 10 feet beam and has a mean draught of 22 inches with a displacement of 12½ tons. The hull is constructed of three skins, the inner being diagonal, and the outside planking of bright mahogany in narrow widths.[6] The keel, which runs from stem to taffrail, is in one length of American rock elm. Deadwood aft has been in this instance entirely abandoned, the object being to assist the steering in narrow bends up the River Thames, and for giving a clear run, and to get greater efficiency from the twin three-bladed propellers, which are built up from steel to a 12 inch pitch and 2 feet 3 inches diameter, rotating outwards, and calculated to revolve

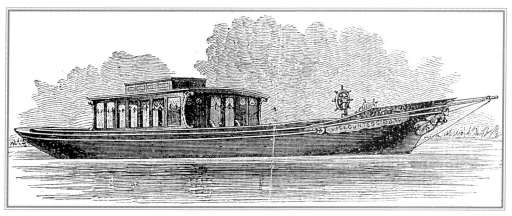

84. *VISCOUNTESS BURY*, **1888**. She was the first and largest commercial passenger electric launch in the world. Length 65½ ft, beam 10 ft.

Electrical Review, 19 October, 1888

at 600 revolutions per minute. These propellers are beautifully made and were provided by Messrs Thornycroft and Co., the well-known torpedo-boat builders of Chiswick.

Mr Sargeant has designed a rudder on an entirely new principle with the object of clearing weeds, obviating stern post dead wood and gudgeons, with facilities for quick removal and easy steering. This rudder will be built of thin steel, galvanised, and slung in a gun-metal trunk. The steering wheel is situated right forward on the deck, as shown in the illustration, so that the man operating has full view of all small craft which so numerously frequent the higher reaches of the Thames in summer. Adjoining the steering wheel will be an indicator communicating with the electrician in charge of the switches controlling the electrical power.

The electrical energy is stored in 200 Electrical Power Storage Company's accumulators of the '1888' type, each of which has a capacity of 145 ampere-hours. The midship section of the vessel being perfectly flat, there will not be any lids to these boxes, so in the event of her taking the ground the acid will not slop over.[7] These storage cells are arranged, one hundred on each side of the vessel, under the seats. The space occupied by them is lined with lead, small drains leading into receivers in case of accident, thus ensuring perfect dryness for the boxes. The cells are computed to hold electrical energy sufficient with one charge to propel the vessel for 10 hours at a speed of six miles per hour, as regulated by the Thames Conservancy bye-laws. There are two 7-inch 'Immisch' motors, which convert the electrical energy into power. These are calculated to develop 7½ bhp at 1,000 revolutions per minute. They are placed under the floor aft, each working direct on to one of the twin propeller shafts. The thrust is taken from a ball-bearing thrust block, which reduces the friction greatly. The switches are fixed, port and starboard, and are two to each motor, one for half and full speed, and the other for going ahead or astern. They are worked by the electrician in answer to bell signals from the man at the wheel. Each propeller can thus be worked independently of its twin companion, and so greatly assist the steering in sharp bends of the river.

In place of the objectionable whistle of the steamers a large and melodious ship's bell is placed on the cabin top and may be sounded electrically by the man steering, the current coming direct from the accumulators. This bell will sound for warning boats and signalling lockkeepers.

All lights for port, starboard, masthead and cabin, lavatories, &c., will be incandescent electric lamps supplied by the accumulators.

Ammeters, voltmeters and suitable resistances are all under the immediate sight or control of the electrician. All the machinery being placed below the floor, leaves a clear space from stem to stern for passengers.

From the illustration it will be seen that the cabin is furnished with a ventilating lantern, and is placed amidships with the lavatories, &c. The upholstering is of crimson embossed velvet, the panelling is of moulded teak, bright varnished throughout, the ceiling being moulded and picked out in gold and white. In the centre is the dining table, and seats run all round the cabin, which is 10 feet long with folding flaps on each side.

The windows are of engraved plate glass, and those of the ventilator amber in colour. The fore and aft parts of the vessel are of bright teak and upholstered with

85. *VISCOUNTESS BURY* AFTER HER REFIT, 1890. *Lock to Lock Times*, July 1890.

J. Cowan

portable seats, so that the accumulators may be easily examined in case of necessity, or at the time of charging.

The carving on the bow boards and figure head, which represents the *Viscountess Bury*, was done in an artistic manner by Mr David Gibb of Limehouse.

The *Viscountess Bury* appeared up river during the summer of 1889, and at Marlow Regatta in July it was noted that 'Immisch's *Viscountess Bury* and Mr Bowen's *Ray Mead*, both electric launches, attracted no little attention, each being well decorated.'[8]

This first year's operations showed that some modifications were necessary or desirable. These were made during the winter of 1889 and included:[9]

Saloon: Lengthened and accommodation materially enlarged and improved to carry sixty or seventy passengers more comfortably.

Motor: Changed to a single motor drawing an average of 45 amps at 164 volts. (Equals 7.4 kw electrical input, which at 72 per cent efficiency would give just over 7 hp output. This compares with the total of 15 hp obtained from the original twin motors.)

Speed: 7 mph. The maximum permitted by the Thames Conservators.

Propeller: A single 19 inch diameter propeller instead of the twin 12 inch diameter propellers.

Batteries: Apparently reduced to 164 cells, divided into two banks connected in parallel.

Steering: Moved from the bow position to the forward end of the upper deck.

86. *VISCOUNTESS BURY* AT DATCHET. From a postcard published prior to 1905.

H. Horsham

87. **THE *VISCOUNTESS BURY* ON A TRIP FROM ELY TO DENVER, 1911**. With her bright varnish and polished brasswork, the '*Vi*' was soon in commission under her new owner, Banham of Cambridge. This photograph was first published in *Ely, Cathedral City and Market Town*, courtesy Mrs D. Rogers, 1972.

Ely Society

88. *VISCOUNTESS BURY AT ELY, 1993*.

E.P. Hawthorne

89. **THE *VISCOUNTESS BURY* BEING TOWED BACK TO ELY FOR RESTORATION BY THE 'VISCOUNTESS BURY TRUST', 1994.**

E.P. Hawthorne

Upper Deck: Although not specifically recorded, the comment on the steering position indicates that this refit must have been the occasion when the saloon roof was converted to an upper deck with a double-sided bench seat fitted over the lantern. In illustrations published subsequent to the conversion, the lantern can just be seen under the seat, the rest of the upper deck being open, sometimes with an awning over, and with ladders down to the fore and aft decks.

The *Viscountess Bury* was in regular use on the Upper Thames during the subsequent decade. On an August Sunday in 1891 several members of the Hygienic Congress took a trip up river from Maidenhead in the 'splendid launch *Viscountess Bury*'.[10] Between 1889 and 1894 she was on charter to the Prince of Wales, who later became King Edward VII. In July 1897 Col. Boxall hired the *Viscountess Bury* for a party to watch the Bourne End Regatta, the launch being 'most effectively decorated with festoons of artificial flowers and foliage'.[11] In June 1901 she was reported passing through Boulter's Lock: 'perhaps the prettiest launch out on Sunday was Immisch's large electric *Viscountess Bury*. A rich profusion of flowers and palms adorned the bow and cabin embedded in green silk and the ladies on board carried green Japanese sunshades. It was a very picturesque affair.'[12]

The *Viscountess Bury* was listed on the Board of Trade Register as an electric boat until 1909.[13] She was then converted to a petrol engine. She was acquired by H.C. Banham in 1910 and taken from the Thames to King's Lynn, a journey not without hazard.[14] Travelling as much as possible by day and within sight of the land, all went well until she left Yarmouth when the weather worsened. She rolled horribly and began to ship water over the bow, but managed to get to the harbour at Wells on the north Norfolk coast. After waiting for better weather, she reached King's Lynn safely. The rest of the journey was accomplished by a combination of good luck and good judgement of the fourteen feet between the mud below and low bridges above required to clear the height between keel and steering wheel.

With her bright varnish and polished brasswork done up, she was soon set to work by Banham. In 1911 it cost sixpence to travel between Cambridge and Clayhithe and she was also seen taking a party from Ely to Denver.[15] In virtually continuous service since then, her last owner was Dan Weller who operated her out of Ely on a 36-mile stretch of the Great Ouse and River Cam.

In 1994 the launch was put up for sale. Her future was secured by Linda Ashton of Stuntney, who with friends from Ely and the author's support, acquired the launch and formed the '*Viscountess Bury* Trust', dedicated to maintaining her as part of Britain's boating heritage and, if possible, restoring her to operate once again as the oldest and, for twenty-one years, the largest electrically driven passenger launch in the world.

90. *ESPERANZA*, RENAMED *THAMES ESPERANZA* IN 1968. Length overall 52 ft, length waterline 45 ft, beam 7ft 6 in, draught 3 ft 9 in. Motor: Mather & Platt 100 volts, 70 amps, 7 kw, 700 rpm. Batteries: EPS forty-two cells with thirty-three plates each. Speed 9 mph. Date unknown.

L. Weaver

ESPERANZA, RENAMED *THAMES ESPERANZA* IN 1968

With clipper bow and counter stern, the 52 ft *Esperanza* has a hull of mahogany on oak timbers, double-skinned and copper-riveted with fore and aft planking outside and diagonal inside; varnished teak decks and saloon which is 16 ft 9 in long with seven lights on each side of bevel edged glass; and canopy over the foredeck.

The first-known record of an electric launch named *Esperanza* is in Lawrence Carr's papers of the Ray Motor Co. at Boulter's Lock, when in 1905 the time sheet for the week ending 19 August for F. Andrews included two hours for charging *Esperanza*. On 9 April 1907 Carr was notified by the owner, Major Charles E. Fenner of Datchet, that he had received a letter from the Thames Conservancy and had replied that all their requirements had been complied with and they could inspect the boat. On 13 September 1909 Carr sent an invoice to Fenner covering the costs for two new boxes for damaged cells in the cabin, repairs to magnets and the loan of a battery. Between 1910 and 1913 Carr evidently looked after the launch all the year round, storing her during the winter, and varnishing, mooring and charging her during the summer and invoicing Fenner as shown in Table 1.

Table 1
Costs of Operation 1909–13

Sept 18, 1909	Includes:	
	Charge 55¾ units @ 1s per unit	£2.15.9
	Supply & fit two new boxes in cabin	£2.7.6
	Repairs to magnets & loan of battery	1.6
Nov 22, 1910	Housing (15 weeks)	£5.12.6
	Cleaning (15 weeks)	£7.10.0
June 28, 1911	Housing for winter 1910 to 1911	£13.10.0
	Charging cells in winter 60 units @ 10d	£2.10.0
	Paint & Varnish	£15.0.0
	Gild names, scroll work, & line round hull*	£2.10.0
	Cleaning 42 cells @ 2s	£4.4.0
	4 A.C. Type E.P.S. cells	£16.0.0
	Set of 48 connectors	£4.16.0
	Charging 167 units at 8d during May & June	£5.15.4
	8 weeks Mooring from May 1st to June 26th @ 7/6	£3.0.0
	8 weeks Cleaning @ 10s	£4.0.0
July 31, 1912	Housing & running account	£41.1.2
Nov 20, 1912	Charging & man's time	£34.14.2
April 18, 1913	Housing for winter, charging cells, rubbing down etc.	£20.8.6

* The account rendered by A. Wheeler (Writer & Grainer) to Ray Motor Co. for this work was £2.0.0.

91. *ESPERANZA* **IN 1911**. Original photograph signed WWF 1911.

G. Banham

At the end of December 1910 Carr's store on Boulter's Lock Island was burnt down and all the contents destroyed.[16] Among the material lost were the fittings for *Esperanza*. In due course these were replaced and on 28 June Carr sent an invoice to Major Fenner for £125 15s for refitting *Esperanza* with 'curtains, carpets, cushions etc.' Among the items were two mats, the purchase of which gave rise to a letter from Hill's Rubber Co. to Carr (opposite). This letter is of significance because it implies that Carr believed that *Esperanza* had been built by Saunders of Goring.

However, there is no record in the very detailed research carried out by Wheeler[17] of a boat named *Esperanza* being built by Saunders. Wheeler's research indicates that prior to 1898, when Saunders built the high speed steam launch *Consuta* in his new hull material, he had built only two electric boats, the 42 ft *Avalon* in 1895 and the *Shamrock* of unknown length and design in 1896. Of course, it was not at all unusual for names to be changed when boats were sold or even hired out for the season and the letter from Hill's Rubber Co. still leaves us with an intriguing mystery, especially as, after 1898, all the recorded Saunders electric launches were built in Consuta material with straight stems. Furthermore, is it correct to assume that steam launch S.L. *Esperanza* as typed in the letter was a 'pen-slip' for electric launch E.L. *Esperanza*?

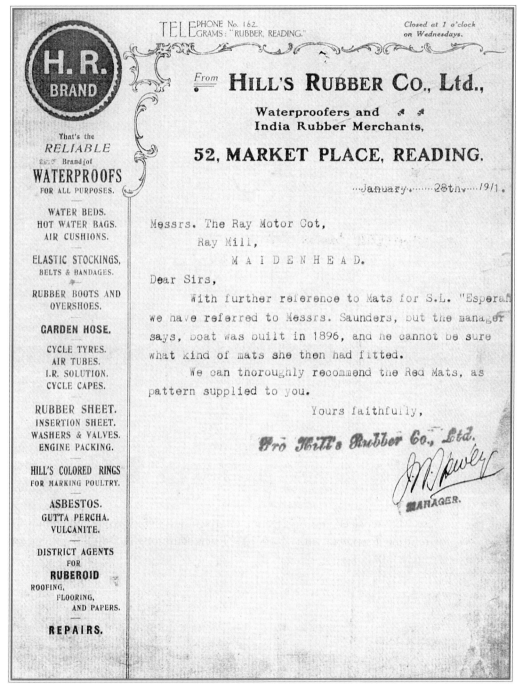

92. COPY OF THE HILL'S LETTER OF JANUARY 1911 TO THE RAY MOTOR CO.

G. Banham

During the refit four new AV33 cells of thirty-three plates each were supplied by the Electric Power Storage Co. Ltd at a price of £16. These were connected to the existing forty-two cells. Space for the new boxes was tight, the existing ebonite boxes being 13 in high, 12 in long, and 9½ in wide; EPS were asked if they could supply boxes to fit into a space of 10½ in high, 15 in long and 11 in wide. It is probable that the EPS Company discouraged this idea because in March 1912 Carr obtained estimates for renewing the whole forty-two cells on *Esperanza*.[18] In April the order was placed with the EPS Company to supply a complete set of forty-two positive and negative sections to be fitted into the existing boxes.

In April 1913 Captain P.M. Brooke-Hitching, who was associated with the Meakes & Redknap boatyard at Marlow,[19] bought *Esperanza* from Major Fenner, complete with the inventory shown in Table 2.[20]

Table 2
Inventory made 15 April 1913
by The Ray Motor Co., Ray Mill, Maidenhead

46	Cells	1	Tiller
1	Spare Propeller		6 Wine Glasses, 4 Tumblers, 4 Large do.
1	Boat Cover	2	Ash Trays
1	Set of 7 Cushions	2	Poles (G.M.) Shoes
2	Back Cushions	2	Boat Hooks do.
	Set of 9 Holland Covers		Flag & Mast
	Spare set of 5 Holland Covers		Burgee & Mast
4	Pillow Cushions	1	Pr. White Lines
2	Red Rubber Mats	1	Pr. Hemp Lines
1	(Cabin) Carpet	1	Set Navigation Lamps
6	Small Carpets		1 Mop, 1 Deck Scrub, 1 Chamois
1	Awning	1	Clock
26	Set of Curtains	1	Barometer
24	Tassels	1	Set Separators for 4 Cells in Lead Lined Boxes
1	Motor	3	Lamp Brackets
1	Amp Meter	3	Fendoffs
1	Controller Switch		4 Volt Fan
1	Table	1	E.C. Bucket
			Signed: George Hearn

Brooke-Hitching asked Carr to get *Esperanza* afloat as soon as possible and spoke of housing her close to Cookham Bridge. However, a few days later he instructed that she be taken up to his place at Riversleigh, immediately above the Marlow Rowing Club premises and just below Meakes & Redknap's boatyard. He mentioned to Carr that he had not decided what to do with the boat and that it depended on some experiments that he 'hopes to make this week'. The launch was sent up the following week complete with its inventory, but unfortunately there is no record of what experiments were made.

There is then a gap in the records of *Esperanza* until 1920.

Between 1920 and 1940 it is said that *Esperanza* was owned by Bond of Maidenhead,

93. *ESPERANZA* AS ILLUSTRATED IN THE GOLDING BROS BROCHURE. Compare this and subsequent photographs with the one taken in 1911 (page 124). The saloon has been moved aft. This raises unsolved questions as to when, why and if it was moved.

G. Banham

who converted her to a six cylinder Wolseley petrol engine. She was then bought by Golding Bros of Windsor who used her as a tripping launch until 1968. While in the possession of the Goldings, she was serviced every year by Tough of Teddington and certified by the Board of Trade.

In 1968 *Esperanza* was bought by Lawrence Weaver, who set about enrolling her on the Register of British Ships. To do so he had to produce a builder's certificate and be able to prove title to the boat.

His first step was to contact George Bond, then in his ninety-fourth year, who said that he remembered working on *Esperanza* as an apprentice when he was eighteen years old. The company had ceased trading and George Bond signed a builder's certificate for *Esperanza*, which states that she was built by Messrs Bond of Maidenhead in 1898.[21]

George Bond also signed a certified copy of the bill of sale, dated 15 February 1945, which showed that Bond's had sold *Esperanza* to Goldings of Windsor for £200. Garrick Golding, in turn, certified in 1969 that Golding Bros had bought *Esperanza* from Bond in 1945 and retained her in their ownership until 1968 when they sold her to Lawrence Weaver. These certificates were accepted by the Registrar of British Ships as sufficient proof of title. Unfortunately, the name was already in use on another vessel and the launch was therefore registered in the name of *Thames Esperanza*.

There is, however, another facet to this story. Bond was one of the builders of double-skinned launches and it appears that there are very few of their boats of this type still in existence, mainly, it seems, because the quality of the wood used for the inner skins was

BUILDER'S CERTIFICATE FOR YACHTS AND SMALL CRAFT.

I (we) ...*Messrs. Bonds* .... *Taplow* of *Maidenhead Bridge Boatyard, Maidenhead* ...... hereby certify that I (we) did build in my (our) yard at .... *Maidenhead Bridge* ...... in the year ...... *1898* ...... the vessel *ESPERANZA* ...... of the following description :-

Whether sail, steam or motor ...... *Electric* ......
Length ...*52 ft* ...... Breadth *7 ft* ...... Depth ...*2' 6"*...
Particulars of Engines (if any) *Bathey driven Electric motors*
Estimated Tonnage (a) Gross ...*11 approx*...: (b) Register .*5 approx*.

I (we) further certify that I (we) built the aforementioned ship for and on behalf of :-

Full names ...... *Ourselves* ......
Address ......
Description or occupation ......

Dated ...*26" day of June 1968.*

George. C. Bond a partner of the firm of Messrs Bonds

NOTE:-
When builders are a limited company this certificate must be given under the seal of the company. When builders are a private company the certificate should be signed by one of the partners who should describe himself as such, e.g. 'A.B., a partner of the firm of Messrs. C.D. & E.'

✗ Now retired and living at - Hawthorn Bath Rd Taplow nr. Maidenhead

94. **COPY OF THE BUILDER'S CERTIFICATE FOR THE ELECTRIC LAUNCH** *ESPERANZA*.

David Roberts

poor and they rotted very quickly. Bond is reputed to have built or owned at least one other boat similar to *Esperanza*. Sir Dhunjibhoy Bomanji, a wealthy Indian merchant, had rented the fine riverside mansion Oakley Court between Bray and Windsor in 1912.[22] In 1920 he bought The Willows nearer to Windsor and used to hire boats to take his guests to Marlow and back. It is said that he saw the *Esperanza* and told Bond that he 'wanted a boat like that'. Two or three years later Bond supplied him with a boat in which he had changed the engine to a Wolseley petrol engine.[23] Named *Lady Frainy*, after Bomanji's wife, she was still afloat in 1932 when 'this most luxurious launch' was described as a 'beautiful creation in immaculate white with a gorgeous canopy'.[24] Although there was a boathouse at The Willows the water was not deep enough to house the *Lady Frainy* and so she was kept at Bond's and taken downstream by one of their skippers to the house when required.

According to one local observer, the *Lady Frainy* was very similar to Kessler's launch *Charlotte* (see page 65).[25] Following the First World War, a number of privately owned boats came on the market and Bond was one of the builders who bought them up and restored or converted them. It is believed that Kessler returned to America before the war and it is therefore quite possible that *Charlotte* became the *Lady Frainy*.

95. ***ESPERANZA* IN 1968 BEFORE WEAVER STARTED RESTORATION**. Lawrence Weaver bought *Esperanza* in 1968, converted her to steam and changed her name to *Thames Esperanza*.

G. Banham

96. *ESPERANZA* **IN 1992**.

E.P. Hawthorne

After Sir Dhunjibhoy's death in 1937, *Lady Frainy* was sold to Mr Olivier, then the owner of Oakley Court, who changed her name to *Olive Branch*. During the Second World War Oakley Court was used by the Free French forces and the *Olive Branch* was seen on one occasion with a distinguished party, possibly including General de Gaulle, and flying the Cross of Lorraine flag. By 1945 her inner skin had rotted and the launch was scrapped.

When Weaver bought *Esperanza*, he found extensive areas of wet rot, a fractured keel and a considerable amount of dry rot, particularly in the stern cockpit. He therefore put in a new inner skin, replaced a third of the outer planking and fitted all new frames, stringers, keel, stern and all internal teak panelling. This was after seventy years of continuous heavy use, mostly as a tripping launch.

Being originally electric, she had a shallow draught sufficient to take a 16 in propeller so Weaver brought in a shipwright from down river to fit a deeper keel aft to take a 30 to 36 in propeller. He also converted her to steam, selling off the Wolseley engine to Phelps at Putney, who put it into an umpire's launch. When all this work was completed, she was used as a private launch operating from Cleeve, near Goring, and on more than one occasion was taken down to the Pool of London.

In 1992 she was put into the Phillips boat auction at Henley and passed into the hands of Roger Angold and David Roberts. Completely overhauled, she was commissioned during 1994 for personal use and occasional charter.

There is one further puzzle about *Esperanza*. Comparison of the photograph taken in 1911 with the Goldings' brochure and subsequent pictures show that the saloon has been moved aft. For some years it has been assumed that this was done to provide more room forward for the installation of the petrol engine, although there is little physical evidence to prove that the saloon has ever been moved.

97. *LADY LENA*, **1904, FROM IMMISCH BROCHURE**. Length overall 41 ft 6 in, length waterline 33 ft 6 in, beam 6 ft 5 in, draught 2 ft.

Capt F.J. Turk, MVO

The mystery remains. Were there two *Esperanzas*? Who built which one and when? What really happened to the original *Esperanza*? Maybe one was run by Bond as a tripping boat, while the other was named *Esperanza* when it came into Major Fenner's possession in 1905. During or following the First World War, the registrations may have been allowed to lapse and, when renewed, the name was switched. Bond bought up Immisch's fleet at Maidenhead in 1914, so there could have been a number of electric launches available to him after the war. Bond could well have run a launch named *Esperanza* until it was sold to Goldings in 1940 and could then have bought the Fenner launch, perhaps bearing a different name, in 1924 for Sir Dhunjibhoy who then named her *Lady Frainy*. Or was the saloon moved?

LADY LENA, NAMED *SILVER STREAM* 1943–63

Lady Lena was built in 1890 by Burgoine of Kingston-on-Thames for Immisch's company, the General Electric & Traction Co. In June 1891 she was licensed to operate as a river service in smooth waters and to carry twenty-four passengers.[26] During June

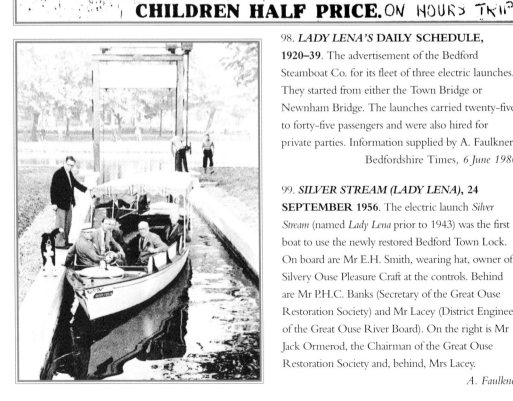

CRUISE
ON THE
"OUSE"
THE ELECTRIC LAUNCHES
"LODORE"   "LADY LENA"   "LORNA DOONE"

Now Running Daily (including Sundays) at frequent intervals :—

Leave Town Bridge for one hour trip 1/-
                          or half   „   „   6d.
    Newnham Bridge for one hour trip 1/-
                          or half   „   „   6d.
CHILDREN HALF PRICE. ON HOURS TRIP

98. *LADY LENA'S* **DAILY SCHEDULE,
1920–39**. The advertisement of the Bedford
Steamboat Co. for its fleet of three electric launches.
They started from either the Town Bridge or
Newnham Bridge. The launches carried twenty-five
to forty-five passengers and were also hired for
private parties. Information supplied by A. Faulkner.
Bedfordshire Times, *6 June 1980*

99. *SILVER STREAM (LADY LENA)*, **24
SEPTEMBER 1956**. The electric launch *Silver
Stream* (named *Lady Lena* prior to 1943) was the first
boat to use the newly restored Bedford Town Lock.
On board are Mr E.H. Smith, wearing hat, owner of
Silvery Ouse Pleasure Craft at the controls. Behind
are Mr P.H.C. Banks (Secretary of the Great Ouse
Restoration Society) and Mr Lacey (District Engineer
of the Great Ouse River Board). On the right is Mr
Jack Ormerod, the Chairman of the Great Ouse
Restoration Society and, behind, Mrs Lacey.
A. Faulkner

100. **LADY LENA, 1993**. Back to her original name but now propelled by steam.

T. Casey

1892 *Lady Lena* was seen in use at Maidenhead and again during May and June 1893.[27] She remained in Immisch's fleet until probably 1914.

In 1919 the Bedford Steamboat Co. bought *Lady Lena* and another electric launch *Lorna Doone* from Maidenhead. Together with their existing steamboat *Lodore*, which the company had operated since 1898 and converted to electric in 1920, these launches ran a regular service along the River Ouse through Bedford.[28] In 1943 the Steamboat Company was taken over by Mr and Mrs E.H. Smith who set up Silvery Ouse Pleasure Craft. However, they bought a problem because, through neglect during the early years of the Second World War, all of the fleet lay submerged in a backwater. Only *Lady Lena* was worth salvaging and, after restoration throughout, she was put back into operation under a new name *Silver Stream*, joining the 25 ft boats *Silver Foam* and *Silver Spray*, both of which were brought from London and fitted out with electric propulsion.[29]

Silver Stream was taken out of service in 1963 and left on the river bank, whence she was rescued by Peter Bridge of Cotterstock near Oundle. Stored for several years, she was bought in 1980 by her present owner Jenkyn Knill. Restored by Terry Hardick of Bath between 1980 and 1982 and converted to steam by Jenkyn Knill himself between 1982 and 1983, she is once again steaming under her original name, *Lady Lena*.[30]

101. *THE ANGLER* WITH KING EDWARD VII AND QUEEN ALEXANDRA ON BOARD, 1905.

H. Horsham

THE ANGLER

Launched in 1902, *The Angler* was the flagship of the Andrews electric fleet. A saloon launch with a length of 45 ft and beam of 7 ft, the hull and superstructure were made of teak and she was very well appointed throughout. The lagging was unusual, being made in the form of panels mounted on horizontal and vertical battens. Each panel was like a picture frame and made in teak. There were no air holes through the panels so the panels were removed every winter to let the air get at the timbers behind.[31]

Like most of the Andrews clipper bow, counter stern launches, she was fitted with a very unusual split rudder hung from the stern post mounted close up to the keel. The propeller shaft ran between the two halves of the rudder, which were connected together by a stirrup, and the propeller was then fitted behind the rudder. This made her very difficult to steer. Apparently, when Goldings owned her, she was unable to come round between the Eton College boathouse and the island opposite: 'So many a time she poked out the windows of the *Windsor Belle*. That's why they didn't use her a lot.'[32] However, this does not appear to have been a problem during her early years.

The Angler was often used by the royal family. For example, in June 1904 King Edward VII and Queen Alexandra visited the Grenfells at Taplow Court one afternoon and in the evening the queen went for a trip in *The Angler*, driven by 'Skipper Slough', as far as the Fisheries at Bray and back.[33] In June 1908 Queen Alexandra journeyed from Windsor to Cliveden Woods; *The Angler* on this occasion having W. Emony[34] as captain and H. Andrews as second officer.[35] That same month it is also reported[36] that E. Andrews received the following instruction from Colonel Legge, equerry to King Edward VII: 'Require your best electric launch – *Angler* is it not – and best man, at the King's boathouse opposite Datchet, 3.30 tomorrow (Saturday) afternoon. State how many boat accommodates and telegraph immediately.' (The best man was Joseph Tindall and the steer hand H. Matthews.) The king and queen cruised from Windsor to Monkey Island.

In 1938 *The Angler* was bought by the tripping firm Golding Bros of Windsor. Andrews had installed a 30 hp Minerva petrol engine, and on Boxing Day of that first winter the engine was taken out and later the saloon was taken off in two halves. She was then towed behind a Salter's steamer down to Tough's boatyard where the Thornycroft 'Handy Billy', a two-cylinder petrol/paraffin engine of 7 to 9 hp, was fitted and bulkheads put in. The 'Handy Billy' was a popular engine for tripping boats; it could run

102. ***THE ANGLER* MOORED ALONGSIDE WINDSOR PROMENADE IN 1946**. Between 1939 and 1969 *The Angler* was used by Golding Bros of Windsor as a tripping launch. Frank (Jock) Golding is standing with his back to the launch and Oddie Golding is facing him.

G. Banham

103. ***THE ANGLER'S* HULL RESTORED, 1994**. Work carried out by David Graham for her owner, Brian Bidston.

B. Bidston

all day on a 'pint of paraffin'. After the war a Mark 1 Morris Navigator engine with a 2:1 gearbox was fitted.

In 1903 *The Angler* was licensed by the Board of Trade to carry thirty-nine passengers. She was used as a hireboat by Andrews until 1938, but by then she had lost her Board of Trade licence and was therefore only permitted to carry twelve passengers. This limitation was still imposed during her first season with Goldings. However, on her return from Tough's boatyard, a handrail and a new 7 in high coaming were fitted and after being tested for rolling to check that no wash came over, she was then relicensed by the Board of Trade to carry thirty-two passengers and two crew.

Early in 1940 she was returned to Tough Bros for some minor repairs, but on her way back to Windsor was ordered to Southend in preparation to assist in the evacuation of the Expeditionary Force at Dunkirk. Jack Golding, who was driving her, was allowed to go to Windsor to tell his brothers and family what was happening. Back on board *The Angler*, he then set off in convoy with the *Em*, *Gerbera*, *Eel* (renamed *Woodland Lily* in 1966), *Marina* and *Windsor Belle*, travelling overnight and reaching Southend Pier early in the morning. By then, however, the emergency was over and the boats were allowed to return to Windsor.

Goldings were able to run their tripping boats – up to Boveney Lock and back for one

104. **EEL, RENAMED *WOODLAND LILY* IN 1966**. She was built around 1903 by Andrews of
Maidenhead. Length 41 ft 6 in. Restored and converted to steam by Lawrence Weaver.

Photograph 1970 by Ron Francis Studios, Camberley

shilling return – until petrol rationing forced them to be laid up. *The Angler* was kept
afloat at Trinder's yard on the mill stream at Clewer under the cover of a tarred hessian
tent. This provided excellent protection and by the end of the war even the varnish work
had not suffered.

When petrol became available again in 1947, *The Angler* was pulled out and the keel
was found to be soft 4 ft from the turn of the stem. The Board of Trade inspector
allowed a steel channel to be bolted on to reinforce the keel sufficiently to get the boat
through the season, at the end of which she was taken to Tough's and fitted with a new
keel. Brought back into commission she was then used by Goldings as a tripping boat
again until 1969. She was usually driven by Dennis, the son of Frank who was one of the
three Golding brothers who had set up the business. She sat well in the water and 'you
could put her nose up against the lock and she would stay on station'.

The saloon was bought after the war by Harrison, who commissioned Trinder to fit it
to another of Andrews electric launches *Bream* which he had bought off Goldings.

Between 1969 and 1992 *The Angler* was owned by David Roberts, who sold her on to
Brian Bidston whose boatbuilder, David Graham, is restoring and reconverting her to
electric propulsion.

EEL, RENAMED *WOODLAND LILY* IN 1966

Built about 1903 by E. Andrews and Son of Maidenhead, the electric launch *Eel* was used as one of the Andrews hire fleet and, like *The Angler*, would have been converted to petrol in the early 1920s. She was bought in 1938 by Arthur Jacobs of Windsor who fitted a Thornycroft 'Handy Billy' petrol/paraffin engine, and installed bulkheads and other items to meet Board of Trade requirements. She looked splendid in a finish of bright varnished mahogany, but after a few years the varnish had deteriorated and she was painted blue. Jacobs sold her to a local garage owner and, in 1966, she was acquired by Lawrence Weaver of Datchet. Drawn up on a very steep slipway at a boatyard at Clewer and 'being a bit soft and not a sound timber amidships you can imagine what shape she was'.[37] As well as restoring her completely, Weaver also converted her to steam and renamed her *Woodland Lily* in 1966.

In 1971 H. Orr-Ewing acquired her and commissioned Michael Dennett at Harris' Boatbuilders Ltd, Chertsey, to replace the mahogany hull and build a new one in carvel iroko. The clipper bow and counter stern were retained, a canvas canopy was placed over the foredeck and the saloon aft was fitted out with two berths. The owner himself refitted the steam plant.

Dimensions: length 41 ft 6 in, length waterline 37 ft, beam 7 ft, draught 2 ft 9 in, speed 8 mph.

105. **WILDER'S LETTER OF 1912 CONCERNING THE *AVONDALE*.**

G. Banham

138

AVONDALE, RENAMED *HERO* IN 1972

The origins of *Avondale* are unknown. Tom Trevethick, the well-known boatbuilder of Lenton near Nottingham, whose experience went back to the early years of this century, considered that the narrowness of the beam and the lack of any underwater perforations in the hull precluded the boat from being anything other than an electric launch. He also thought that the form of construction suggested that she was most likely built by Andrews of Maidenhead. If this was so, she could not have been built before 1898, the year in which Andrews commenced his electric launch activities by building *Bleak* and *Gudgeon*. At Cookham Regatta in 1901 a launch *Avondale* was reported to have been moored along the bank upstream of the bridge, having been hired by Col. Hunsiker.[38] If this launch was electric, then she would have been built between 1899 and 1901. Dimensions: length overall 35 ft, length waterline 27 ft, beam 5 ft 8 in, draught 2 ft.

Positive proof of the existence of the electric launch *Avondale* is provided by the letter (reproduced opposite) from Wilder to the Ray Motor Co., showing that she was owned in 1912 by Harry Wilder of Maidenhead who was using her as a tripping boat.[39] Subsequently, she was owned by Mr Hill of Windsor and then by Eric Haynes of Old Windsor who ran her until about the 1950s.

106. *AVONDALE* **PHOTOGRAPHED IN 1992, RENAMED *HERO* IN 1972**. A 35 ft Andrews launch with a LWL of 27 ft, beam 5 ft 8 in, draught 2 ft.

E.P. Hawthorne

The launch was derelict in the late 1960s and acquired in 1969 by C.J.B. Stirling.[40] Tom Trevethick undertook a major rebuild. The keel and the carvel hull of teak planking were found to be the original and sound, but the oak ribs, decks and internal fittings all had to be replaced. When Christopher Stirling acquired *Avondale* she was fitted with a Stuart Turner petrol engine which was then replaced by a steam engine and Merryweather boiler. At launching, her name was changed to *Hero*. Later she was owned by John Player & Sons who used her for advertising purposes. During this period, the stern was damaged by a falling crane and required new planking locally.

In 1983 she was re-acquired by Christopher Stirling and three years later she was bought by Terence Casey, who fitted the rigid canopy. Today she is frequently seen cruising along the Cookham and Spade Oak reaches at Bourne End.

Hero is well known to television viewers, having featured in the BBC television series *The Onedin Line*, and in 1973 she was used in the filming of ATV's series on the life of King Edward VII.

TENCH

Built by Andrews of Maidenhead between 1900 and 1903, the hull of *Tench* is thought to have been very similar to those of the *Bream*, *Barbel* and *Pike*, all of which were 30 ft length.[41] During the 1980s *Tench* was found in a derelict state lying in the Essex marshes.

107. ***TENCH* UNDERGOING RESTORATION, 1993**. Probably built between 1900 and 1903, this 30 ft Andrews launch was discovered in a derelict state during the 1980s. Now owned by Dick Goodall of Wargrave, she is being restored by David Brownjohn of Sonning Common.

Dick Goodall

Now owned by Dick Goodall of Wargrave, she is being restored by David Brownjohn of Sonning Common. Only part of the keel and some planking have been of any use. None of the nails was sound and all had to be replaced.

ABEL, RENAMED HUMBLE IN 1960

It is believed that *Abel* was originally built as an open electric launch in 1902 by a boatbuilder in the Kingston area. The hull is mahogany on oak frames and is very similar to that of the launch presented by Mr Palmer, of the Huntley & Palmer biscuit company, to the National Maritime Museum. Dimensions: length 52 ft, beam 8 ft 3 ins, draught 2 ft, speed 7 mph. Motor 3 kw 36 volt Nelco, two banks of twelve 6 volt batteries. Duration: cruising 14 hours, full speed 11 hours.

During the Second World War she was used as a fire tender in the London Docks. She was fitted with a diesel engine as the propulsion unit and a steam-driven fire pump which produced a jet of water powerful enough to reach the roofs of the warehouses.

Golding Bros, the hireboat operators at Windsor, bought her in 1950. The fire pump was removed and the boat fitted out to take thirty-six passengers on side seating.[42] With the elder Golding brother, Dennis, at the helm, the open launch took passengers from the promenade at Windsor on what was described in their brochure as a '90 minute trip to the "Old World" village of Bray. Made famous in song by the antics of the renowned Vicar.'

In 1960 the Golding brothers decided to change the boat's name and call her after

108. *ABEL,* **RENAMED** *HUMBLE* **IN 1960**. Length 52 ft.

E.P. Hawthorne

109. *MAGNOLIA*. This 40ft launch was built in 1902 by Sam Saunders at his East Cowes boatyard. She had a speed of 10 mph.

Ray Wheeler

110. **THE 40 FT *MAGNOLIA*, RENAMED *MAJESTIC***. Built by Sam Saunders in 1902 and now owned and recently restored by Chas and Julie Newens.

Chas Newens

their grandmother who many years earlier had been known and nicknamed as 'Humble by nature, Humble by name'.

In 1981 *Humble* was bought by John Morrell and Patrick Kelly who commissioned Peter Freebody of Hurley to refurbish her and fit a saloon designed by John Morrell to be similar to that on Palmer's launch. In 1989 she was reconverted to electric propulsion by Rupert Latham of the Steam & Electric Launch Co. During the conversion the old engine bed was found, giving rise to the suggestion that the original engine was probably electric.

MAGNOLIA, RENAMED MAJESTIC

This launch is one of the three remaining hulls built by the Consuta method developed by Sam Saunders. She is still in excellent condition with her hull in original unrestored form. Forty feet long and six feet beam, she was built in 1902 at the new works at Cowes for the Jesse Boots family of pharmaceutical fame and was fitted with a Saunders electric motor which gave her a speed of 10 mph.[43]

In due course she was converted to petrol and her name changed to *Majestic*. Her present owners are Chas and Julie Newens who restored her to a very high standard and installed a 165 hp General Motors petrol engine which gives her a speed of over 18 mph. She is frequently used as an umpire's launch at Henley and on the Tideway and as a luxurious hire launch.

MARY GORDON

Built of teak and launched in 1899 by Mary Gordon, wife of John Gordon, the Lord Mayor of Leeds, this electrically propelled boat could carry 75 adults or 120 children and was operated on the Waterloo Lake at Roundhay Park in Leeds.[44] Mr W. James of Seacroft Gardens, Leeds, recalls that when he was a passenger in 1904, she was battery operated. During the early 1920s she was sold to Stephen Askew, a Wakefield cinema proprietor, who moved her on a wagon drawn by six horses from the Waterloo Lake to the 'Potato Basin' on the River Aire in Leeds and then drove her to Wakefield for a refit and installation of a 'new petrol engine'. Askew personally ran the boat on Sunday trips lasting half-an-hour between Chantry Bridge and Kikthorpe Weir on the River Calder.

A few years later she moved to York where she was operated on the River Ouse. In 1947 she was sold to Mr W.R. Hendry of Lincoln who restored her and ran her as a tripping launch on the Lincoln Canal. Her engine was still the Model T Ford engine installed thirty years earlier. A handbill stated that the *Mary Gordon* provided lovely trips on Lincoln's only passenger boat with music aboard and called at Ye Olde Pyewipe Inn for a gentle refresher.

'Skipper' Ross Hendry operated her until 1957, keeping her at Brayfield Pool in Lincoln and running her up the Fossdyke to Saxilby. Derrick Davison bought her with the intention of reribbing her, fitting new decks and installing a 1912 replica 15 hp steam engine and then operating her on the River Trent. However, during the early 1980s, Mr Davison sold her on to Graham Mackereth. In 1987 she was sold again, this time to David Lawrence of Aberford who planned to restore and operate her again on Waterloo Lake. This project was not followed up and she was once again saved from the scrap heap by Graham Mackereth of Runcorn in the hope of setting up a project to restore her.

CANOES

Canadian canoes were imported from the beginning of the nineteenth century and were exhibited and won medals at the Colonial Exhibitions in London in 1883 and 1886. The original canoes varied from 11 to 19 ft. When the electric launch became popular in the 1890s, boatbuilders would have been very familiar with the design and construction of canoes and some of them would have probably fitted out their canoes with an electric motor and batteries. The hull design was ideal and by stretching the length to 25 ft a craft could be obtained which was sturdy, stable and big enough to carry the electrics and up to eight passengers in comfort. It is, therefore, very surprising that there are virtually no extant records of the electric canoes that were built before 1920.

Sam Saunders of Goring was one of the principal importers of Canadian canoes, but there is no record that he built any electric canoes. In fact, it is not known who was the first builder on the Thames to launch an electric canoe. Woodhouse & Rawson at Eel Pie Island advertised in 1892 as builders of the 'Patent Electric Canoes' but there is no mention of any more than the first two demonstration boats being built.[45] Neither the Immisch Launch Co. nor the Thames Valley Launch Co. mention canoes in their brochures published in 1900 and 1902, although the TVL Co. advertises an electric skiff for sale at £90. Similarly, no reference to canoes has been found in the *Maidenhead Advertiser* until 1913.

There may have been more interest in building electric canoes after the turn of the century. Although petrol engines took over as the propulsion unit for launches, they may well have been too heavy and bulky for fitting into canoes and electric propulsion may have been a feasible alternative. Nevertheless, records are sparse. For example, it is believed that Bond of Maidenhead built the canoes which later were named *Beazie* and *Juliana*, and Meakes & Redknap of Marlow built the canoe which is now known as *Princess Beatrice*. In 1913 it was reported that Bond had sold an electric launch and an electric canoe to Sir John Jackson, the well-known government contractor, who was taking up residence at Henley.[46]

The Ray Motor Co. records include invoices for charging up Lord Louth's electric canoe *Slug* in July 1913 but give no details about its origin. In 1913 Carr also appears to have been working on the design of an electric canoe for which a calculation of its displacement was among his records, but he did nothing further until 1919.

In June 1914 the *Maidenhead Advertiser* carried a report that 'the increased popularity of the electric canoe amongst the wealthy users of the river has been a feature of the season. Two years ago, Mr Ernest Dunkels' *Vixen* and the late Mr Harry King's *Merry Widow* were the only craft of the kind in this neighbourhood. But now they are found in great numbers. We are told that the demand for them this year was very great and boatbuilders were able to command a good price.'[47] The *Vixen* was among the electric boats which had passed through Boulter's Lock on Ascot Sunday in 1913 and she followed the 1914 Long Distance Swim from Cookham to Boulter's Lock which was won for the third year running by Mr H.E. Hewens in the time of 39 minutes 30 seconds.[48]

Undoubtedly electric canoes were built before 1914 but the 1920s marked their heyday.[49] The following are representative of the type of electric canoe which was built before 1914:

111. **PRINCESS BEATRICE, 1990**, previously named *Halcyon*. Immediately behind *Princess Beatrice* is the canoe *Sandpiper*. Further behind is the 30 ft steam launch *Victoria*, built in 1906 by Sam Saunders in his lightweight material Consuta, and which the owner is presently converting to electric propulsion. Length 25 ft, beam 4 ft 2 in, draught 1 ft, speed 7 mph.

E.P. Hawthorne

PRINCESS BEATRICE, ALSO NAMED HALCYON

Princess Beatrice was designed by Lynton Hope and built by Meakes & Redknap of Marlow in 1907. She was owned for fifty to sixty years by Dr Grace of Ludham, during which time she was named *Halcyon*. Rescued in 1990 from the mud at Ludham Bridge Marina, where she had sunk, she was restored and fitted with new electrics by Guy Wootten of Cookham Dean.

The hull is double-skinned, the outer being carvel mahogany over diagonal teak. This construction is rare for a canoe. She was refitted during the 1980s with a 48 volt 2 kw Nelco electric motor and eight Oldham Crompton 6 volt monobloc batteries with a capacity of 175 ampere-hours.

BEAZIE, ORIGINALLY MAY HAVE BEEN NAMED AEGINA

With mahogany carvel hull, this 25 ft 3 in electric canoe was reputed to have been built in 1908 by J. Bond of Maidenhead and acquired by Mrs Lowenadler in 1916.[50] A new motor, made by Submersible and J.L. Motors Ltd of Southall was fitted in 1920. The nameplate on the motor states that it is semi-enclosed series wound, built in 1920, 2.5 bhp with a rating of 7 hrs and running at 650 rpm when supplied with 33 amps at 70 volts. At the same time, fifty-five new nine plate cells, type HFP4, were supplied by the firm of Pritchett & Gold and EPS Co. Ltd. These had a capacity of 290 ampere-hours at the five hour rating.[51]

112. *BEAZIE*, **REPUTEDLY BUILT IN 1908, AFTER RESTORATION, 1990**. This canoe may originally have been named *Aegina*. Restored by Rupert Latham (sitting in stern) at the Steam and Electric Launch Co. and used as a mould for his successful GRP electric canoe.

Photograph by Robin Gates

113. *CYMBA*, **1992**. Incorporating some of the planking from the original, reputed to have been built in 1908, this canoe was built in 1992 by Peter Freebody of Hurley.

Peter Freebody

114. *JULIANA*, 1994, REPUTEDLY BUILT BY BOND OF MAIDENHEAD ABOUT 1910.

E.P. Hawthorne

In 1946 the celebrated stage and film actress, Beatrice Lillee, Lady Peel, bought a magnificent riverside house close to Marsh Lock, Henley-on-Thames, and with it the electric canoe. The canoe was renamed *Beazie* after the name given to Beatrice Lillee by Ivor Novello. In 1990 the canoe was restored by Rupert Latham and his staff at the Steam & Electric Launch Co., who also used it as the master pattern for their very successful GRP hulled electric canoes.

JULIANA

This 25 ft 10 in electric canoe is believed to have been built by Bond of Maidenhead about 1910. She was constructed with 4 inch mahogany planks on steamed oak timbers at approximately 5 inch centres. She was owned and operated as an electric canoe by the Guards Club at Maidenhead until it closed down during the 1960s. Her new owner converted her to a petrol engine and, in 1989, carried out major restoration. Still in very good condition, she was auctioned at the Phillips Boat Auction at Henley in 1994.[52]

Chapter 12

ELECTRIC PROPULSION SYSTEM

The pioneers of electric boating during the 1880s gave detailed descriptions of their novel electrical systems in lectures to professional institutions. However, by the time of Immisch's second season in 1890, the basic form of the propulsion system for electric boats had settled into a pattern which persisted throughout the next twenty-five years. The ideas of gearing between motor and propeller, of twin motors, and of switching in random numbers of batteries as the boat's journey progressed had been tried out and found unsatisfactory. By 1890 batteries were wired up as banks of cells which could be operated in series or parallel; the motors were directly connected to matched propellers; and the control system used either plain or drum mechanical switches.

Boatyards and electrical equipment manufacturers then concentrated on improving the performance and reliability of the components of the system. As today, they drew heavily on the technical developments occurring in other industries, particularly tramways and trains. Consequently, specific information on boat electrics dwindled as is shown in the following sections which highlight some of the equipment used.

MOTORS

The motors used in electric launches were primarily designed for general industrial use and incorporated the minimum of adaptation to the special requirements of the boatbuilder, although some, notably Rowland Edwards of the TVL Co. and Sam Saunders at Goring, occasionally used motors of their own design. Consequently, there is usually little reference to the detailed design of the motors in the boating reports and journals, the writers mostly confining themselves to a simple description of the installation and often not even mentioning the name of the motor manufacturer.

Reckenzaun's *Electricity*, the first electrically propelled boat with commercial potential to be launched on the Thames, was fitted with two Siemens D3 motors driving a 22 in diameter propeller. Either or both of the motors could be switched into the circuit at will. During the first run of this 25 ft launch on 28 September 1882, the motors drew 24 amperes at 96 volts, corresponding to an input power of 2.3 kw.[1] The motors ran at 950 rpm and were geared down to 350 rpm at the propeller.[2]

The Siemens D3 motor had a length overall of 28 in, width of 23 in, height of 10 in and weighed 316 lb. The total weight of the two motors, countershaft supports and pulleys was 812 lb and Reckenzaun decided to replace them with a single Siemens D2 motor, fitted with reversing gear but driving direct on to the propeller shaft. The weight was reduced to 658 lb and the total space occupied by the motor was reduced to only

30 in long, 28 in wide and a height of 15 in. Reckenzaun was also aware that it was possible to improve the boat's performance by ensuring that there was a proper match between motor and propeller. Thus he carried out a number of experiments on different propellers and achieved his designed speed with a two bladed 18½ in diameter propeller running at 813 rpm.

In 1883 Messrs Yarrow & Co. launched their 40 ft 'electrical steam launch', as *The Electrician* magazine described it.[3] This was fitted with a Siemens D2 motor which, although capable of producing 8 to 9 hp, probably only developed 7 hp when supplied with 40 amps from eighty Sellon-Volckmar battery cells.[4] In fact, its measured efficiency was 78 per cent and its output power to weight ratio was 351 ft-lb/min per lb weight (in other words about 17 watts per kg).[5] As in *Electricity*, the motor was directly coupled to the propeller which was two bladed of 19 in diameter and running at 675 to 750 rpm. On a trip from Temple Pier to Greenwich on the tidal Thames, the input supply achieved was 41.22 amps at 112.5 volts (when using sixty cells), corresponding to a motor input power of 4.64 kw and this gave a speed of 6 to 7 mph. Using eighty cells, an output power of 7 hp was obtained.

Reckenzaun also noted that a 20 ft electrical launch would accommodate at least as many people as a 30 ft steam launch and that 'little difficulty should be encountered in charging the cells, and this is merely a question of detail'. The industry is still looking into this little point of detail! The motor itself tended to overheat, but this was attributed to passing excessive currents through it in order to achieve the best possible speed. This caused the insulation, usually cotton or silk, to break down and Yarrow suggested that asbestos or some other non-conductor should be used. He also pointed out that the motors were designed for stationary use for lighting, where weight was no object and a reduction in weight would be beneficial.

The fourth electric boat to be built on the Thames was the 25 ft *Australia*. This was fitted with a Reckenzaun motor which was substantially lighter, weighing 390 lb and producing a maximum output power of 6 hp. On a trial run, the motor took a current of 37 amps supplied from fifty EPS cells at 100 volts.[6]

The 36 ft *Volta*, launched in August 1885, had two Reckenzaun motors arranged in line and direct coupled to the 20 in diameter three-bladed propeller running at 600 rpm.[7] The motors were series wound, the resistance of the field magnets being 0.2 ohms and the armature 0.16 ohms. They weighed 448 lb each. The normal supply was 28 amps at 120 volts, giving 4.5 hp. By coupling the motors in parallel, the current could be increased to 90 amps and the speed to 1,000 rpm, when the motors would develop about 14 hp. At that power the boat made 12 to 14 knots.[8] This power could not be maintained for long, but would be useful in emergencies.

The *Countess*, owned by the Elieson Co., had its second trial in the Albert Dock in October 1887. With a length of 90 ft she was then the largest electric boat to have been built. She was fitted with a 20 hp Crompton motor running at 1,000 rpm. A very complicated gearing system was used to bring the motor rpm down to 200 at the propeller, which was 3 ft 6 in diameter with a pitch of 5 ft 6 in.[9]

The launches built for Moritz Immisch from 1888 were, of course, fitted with Immisch motors. An Immisch advertisement in 1887, similar to that in 1889 (see page 150), states

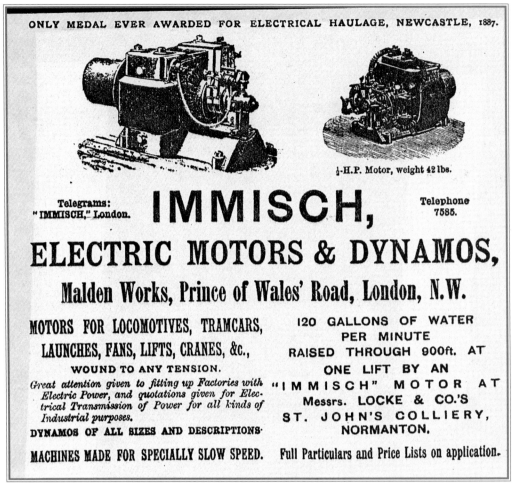

ONLY MEDAL EVER AWARDED FOR ELECTRICAL HAULAGE, NEWCASTLE, 1887.

¼-H.P. Motor, weight 42 lbs.

Telegrams:
"IMMISCH," London.

IMMISCH,

Telephone
7585.

ELECTRIC MOTORS & DYNAMOS,

Malden Works, Prince of Wales' Road, London, N.W.

MOTORS FOR LOCOMOTIVES, TRAMCARS, LAUNCHES, FANS, LIFTS, CRANES, &c.,
WOUND TO ANY TENSION.

Great attention given to fitting up Factories with Electric Power, and quotations given for Electrical Transmission of Power for all kinds of Industrial purposes.

DYNAMOS OF ALL SIZES AND DESCRIPTIONS.

MACHINES MADE FOR SPECIALLY SLOW SPEED.

120 GALLONS OF WATER
PER MINUTE
RAISED THROUGH 900ft. AT
ONE LIFT BY AN
"IMMISCH" MOTOR AT
Messrs. LOCKE & CO.'S
ST. JOHN'S COLLIERY,
NORMANTON.

Full Particulars and Price Lists on application.

115. **IMMISCH MOTORS ADVERTISEMENT, 1889**.

Electrical Directory, 1889

that the company had received the highest award for electric motors at the International Inventions Exhibition in London in 1885 and also referred to motors for launches. The earlier advertisement was published a year before he launched his first electric boat and shows that he was aware of the progress being made in electric boating and was interested in selling into this new market. His launch business, set up in 1888, provided the opportunity to demonstrate his motors. For example, the *Viscountess Bury* was fitted with two 5½ kw Immisch motors which were replaced the following year, presumably because less power was actually needed, by a single 7½ kw motor taking on average 45 amps at 164 volts. His first five launches, built by Tagg, were fitted with his smaller motors of about 2 kw.

Other boatbuilders who took an interest in electric boats bought motors from other manufacturers. Sargeant, who had fitted Immisch motors in the *Viscountess Bury* and the

116. SAUNDERS 3 KW MOTOR.

R.L. Wheeler

Ray Mead, would have fitted motors made by the firm Woodhouse & Rawson, when he was taken over in 1890. Certainly a 3.75 kw 'W. & R.' motor was fitted in *The Bonnie Southport* launch in 1892.[10] Sargeant was also reported to be building a launch of 75 ft length, 13 ft beam and 16½ tons displacement.[11] This was to achieve a speed of 8 knots when driven by a motor operating at the very high figure of 400 volts and giving a propeller speed of 650 rpm. Unfortunately, there is no record of whether this launch was ever built.

This was still the period during which motors and controllers were more or less hand-made and therefore an individual with ideas could get them altered or made to his own design. For example, Edwards at the Thames Valley Launch Co., in conjunction with Septimus Beevor, designed motors which were fitted into his launches. After the turn of the century the TVL Co. appear to have used Newton motors. These were manufactured by the Newton Electrical Works at Taunton, which was founded in July 1896 with a capital of £32,650 held by eighteen shareholders and with Mr F.M. Newton as Chairman.

The Saunders company also used motors made to their own design. These were 'arranged to run at a wide range of speeds, without the use of any external resistances, and at constant volts, thus avoiding the running of the battery in separate groups. The motors have two commutators of hard copper, of large dimensions, to ensure cool running, and are fitted with carbon brushes. The armatures are slot wound, ensuring long life and good permanent insulation which is not liable to damage from mechanical shock. The motor shaft runs in self-oiling bearings, the after one forming an efficient thrust bearing. The motors are double wound so as to form practically two series motors.'[12]

Carr at the Ray Motor Co. obtained an estimate in March 1901 for a Newton T2 motor to be fitted into a 22 ft launch for Mr S. de Lissa. It was one of the T type range shown in the Newton advertisement dated 1902. Output was listed at 1 to 4 bhp for motors within the same dimensions, the higher output corresponding to a specific weight of 112 lb/hp.[13] Newton continued to make this type of motor for many years. One version of it was fitted in the canoe *Gena* built in 1920 and is still in use. Other versions were fitted in the canoes acquired or built by Messums at Bray and bought by Peter Freebody of Hurley when Messums closed down in the 1970s.

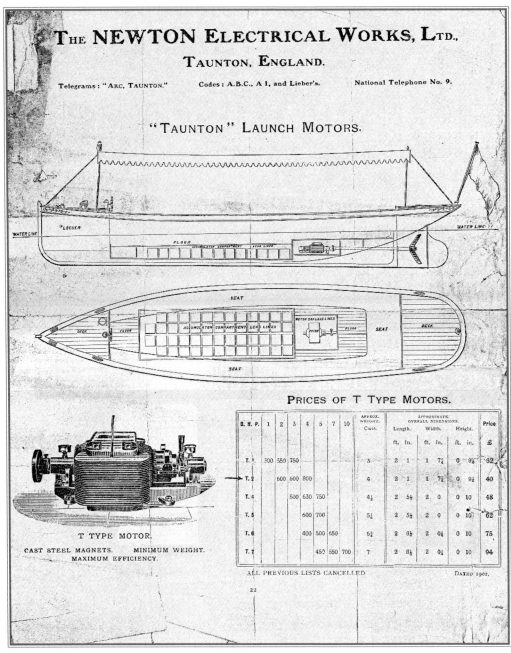

THE NEWTON ELECTRICAL WORKS, LTD.,
TAUNTON, ENGLAND.

Telegrams : "ARC, TAUNTON."   Codes : A.B.C., A 1, and Lieber's.   National Telephone No. 9.

"TAUNTON" LAUNCH MOTORS.

PRICES OF T TYPE MOTORS.

B. H. P.	1	2	3	4	5	7	10	APPROX. WEIGHT. Cwts.	Length. ft. in.	Width. ft. in.	Height. ft. in.	Price £
T. 1	300	550	750			—	—	3	2 1	1 7½	0 9½	32
T. 2		600	600	800				4	2 1	1 7½	0 9½	40
T. 4			500	630	750			4½	2 5½	2 0	0 10	48
T. 5				600	700			5¼	2 5½	2 0	0 10	62
T. 6				400	500	650		6¼	2 8½	2 0¼	0 10	75
T. 7					450	550	700	7	2 8½	2 0¼	0 10	94

ALL PREVIOUS LISTS CANCELLED   DATED 1902.

22

T TYPE MOTOR.

CAST STEEL MAGNETS.   MINIMUM WEIGHT.
MAXIMUM EFFICIENCY.

117. **NEWTON MOTORS, 1902, AS USED BY THAMES VALLEY LAUNCH CO. AND RAY MOTOR CO.**

G. Banham

118. TYPICAL ELECTRIC MOTOR OF THE 1900s: THE COMMUTATOR END.

E.P. Hawthorne

119. TYPICAL ELECTRIC MOTOR OF THE 1900s: THE DRIVE END. This motor was demonstrated by Peter Freebody at the 1993 Traditional Boat Rally at Henley. He had acquired it from Messum's at Bray when they closed down and it is probably a T-type Newton motor.

E.P. Hawthorne

The Submersible & J.L. Motor Co. appears on the electric boat scene from about 1910 onwards. A drawing of one of their motors was sent to Messrs Meakes & Redknap in December 1913.[14] The drawing itself appears to have been produced in March 1912 and shows an F1 type producing 2 hp at 60 volts and 32 amps and running at 700 rpm. In 1919 Carr and Horsham at the Ray Motor Co. acquired an installation drawing of an F4 type motor giving 2½ hp at 650 rpm. It refers to a 1914 design but was issued in December 1919 under the name of the Submersible Motors Ltd, the J.L. presumably having dropped out during the war.

The canoe *Beazie* was refitted in 1920 with the same size of Submersible Co.'s motor. It was described as a semi-enclosed type with a rating of 7 hours at 70 volts, 33 amps, 650 rpm with an output of 2½ bhp. Short Brothers (Rochester & Bedford) Ltd acquired an identical motor for installation in their 25 ft canoe, which they introduced to the market in 1921.

All the motors used in electric boats were series wound and usually two pole. The motors fitted in the early boats drove the propellers through gearing, but it was soon realized that it was more efficient, and probably quieter, to use slower running motors connected directly to the propeller shaft.

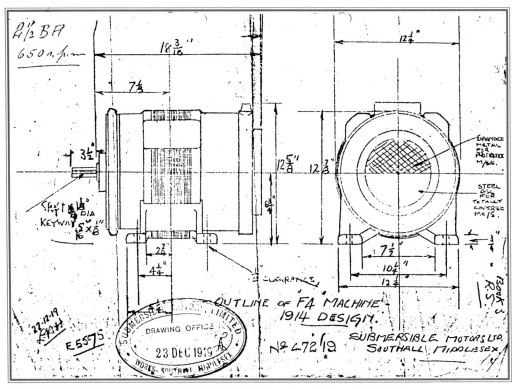

120. **SUBMERSIBLE MOTORS LTD: F4-TYPE MOTOR**. Although designed before 1914, this motor was fitted in many of the electric canoes built during the early 1920s.

G. Banham

These launch motors seem to have required very little maintenance. Apart from being slow speed, they were very substantially constructed, with the result that (as shown in the Ray Motor Co. records) it was only necessary from time to time to turn up the commutators and fit new brushes.

The first outboard motor ever fitted to a boat was that used by Gustave Trouvé in 1881, when he demonstrated the first successful electric boat on the lake in the Bois de Boulogne in Paris. Since then no real attempt seems to have been made to develop an outboard electric motor until the 1950s.

CONTROLLERS

The controllers used on electric boats owed much, like the motors, to the designs evolved for industrial applications and particularly tramcars. Boats had the added complication of requiring switching between ahead and astern at a moment's notice.

Speed regulation was obtained in a number of different ways.

The earliest electric boat *Electricity* was fitted with two motors and a belt and pulley gearing system between the motors and the single screw propeller. Control was exercised through four separate mechanisms:[15]

1. A switch to pass the current from the batteries to either or both motors.
2. A commutator to switch into the circuit additional cells to add to the basic forty cells until a total of fifty-four was reached.
3. An Addyman's friction clutch to bring one of the motors into or out of gear with little shock.
4. A lever by means of which one of two pairs of brushes could be brought against the commutator thereby altering the direction of rotation of the motor to give ahead and astern power. One pair had an angular lead forwards and the other backwards.

This was a complicated system and within a couple of months it was substantially modified. The two motors were replaced with a single larger motor drawing a maximum of 43 amps at 92 volts from forty-six cells.

The control system was further simplified in Yarrow's boat which had a single motor connected directly to the propeller.[16] The motor was a Siemens and, like *Electricity*, was fitted with two pairs of brushes giving ahead or astern and operated through a cable by a lever mounted beside the steersman. He also used a switch which had four positions: off or drawing current from forty, sixty or eighty cells. This system was designed to take a maximum of 42 amps at 112 volts from the sixty cells, and by bringing in the extra cells a duration of five to six hours at a constant cruising speed could be obtained.[17] Yarrow pointed out that the Board of Trade limit for 'perfectly safe operation' was 200 volts, and since the maximum that could be developed on the launch was 120 volts it was not 'in the least degree dangerous to life'.

By 1885 the control system had been even more simplified. The *Volta* was fitted with two motors in line and the switching was arranged so that the current passed through the motors either in series or in parallel or through only one motor. This gave a power

121. **DRUM CONTROLLER, 1918**. A standard reversing controller giving five speeds. Arc shield open and fitted, lower left, with magnetic blow-out coil.

W.P. Maycock

output to the propeller of 4, 7 or 12 hp.[18] For reversing, the system of switching over from one pair of brushes to the other was scrapped and instead the current through the field magnets was reversed.[19]

The *Lady Cooper*, launched in 1888, had a similar control system, although the reporter described it as of a peculiar design intended for tramcars as well as boats.[20] The batteries could be switched in parallel or series to the single motor, and astern power was probably obtained by reversing the current through the field.

A description of the controls for the *Delta*, one of Immisch's first five electric launches, refers to three control handles: one for turning the current on and off, the second for full

122. **SAUNDERS CONTROLLER, THE DRUM TYPE PATENTED BY SAUNDERS**. The batteries were always in series and the motor, being double wound, effectively acted as two series motors. The controller varied the connections between the motor armatures and fields, thereby giving a range of speeds.

R.L. Wheeler

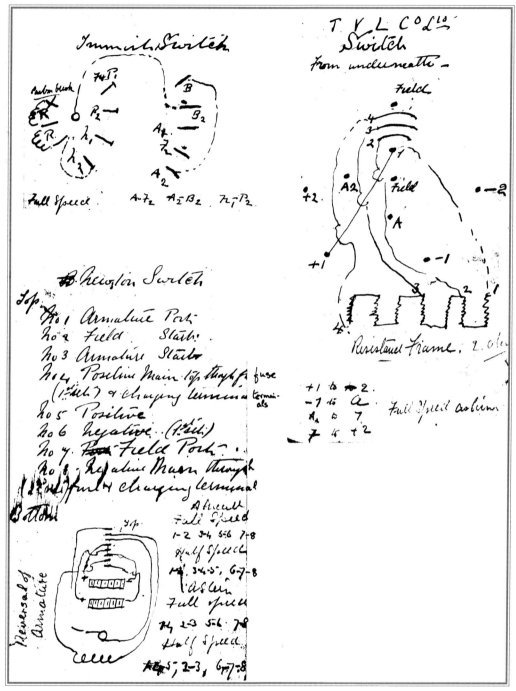

123. **CONTROLLER WIRING: 1**. Sketches from Carr's notebook while with the Thames Valley Launch Co. The Immisch switch appears to have two resistances in the field winding. The Newton switch seems to have been the drum type. The TVL switch is probably also a drum type and had three resistances in the field winding.

G. Banham

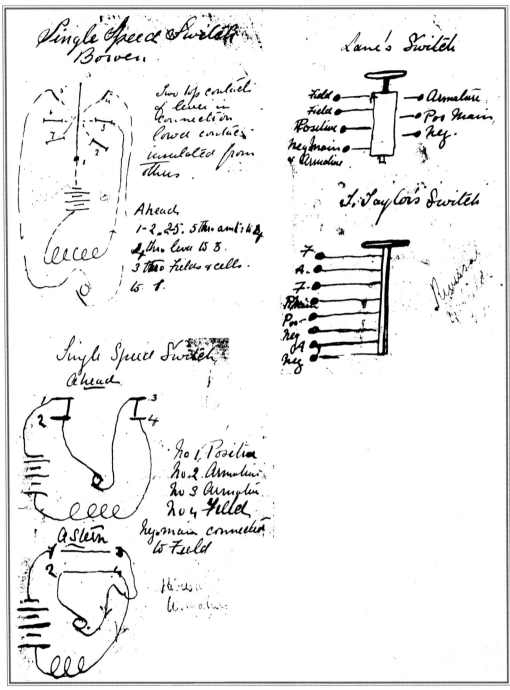

124. **CONTROLLER WIRING: 2**. More of Carr's sketches. Bowen's switch appears to have been a drum type. Lane's and T. Taylor's were drum type. The single speed switch may have been the one used on small boats.

G. Banham

or half-speed, and the third for going ahead or astern.[21] The first was mechanically connected to the other two so that they could not be moved without first cutting off the current. This system became known as the 'Immisch' type. Fusible cut-outs were also in the circuit so that the motor was prevented from burning up if the propeller became jammed by weeds or ran aground.

William Sargeant, the builder of the big electric launches such as the *Viscountess Bury*, patented a single lever control for a 75 ft launch which he was building in 1892. This was arranged to give full- and half-speed ahead and the same astern.[22] It was said that the potential was 400 volts, although this seems very doubtful in view of Yarrow's comment that the Board of Trade's maximum permissible voltage allowed on boats was 200 volts.

A report on the Immisch fleet in 1898 mentions that the 'Immisch' switch had been replaced by the 'Moy' type single lever control, which gave the same five positions: off, half and full ahead, and half and full astern.[23] The batteries were connected in parallel for half-speed and in series for full-speed.

Every motor manufacturer and some of the electric boatbuilders had their own designs of controllers. The systems for the smaller boats were similar to the 'Moy' system. The more elaborate high voltage systems adopted much of the switching technology developed for tramcars, suitably modified to produce ahead and astern operation. These used a drum controller design which produced increases in the motor speed by switching out a set of resistances in the field coil circuit, thereby giving scope for a wide range of speeds. There were, of course, a number of variations on the theme, as can be seen from the sketches in Carr's working notebook which illustrates the wiring on several of the controllers fitted to launches under his care. Saunders, up at Goring, also developed and patented his own controller, which was an adaptation of the drum controller. Saunders insisted that batteries should never be run in parallel and his controller was designed to make use of the double wound armature in the motors that he used.

The major problem with the earlier controllers was sparking at the contacts as the lever was moved from one position to another. This was due in part to the high voltages employed and much effort was expended in overcoming the problem. For example, the Thames Valley Launch Co. developed its own switch, the 'Beevor-Edwards', and claimed that because the 'make and break' were independent of the main switch, there was no sparking 'thus removing the danger of burnt contacts, which so frequently leads to trouble in other forms of controller'.[24]

The simple switch and the drum controller remained the basic control system types for electric boats right up until the 1970s when the MOSFET (metal-oxide field-effect transistor) electronic system, giving completely variable speed, came into use.

BATTERIES

The key to successful electric boating in the 1890s and 1900s was, as now, the batteries (or accumulators as they were called at that time). The first electric boat, designed and built in 1839 by Professor Jacobi, emitted such a cloud of toxic fumes that its first outing was terminated after a short distance, never to be repeated. The first battery cell using the lead acid principle was invented by Gaston Planté in 1859, but the process and time taken to 'form' the cell and get it up to its operating condition precluded its use in practical applications.[25] This 'forming' problem was not overcome until Fauré devised a method of production of the lead plates which cut the forming time down to two or three charges.

Major improvements in the Fauré cells resulted from work by Swan and by Sellon and Volckmar of the Electrical Power Storage Co. at Millwall on the Thames in the Port of London. They devised the idea of making a perforated plate with holes into which red lead paste was forced. These plates were then placed with separators between into a box filled with sulphuric acid. These boxes were called a 'cell' and, when fully charged, supplied current at 2 volts. In one application these plates were fitted into rectangular lead-lined wooden boxes of 827 cubic inches capacity and weighing 80 lb. Each box, or cell, contained sixteen plates and was known as a 'one horse-power' cell, in other words capable of storing energy equivalent to 1 hp for one hour. These cells were found to have an average output of 32 amps at 2 volts over a nine-hour period of discharge, corresponding to a capacity of 288 ampere-hours and a specific energy of 21 wh/kg.[26] Nowadays, traction batteries are usually made up of three or six cells fitted inside a single casing or 'monobloc', giving 6 or 12 volts respectively and having a specific energy of 35 to 80 wh/kg.

In 1882 single cells were used by Anthony Reckenzaun, Sellon and Volckmar in the Electrical Power Storage Co.'s boat *Electricity*, the first electric-powered boat built in the UK.[27] This was taken on its trial trip on 28 September 1882. Forty-five cells of about 10 in cube and calculated to supply power for six hours at the rate of 4 hp were stowed fore and aft under the floor and seats. In practice, they supplied about 2.3 kw at 24 amps and 96 volts to each of two D3 Siemens motors.[28]

In a general report of the tests of *Electricity*, Reckenzaun reported that each cell weighed 56 lb, had a capacity of 350 ampere-hours and gave a fairly constant current for 7½ hours.[29] Each cell was made up of forty plates of lead, each 7½ in long by 5¼ in wide, and weighing 15 oz, placed vertically in an ebonite box. The plates were separated by narrow india-rubber strips and the box was filled with dilute sulphuric acid.

A year later, in July 1883, Yarrow of Poplar in London launched a 40 ft galvanized steel boat with 6 ft beam. Fitted with a Siemens motor under the floor at the stern, she had eighty Sellon-Volckmar cells. These were placed, seven on each side, under the seat and the rest under the floor. On her trials a maximum speed of 8 mph was achieved, with a current of 41.22 amps at 112.5 volts, equivalent to 4.63 kw. The speed controller was a switch bringing in the current from forty, sixty, or the full eighty cells.

A.F. Yarrow gave a lecture[30] about his electric launch in which he describes the cells as follows: Each cell measures 9½ in long by 9 in wide by 7½ in deep; the cell itself can be of glass, porcelain, or of any material not attacked by acid. Into each of these are placed eighteen pairs of plates. . . . The positive plates are pasted with red lead, and the negative plates are pasted with litharge.[31] They are first subjected to the process of 'forming' – that is to say, by means of an electric current the red lead becomes peroxide of lead – a substance of a chocolate colour – the litharge of the negative plate is reduced, and becomes spongy lead. The plates are immersed in the cells previously referred to, containing diluted sulphuric acid in the proportion of one of acid to four of water. The

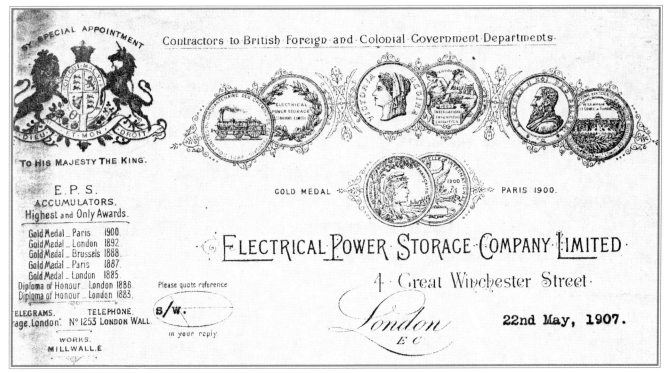

125. BATTERY SUPPLIER FOR ELECTRIC BOATS FROM 1882 ONWARDS.

G. Banham

lead casting or grid has numerous square dove-tailed holes, which are filled or pasted with the oxides of lead. These dove-tailed holes serve as a convenient means of keeping the red lead and litharge in close electrical contact.

It was found that during the first three hours of use of the fully charged accumulators, the boat speed dropped by about half a mile per hour. To overcome this, only fifty or sixty of the cells were connected up and, as the current fell off, other cells were coupled up. This enabled the boat to be kept running for five to six hours. If full power was required all the cells were brought into the circuit.

Reckenzaun was a realist. Although he showed that, theoretically, a fully oxidized lead-acid battery should enable the boat to travel for 82 hours, he pointed out that this was quite impossible: 'we might as well dream of getting 5 hp out of a steam engine for 1 lb of coal per hour'. He concluded his talk by saying, 'Whether electricity will ever rival steam remains yet to be proved; we may be on the threshold of great things; the premature enthusiasm has subsided and we enter upon the road of steady progress.'[32]

Towards the end of the 1880s the perforated lead tube was replaced by an asbestos sheath, which made the plates more robust and improved the capacity to weight ratio. This was followed towards the end of the century by the introduction of the ebonite tube, which had the same mechanical strength as the asbestos sheath but used thinner sections and improved the performance of the plate.

The Electrical Power Storage Co., in particular, had built up a strong position during the 1880s in the field of traction batteries. Based on these developments and its experience with the boat *Electricity*, the company launched a new electric boat *Lady Cooper* just in time for the Oxford and Cambridge Boat Race in 1888. She was fitted with sixty-six cells of EPS Co.'s new improved traction or 'T' type. The cells contained twenty-three plates giving a maximum of 40 amps at which rate of discharge their capacity was 175 ampere-hours.[33]

During the latter half of the 1880s a number of trials of battery-operated electric trams were carried out.[34] These usually involved replacing a horse-drawn tramcar and running the test tram over short distances. One of the most extensive trials was that of Immisch's Electric Traction Co., which replaced five horse-drawn trams on the North Metropolitan Co.'s line from Canning Town to Barking. Started in 1889, these trials went on for two or three years, demonstrating that the batteries could stand up to the vibration and rough conditions of the tramways. After running 40,000 miles during one seven-month period, it was reported that the cell plates had stood up to the rough usage much better than expected, the main fault being burning of the lugs to the cross bars.[35] It was this progress in improved battery robustness and life that encouraged Immisch to start up his electric launch company in 1889, and each of his first five electric launches, ordered from Tagg & Son at East Molesey, were fitted with two hundred EPS Co. cells.

Other companies began to enter the battery business. In 1891, for example, the Chloride Electrical Storage Syndicate was formed and its battery production started in 1893 at Clifton, Manchester.[36] The Epstein Electric Storage Co. made the seventy cells which were fitted in the Woodhouse & Rawson electric pinnace *Electric* launched in 1891. Immisch himself had a shareholding in the Lamina Accumulator Co. and there is also mention of Leitner cells made by the Accumulator Industries Ltd, such as those fitted by the Thames Valley Launch Co. in some of their boats.[37]

Nevertheless, the Electrical Power Storage Co. maintained a strong position in the electric boat field throughout the 1890s. In 1898 it was reported that the largest electric launch in the Immisch fleet, the 65 ft *Viscountess Bury*, was equipped with one hundred and sixty T-23 EPS Co. cells and the smallest, the four-seater 22 ft *Celia* had twenty-two of its B-15 type of cell. In fact, in eighteen launches of the fleet, the majority of the cells used were of the B type, the remainder being of Epstein or Lamina manufacture.[38]

Right up to the 1930s the batteries for electric boats were built up from individual 2 volt cells connected in series or parallel and numbering enough to give the required motor voltage. The construction of the cells was such that the plates and separators could be dismantled and replaced and this meant that the boatyards could repair damaged cells on their own premises.

Plates were damaged mainly because owners were lax in getting their cells recharged. In July 1899, for example, Carr of the TVL Co. at Boulter's Lock, Maidenhead, was writing to Mr Stearn, the owner of *Little Nell*, that he couldn't get any charge into the cells because they were run right down to a specific gravity of 1100 and the thirty cells only produced 40 volts. Sometimes plates suffered mechanical damage and we find Carr

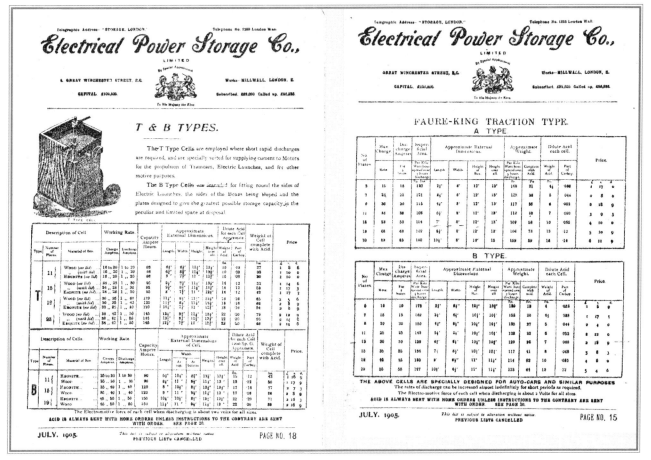

126. **TRACTION BATTERY SPECIFICATIONS, 1905**. The T-type batteries were said to have been used in the *Viscountess Bury* and other large launches in the Immisch fleet. The B-type batteries were specially designed to fit along the sides of electric launches, the sides of the boxes being narrower at the bottom than at the top, and may have been fitted in Immisch's 22 ft launch *Celia*. The A and B Fauré-King types on the right were recommended for use in electric cars and launches.

G. Banham

writing in March 1900 to Mr Atkins, the owner of *Asthore*, to say that the cells needed thorough cleaning and possibly replacing of four cracked positive sections. In 1901 Carr's records of cell renewals included ten E-25 EPS Co. positive sections; nine E-19 EPS Co. positive sections; one 7-plate Epstein positive section; three 7-plate Epstein boxes 4 in x 9 in x 11 in; and five hundred glass separators for small Chlorides.

Cells and the acid carboys must also have been damaged during transit to the boatyards, but this does not seem to have been noted as a problem until after the First World War. For example, during the June 1919 refit of *Mina* some of the new positive plates ordered from the EPS Co. were found to be damaged because they had been badly packed. This was unusual as Carr told Mr A.F. Ross, the owner, that the EPS Co. staff 'are usually most careful'. In December that year Carr ordered sixty AXE8 cells from Chloride Electrical Storage Co. for delivery in February the following year. On their arrival he found that out of the four cases, one had been damaged and that five boxes in that case had been broken and one set of cell and cell connectors were missing.

The EPS Co. made an attempt to meet the boatbuilders needs, and its catalogue, issued in July 1905, listed details of the T and B types of cells. The B type cells were 'intended for fitting round the sides of electric launches, the sides of the boxes being sloped and the plates designed to give the greatest possible storage capacity in the peculiar and limited space at disposal'. The ebonite cells were 10½ in wide at the top and 8¾ in at the bottom and the 19-plate cell had an energy/volume ratio of 14.2 wh/l compared with 22.8 wh/l for the standard E-19 traction cell. The T type was designed for short rapid discharge and was 'especially suited for supplying current to Motors for the propulsion of Tramcars, Electric Launches, and for other motive purposes'.[39]

It was, of course, possible for the boatyards to change the plates in a cell. However, this often resulted in a launch's cells becoming unbalanced, with ones containing old plates being connected to cells with new plates. The accumulator companies disapproved of this practice; in 1907, for example, the EPS Co. were writing to Carr to say that 'as the negatives had been in use for 6 or 7 years, it is rather doubtful if they would be in sufficiently good condition to warrant your putting new positives to work with them'. In any case, a cell life of seven years was a very good achievement.

Cell costs are difficult to pin down. Kempe's *Pocket Book*[40] of 1892 quotes that the launch *Magnet*, designed by Reckenzaun, was fitted with fifty-six cells of 155 ampere-hours capacity at a cost of £2 per cell. In 1905 the EPS Co. catalogue was quoting £2 14s 6d for a 23-plate E type cell with a capacity of 150 ampere-hours. Fauré-King A Type 11-plate traction cells of 190 ampere-hours were quoted in the same catalogue at a price of £3 9s 3d, and similar cells were quoted in 1919 at about £3 10s.[41]

An interesting comparison of cell costs was given by the estimates received by Carr in 1913 for a complete new set for the electric launch *Esperanza*. One estimate was for forty-six Edison AV33 Type cells giving 570 ampere-hours at 92 volts. Another estimate was for forty-six Fors cells manufactured by the Callendar Cable & Construction Co. The cost and weight for the Edison and Fors cells were £1,125 and 6532 lb versus £320 and 3680 lb respectively. In the end the owner, Major Fenner, decided simply to replace some of the existing plates and boxes at a total cost of about £116.

In June 1913 Carr invoiced the Maidenhead and District Boating Co. £46 10s for supplying thirty special 15-plate horizontal traction type sections of 157 ampere-hours capacity complete and fitted in their launch *Santarello*. During the following month, the Hart Accumulator Co. quoted £45 7s 6d for the supply of thirty 11-plate 'CT' Type cells of 187 ampere-hours capacity complete in ebonite boxes with lids, acid and connections.

In May 1913 the 30 ft electric launch *Mina* was fitted with twenty-five E.L.19 Moting type positive sections, ebonite sheet separators and cell connectors, five new positive sections and acid for a total sum of £24 14s 4d. In June 1919 *Mina* had twenty-eight accumulators cleaned and filled with fresh acid. By July, however, new positive plates had to be ordered. These were damaged in transit and, in February 1920, Carr ordered a complete replacement set of thirty-six 11-plate FKA type positive and negative sections, separators, grids and acid to fit into the existing ebonite boxes at a cost between £98 and £112.[42]

During 1920 Carr provided twenty-four FK 5-plate positives with new separators, acid and fitting to existing boxes for £80 15s for Mr H. Stanley's electric launch *Whip*.

Rationalization of the battery industry was inevitable. By 1920, for example, the Electrical Power Storage Co. had absorbed the Premier Accumulator Co. and then merged with another company to form Pritchett & Gold and EPS Co. Ltd.[43] This company was still supplying batteries for electric boats in 1937 when forty Fauré-King 11-plate cells were fitted in Bond's 28½ ft electric canoe *Victoria*.

CHARGING

As early as 1884 Anthony Reckenzaun of the Electrical Power Storage Co. pointed out that 'it is hardly probable that anyone would lay down a complete plant, consisting of a steam or gas engine and dynamo, for the sole purpose of charging the boat cells, unless such a boat were in almost daily use, or unless several boats were to be supplied with power from one station. In order that electric launches may prove useful, it will be

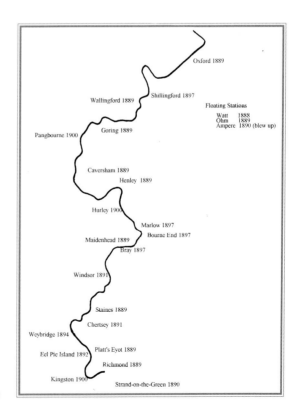

127. **CHARGING STATIONS ON THE THAMES**. Dates are when first report of the existence of a charging station has been noted.

E.P. Hawthorne

M. IMMISCH & CO.'S

Electric Charging Stations
AND
Electric Pleasure Launches
ON THE THAMES.
SEASON 1889.

MESSRS. M. IMMISCH & CO. have now established
SIX ELECTRIC CHARGING STATIONS
on the River, situated as follows: at RICHMOND, PLATT'S EYOT,
Hampton (Head-Quarters and Principal Station), STAINES, MAIDEN-
HEAD, HENLEY, READING, and are prepared to sell or let on hire

ELECTRIC PLEASURE LAUNCHES.

For Regattas, Fêtes, or Parties, Two Self-Propelling Charging Stations will
be available, and can be moved to any part of the river, either for re-charging
Launches or for supplying Electric Light.

One day's notice will ensure a Launch being sent to any landing place on the
river between London and Oxford.

Orders for the Hire of the Launches will a'n be taken by all the principal Boat Builders up the River.

Full Particulars, Estimates, &c., on application to
M. IMMISCH & CO.,
Malden Electric Works, Kentish Town, LONDON, N.W.

128. **AN ADVERTISEMENT IN SALTERS GUIDE, 1889, SHOWING AN IMMISCH FLOATING CHARGING STATION**. One of the three floating 'hulks' which Immisch commissioned William Sargeant to convert into charging stations and which first appeared at Henley Regatta in 1888.

J. Cowan

desirable that charging stations should be established, and on many of the British and Irish rivers and lakes there is an abundance of motive power in the shape of steam or gas engines, or even waterwheels.'[44]

It was Moritz Immisch who put this idea into practice by realizing that success in developing an electric hireboat business was dependent on simultaneously setting up a widespread system of charging stations. This was why he and a party of friends made their first appearance on the Thames in a 'roomy hulk' moored at Mortlake and from which they watched the Boat Race of 1888.

The hulk was Immisch's first purchase and was destined for conversion into a floating charging station. Subsequent to the Boat Race, it was fitted out by William Sargeant with an adapted steam locomotive boiler driving one of Immisch's dynamos. The capacity was 15 kw, sufficient to charge the six launches which Immisch planned to have at Henley during the following year.

In April 1889 Electric Charging Station No. 1 was stationed above Boulter's Weir. This was Immisch's hulk moved into position for the first river event in the calendar – Ascot week. In the same month Mr Bowen of Ray Mead Hotel, Maidenhead, took delivery of his large 60 ft electric launch *Ray Mead*.[45]

In June 1889 the electric launch *Volta* was recorded as having charged up at Immisch's headquarters at Platt's Eyot on a trip from Hampton Court to Chertsey and back to Richmond.[46] Another charging station had been placed at Kew Bridge and a third was to be constructed above Richmond Bridge.[47]

September 1889 saw a trip in Immisch's launch *Eta* which set off on a Saturday from Hampton. On board were Mr A. Rawlinson of Brighton, Mr Saunders of the Miller of Mansfield Hotel at Goring and Mr Volk, the Manager at the Platt's Eyot works. After fourteen hours, they had travelled 26 miles and stopped overnight at Maidenhead while the launch was charged up. A short trip to Medmenham and back occupied the Sunday, but on the Monday, they did the 34 miles to Goring where the batteries were recharged overnight, presumably at the Goring Mill boatyard where Saunders' relative, Sam, would later be building electric launches using his patented Consuta laminated-wood system for the hulls.[48] On the Tuesday they travelled to Oxford and back to Abingdon, where they stayed overnight but without recharging the batteries. The following day they had lunch at Goring during which the batteries were put on charge (there is no record of the duration of the charging period!). This meant that the launch covered the 60 miles from Goring to Oxford and back without recharging. That night was spent at Reading and on Thursday Maidenhead was reached at 1 p.m. This was quite an expedition, 124 miles being covered with two overnight charges and one lunchtime charge.[49]

Another trial of one of the new electric launches was undertaken by Professor Forbes.[50] He hired the launch *Delta* from Immisch for the summer and kept a record of its performance: 'The house which I occupied was at Bray, just below Maidenhead, and each night I took the launch by myself, towing a boat behind, up to the charging station (which was not a mile away). I left it there to be charged during the night, and by breakfast time the launch was outside ready charged, with a sufficient supply to last me the whole day. I may mention that I never exhausted the complete charge of the batteries in my launch during the whole time. I generally went out shortly after breakfast, spent the whole day on the river, very often coming home at eight o'clock, and afterwards taking it up to the charging station in the evening; and certainly forty miles was not by any means enough to exhaust the supply of electricity on the launch.'

Professor Forbes had ideas about charging. His account continues: 'It may be also added that on the Thames it is easy to secure a sufficient number of charging stations. At present there are four or five at easy distances apart. Eventually there can be little doubt that the hotels on the river will find it financially a good plan to be lighted electrically, and then this power which they have on the premises can be used during the night for charging the storage batteries of launches.'

Another of his suggestions for charging stations was certainly original: 'I would suggest that there is a very large field open in the future – if somebody could be got to organise it, for the delight of those who wish to use these extremely convenient launches on the river – namely, that, in order to supply the enormous demand which will certainly exist after a few years for charging stations, negotiations should be opened by somebody who has the energy to do so with the Thames Conservancy and also with the mill owners – which exist at nearly all the weirs – so as to establish charging stations with water-power at nearly every one of the weirs on the part which the launches frequent, and thus to establish what would undoubtedly be a most perfect method of launching in any part of the world.'

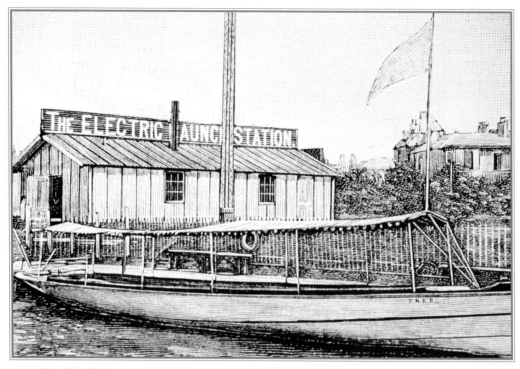

129. **ELECTRIC CHARGING STATION AT EDINBURGH**. It was probably built for the International Engineering Exhibition in 1890.

An even more novel idea for overcoming the problem of the trailing wires from bank to boat was put forward to the London County Council. During June 1900 the Council debated a proposal to set up an electric river service equipped with launches carrying 100 to 150 passengers. In a leading article, *The Electrician* proposed that trucks of charged cells could be wheeled on to the boats and automatically connected, 'as is done, for example, in the Birmingham battery system'.[51]

During the following ten years, charging stations were steadily installed at various places along the river:

1888: Immisch stationed his first floating charging station just below Kew.[52] In July, the station was towed up to Henley for the regatta, moored opposite the steward's barge, and after dark was used for a display of arc and incandescent lighting.[53]

1889: Immisch states there are charging stations at Richmond, Hampton, Staines, Maidenhead, Henley, Reading, Wallingford, Oxford. It is possible that some of these were really the floating stations, named *Watt* and *Ohm*.[54]

1889: *Eta* charges up overnight at Goring (probably at Saunders boatyard).

130. **IMMISCH FLOATING CHARGING STATION**. An Immisch barge travelling under its own power to a regatta where it would be used as a charging station. It is towing four of his electric launches. This photograph was published as a postcard prior to 1905.

H. Horsham

1890: Immisch: The only shore station was at Platt's Eyot. The *Watt* went up to Henley and the other large floating station, *Ohm*, was at Maidenhead. The boiler of the third, *Ampere*, blew up and does not appear to have been replaced. During this year there were fourteen electric launches on the Thames.[55]

1891: Woodhouse & Rawson United Ltd install a permanent charging station at Chertsey. Presumably they already had a charging station at their yard, which they had bought from Sargeant, at Strand-on-the-Green.[56]

1892: Sargeant installed a 100 hp engine and two shunt wound dynamos at his new yard at Eel Pie Island. These provided twelve circuits totalling 200 amps at 100 to 300 volts. The dynamos were also used to provide power for the workshops.[57]

1897: Immisch advertised stations at Hampton, Chertsey, Weybridge (probably the TVL Co. station), Windsor, Bray Lock, Marlow (Meakes & Redknap?), Henley, Reading, Shillingford, Oxford. Robert Shaw & Sons advertised electric launches and charging facilities at Great Marlow and at Bourne End.

1898: Immisch was reported as still having the two floating stations, the *Ohm* and the *Watt*. They were fitted with marine engines connected, by spur gear and clutch respectively, to a 160 volt 60 amp Immisch dynamo.[58] The charging station at Platt's Eyot had a 25 hp John Fowler & Co. steam engine connected by link belting to two Immisch dynamos developing 50 amps at 250 and 365 volts. There was another stationary charging station at Bray with a 25 hp Marshall engine connected by link belts to three Immisch dynamos giving 50 amps at 350, 250 and 160 volts respectively; and also a 10 hp marine engine direct coupled to a Paterson and Cooper dynamo giving 35 amps at 160 volts.[59]

1900: Thames Valley Launch Co. had stations at Weybridge, Maidenhead (Boulter's Lock), Hurley (at the mill in the backwater of the lock cutting), Henley (on Rod Eyot previously belonging to the Upper Thames Electric Launch Co. Prior to that TVL had a station at Marsh Lock), Pangbourne (adjoining Whitchurch Bridge), Shillingford Bridge, Oxford (by arrangement with the Oxford Electric Lighting Co.).[60]

1900: Other charging stations were installed at Kingston (Immisch?), Staines, Maidenhead (presumably Bowen had a charging station at his yard next door to his Ray Mead Hotel), Bourne End (?), Goring (Saunders Goring Mill boatyard and Springfield Works), Henley (1896 Kerbey Bowen on the Eyot just above Henley Bridge).[61]

1902: TVL added two more charging stations, making eight in total, at Windsor and Reading.[62]

1932: Salter's Guide to the Thames listed J.G. Meakes Ltd at Marlow and Townsend Bros at Bourne End as having electric charging stations. Hobbs & Sons at Henley, Red Lion Hotel at Henley, H. Wilder and Bond at Maidenhead are listed as hiring electric canoes and, presumably, charging facilities.

The Electrician of 30 May 1890 was greatly impressed by Immisch's developments and suggested that electrical power could be adapted for houseboats which were getting more numerous and larger every season: 'An electrical plant would be an immense advantage to these floating dwellings and there would be much saving of steam and horse traction. It only remains for some ingenious mind to make the first experiment and show the way.' Eventually houseboats were equipped with electric lighting but electric propulsion remained a pipe dream.

During the 1890s electricity was beginning to supplant gas as the means of lighting houses. Often, a boatyard with an interest in electric boats would sell their expertise during the winter months by fitting lighting installations in the local houses. For example, Carr at the Thames Valley Launch Co. depot at Boulter's Lock carried out a fair amount of electrical work in houses throughout the Maidenhead area.

Initially, these private lighting installations were self-contained, with dynamos being used to provide the power. Some of the riverside houses used their dynamos, which produced direct current, to charge up their boats as well. In fact, in some parts of the country private systems were in use for a long time. For example, the lighting at the Landore Hotel at Keswick in the Lake District was being supplied in 1903 by power from a dynamo driven by a water turbine and some of the power was used to charge up an electric launch running on Derwentwater.[63] However, on the Thames it was common practice for the summer season residents to keep their boats at a boatyard with a charging station. The specification and costs of such a station were described by F. Reckenzaun in the 1892 edition of Kempe's *Electrical Engineer's Pocket Book*.

An indication of the charging requirements for launches is given by the invoice for May and June 1911 rendered by Carr at Boulter's Lock to Major Fenner, owner of the 52 ft launch *Esperanza*. She was fitted with a 7 kw motor and a total battery capacity of 450 ampere-hours. The launch was charged up on ten days over a period of nine weeks. The amount of a charge was 8 units (kwh) on two occasions, 15 on another two, 20 on five, and 30 units on one occasion. The total was 175 units which at a cost of 8*d* per unit totalled £5 16*s* 8*d*.

During 1919 Mr A.F. Ross moored his 30 ft launch *Mina* at Carr's boatyard and ran up a charging account in the four months from June to September of 37.8, 22.4, 55.2 and 19.6 units (kwh) respectively. The total of 135 units cost £6 15*s* 0*d* at 1*s* per unit.

Setting up the charging procedures involved rather more than the present-day plugging into the mains and switching on, as these comments from Carr's notebook of about 1900 indicate:

> *Riversdale*. Charges in series when switch is off and springs from brushes removed – in parallel when ½ ahead or astern. At half-speed require 30 amps for 38 cells. It seems that this boat may have been charged at the same time as *Water Nymph* which at full-speed setting needed 30 amps for 26 cells. 'When charged together, the voltmeter ought to read 110 volts before cutting in.' [There is also a note that if the house cells are to be charged at the same time, six of the boat cells would need to be cut out.]

> *Iverna*. 60 amps from 38 cells. Charging terminals in bow. The stern cells each side to be bridged and springs from motor removed and brushes pushed back to disconnect motor.

> *Frou Frou*. 35 amps from 14 cells. When charging remove one brush as armature leaks.

In 1902 the TVL Co.'s price for charging was 1*s* 6*d* per unit (kwh). This was reduced to 1*s* per unit for boats which were hired for the season or moored at their yards, and even this was discounted to 8*d* per unit for launches built by the company.[64] The price of 1*s* per unit was invoiced to Major Fenner in September 1909 for his launch *Esperanza* but in June 1911 the price to Major Fenner had gone down to 8*d* per unit. In 1919 Mr Ross, the owner of the 30 ft launch *Mina*, was charged 1*s* per unit. However, in 1920 there was an increase to 1*s* 3*d* per unit, a figure that was invoiced to Sir Bernard Oppenheimer, who had just bought the launch *Mina*.

Chapter 13

HANDING ON THE TORCH: THE INTER-WAR YEARS 1918–39

The electric boating business emerged from the First World War years in sorry shape. The construction of new electric boats had declined rapidly from about 1904 onwards and many of the existing craft had been converted to petrol or oil engines. Coupled with the virtual close-down of the leisure boating business during the four years of the war, this meant that there was neither the interest nor the technology to justify the boatbuilders in re-entering the electric boat market. Except, that is, for a handful of yards who felt that there might still be a future for the electric canoe.

Of these, the Ray Motor Co. and Bond at Maidenhead, Meakes of Marlow and Hobbs of Henley were the main suppliers on the Thames.

Mr Carr at the Ray Motor Co. had toyed in 1913 with the idea of building an electric canoe and worked out a specification for one of 25 ft length (Table 1). His record books make no mention of actually building a canoe at that time, presumably because he did not receive an order before the war clouds appeared on the horizon. However, when Horsham returned in 1919 to work with him again, they decided to go into the electric canoe business more seriously.

Thus, on 23 January 1920, Lee and Enomy were despatched to London to buy £54 10s worth of timber. On 5 February Carr paid £45 for a 70 volt 2½ hp series wound motor complete with thrust bearing and flexible coupling. This was followed on 22 April by the purchase of sixty Chloride Exide AXE8 cells complete with acid for £134.[1] The first canoe was constructed by May that year and sold for £460 to Mr Anagnos, who named her *Aris*.[2] By 1922 she had been bought by Mr Courtney, who changed her name to *Bunting*.

During the next two years Horsham built similar canoes, two of which, named *Gena* and *Genetta*, were for Carr's own hire fleet. In 1923 Carr wrote to Utopia Ltd, saying that he had five second-hand canoes for sale, and in 1924 he himself bought *Bunting* back, changing her name to *Genella*.

Of Carr's three canoes, *Gena* is still in use. She is one of the few electric boats which, except for batteries, has remained in her original condition since she was launched just over seventy years ago in 1922.[3] With a length of 25 ft, beam of 4 ft and draught of 1 ft 3 in she had a speed of 8 mph and could carry six passengers. She still has her original brass fittings and 72 volt 2 hp series motor which was made by the Newton Electrical Co. Ltd. It is believed that forty-eight accumulator cells were fitted, but the present batteries comprise twelve 6 volt Oldham Crompton semi-traction batteries weighing 900 lb. The original controller comprised rotary speed and separate reverse

131. **GENETTA**. Built by the Ray Motor Co. in time for the 1922 season, *Genetta* was often hired out to members of the Guards Club in Maidenhead.

G. Banham

switches made by Lane of Staines in 1923. The camping cover was originally supported on two cane hoops and probably left the decks exposed. Subsequently, a new cover on five cane hoops was fitted so as to encompass the entire boat, and new cushions were made in modern Bentley green velvet Dralon.

After Carr handed over the company to Horsham and his colleagues, *Gena* continued to be operated by Horsham & Sons until Bill Horsham died in 1952. Bill's son Tom inherited the business and retained the canoe until she was sold in 1963 to a personal friend, George Bailey, who lived across the road and subsequently moved to the Oxford–Banbury canal. Her present owner is Robin Newlands, President of the Thames Vintage Boat Club.

In 1919 there was a natural need for many companies to find new areas of activity to replace their contract work for the armed services; Short Brothers, the famous seaplane manufacturer was such a company. They built a 25 ft electric canoe for an exhibition and evidently sold a few. Described as really luxurious craft, they were priced at £475. However, the prospects cannot have been encouraging because in March 1921 the company wrote to a potential customer offering him one of the canoes for £350 and saying that this price was reduced in order finally to clear the stock.[4]

132. **GENA, 1922**. *Gena* is one of the few electric boats which has remained in her original condition, except for batteries, since she was launched in 1922 and is now owned by Robin Newlands.

G. Banham

133. **GENA, 1990**.

E.P. Hawthorne

LUXURIOUSLY fitted Electric Canoes are a speciality of Short Bros. These canoes are fitted with a $2\frac{1}{2}$-h.p. electric motor and are handsomely upholstered with corded velveteen in rose, green, or blue. The decks are covered with Wilton Pile carpets, and they are the acme of river luxury and comfort.

Electric Canoes are ideal for river work, being clean and simple to handle. The illustration gives an idea of the handsome lines of the Short Canoe, but to be fully appreciated it should be seen gliding noiselessly amid the sylvan beauties of the river.

134. **SHORT BROS ELECTRIC CANOE**. The aeronautical firm Short Brothers of Rochester entered the electric canoe market in 1921 as a diversification from war work. Their venture was shortlived and they had stopped production within a few years.

G. Banham

Sometime prior to 1928 Hobbs of Henley produced a brochure advertising electric canoes for hire. There appear to be no records of any being built and the advertisement in the same brochure, illustrating a very graceful 25 ft petrol motor canoe, specifically mentions it as 'having the advantage over the Electric Canoe of unlimited radius'.[5]

Bond of Maidenhead also started to build electric canoes again after 1918 and maintained a fleet for hire until 1955. George Banham well remembers the wires trailing down over the balcony from the charging box in the boathouse to the boats below.

During the inter-war years the electric canoe continued to be used by a few private owners. Lord Astor, for example, maintained *Liddesdale* and even went out to tender for a replacement in 1934. Members of the Guards Club at Maidenhead continued to hire electric canoes from both the Ray Motor Co. and Bond until 1945 and 1955 respectively. Other boatyards, such as Messums at Bray, possessed canoes for hire, but very few new ones were built, although in 1937 Bond did build a 28½ ft canoe named *Victoria*, the report in the *Motor Boat* mentioning that this was the first electric boat to be built on the Thames for many years.[6]

It is possible that the only electric launches built during this period were those from Thornycroft, who had taken over the Immisch Launch Co. just before the war. In 1924 this yard supplied thirty 25 ft launches for use in the British Empire Exhibition at Wembley, but there are few records of any other new building. It is clear that the private owner in general had lost interest in electric boats and taken to the new fast, longer range petrol boats, leaving only a few electrics on the river, such as the 41 ft launch *Whip*, which was fitted with a Newton motor and twenty-four cells.

Whip appears in the Ray Motor Co.'s books[7] in February 1918, when Carr wrote to Mr Geo. Sanders enclosing an estimate of £14 10s for twelve new positive sections and wood separators to be purchased from the Electrical Power Storage Co. and pointing out that Sanders must get a permit from the Ministry of Munitions. It seems that nothing happened until November 1919 when Carr wrote to a Mr Stanley saying that he had heard from Mr George Sanders that Stanley wished to have the boat stored for the winter. Carr quoted 3s 6d per ft plus £1 15s for keeping the battery charged.

In April 1920 Carr gave Stanley an estimate for fitting out *Whip*, which included cleaning down and varnishing for £35 and buying and fitting twenty-four new FK 5 plate positive sections for £80 15s. However, Mr Stanley did not follow this up and must have put the boat up for sale. In August Carr wrote: 'Not had one enquiry this season. . . . The weather has been so bad that river business of every sort has suffered in consequence.' There were no buyers during the winter either, until in May 1921 Carr wrote to Stanley that 'Mr Bliss has been to see boat. We will certainly help to sell her but meanwhile money is a bit tight with us and we should find your cheque very useful just now.' That potential sale fell through and once again there was a long delay until September 1922, when the launch appears to have been sold to Mr J. Brimpton of 22 Hatton Garden, London.

The new owner cannot have been too interested in getting afloat for Carr had to write to him in the following February pointing out that the *Whip* 'is lying at our wharf. Rent owing is £59.10.0. Nothing has been done to it since 1919.' In August 1923 Carr writes again: 'We are anxious to know what you intend to do with your launch *Whip*. Nothing whatever has been done to the launch since 1919, consequently she is getting very bad

135. **WHIP**. A pre-1914 launch which was moored at the Ray Motor Co. yard from 1918 until 1923 waiting for a buyer.

Maidenhead Library

and will soon deteriorate into an absolute wreck.' That is presumably what happened for nothing further is heard of *Whip* and Carr was probably left with another bad debt.

San Martin was another electric launch which was kept in commission during this period. She was carvel built using cedar on ash frames with mahogany topsides, brass fittings, a motor described as 'sausage shaped' and is said to have been built about 1890. During the late 1930s she sank at her moorings where she was rescued by C.P. Murch of Bourne End. He repaired her and fitted her out with ten 6 volt 125 ampere-hour batteries which gave a cruising time of six hours. The controller was a switch with two speeds forward and two astern supplying 4 and 20 amps to the motor.

In 1955 she was bought by Mr Martin and in 1960 by Mr Blenner-Hassett, both residents on the Spade Oak Reach at Bourne End. In 1974 she was bought by Mr W.D. Davies of Goring-on-Thames, who sold her in 1984 to Peter Freebody of Hurley in whose yard she now awaits possible restoration or replication.[8]

136. *VIRGINIA*. This launch was operated for several years by Turks Boatyard, Cookham, after acquiring her in 1918. The driver is Bill Rippington, Senior.

H. Horsham

137. *SAN MARTIN*, **SAID TO HAVE BEEN BUILT ABOUT 1890.**

G. Banham

138. *SAN MARTIN, 1943*. C.P. Murch of Bourne End rescued and restored *San Martin* during the late 1930s. He is shown driving her along the Spade Oak Reach at Bourne End.

J. Murch

Some of the old electric launches, converted to petrol or oil engines, continued to be used as hireboats. For example, the famous 65 ft *Viscountess Bury*, which had been moved from the Thames to King's Lynn and converted to petrol, ran between Cambridge, Ely and Denver. Andrews at Maidenhead converted at least five of their old electric launches to petrol and kept them going until they were sold off in the late 1930s.

Bond at Maidenhead may have kept some electric launches in commission for a few years. After the First World War there were a number of launches going cheap and he is understood to have bought up some of the pre-war electrics, such as *Charlotte*, and converted them to petrol. Although an advertisement in Salter's Guide in 1936 mentions electric launches for hire, it is not clear what or how many launches the company had and certainly by 1937 all their old electric launches had been converted to petrol.[9]

Surprisingly, the Bedford Steamboat Company bucked the trend and changed from steam to electric launches. In 1919 two electric launches were bought from Maidenhead, the *Lady Lena* and *Lorna Doone*. The former launch had been built in 1890 and was operated as an electric hireboat by the Immisch Electric Launch Co. until 1914.[10] Even more enterprising, the steam launch *Lodore*, with which the company had started its operations in 1898, was converted to electric. These three launches operated a regular

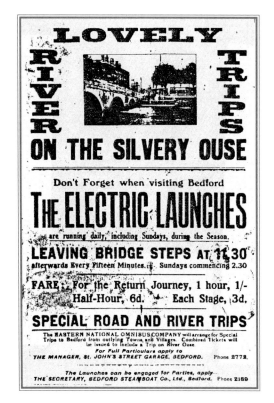

139. **THE BEDFORD ELECTRIC LAUNCH FLEET**. The Bedford Steamboat Co. carried on the torch of electric boating by changing from steam to electric tripping boats from 1919 until 1943 when its successor, Silvery Ouse Pleasure Craft, continued with electric boats until 1976.

Bedfordshire Times, *6 June 1980 and A. Faulkner*

service along the River Ouse until 1939. During the war the boats were not used and steadily deteriorated until they sank. In 1945 *Lady Lena* was raised, restored, renamed *Silver Stream* and put back into service with two other launches, *Silver Foam* and *Silver Spray*, both of which came from London and were converted to electric propulsion. These boats were replaced during the early 1960s by two launches, which were also converted to electric, and these kept the service going for many more years.

The inter-war years, punctuated by the depression, were therefore a period of stagnation for the electric boat business, which was kept going only by the low-key efforts of some boathirers and a few private owners.

Table 1
Ray Motor Company Canoe Specification

Among the Ray Motor Co. records there is an undated specification for a canoe as follows:[11]

Specification

25 ft Electric Canoe

Hull	To be built Clinker of Cedar bright	
	Keel	Pitch Pine
	Stem & Stern	Canada Elm bent to shape
	Deadwood	Oak tapered from throat

	Timbers	Canada Elm on Oak
	Gunwale	" " " "
	Bresthooks	Mahogany rounded up
	Decks	Mahogany, double broken joints
	Deck beams	Pine
	Combings	Mahogany, bent to shape
	Rubbing board & fillets	Mahogany
	Floor Wrongs	Pine to floor level
	Floor	Spruce cleated
	Cell Floor	Yellow deal
	Backs	Four Mahogany. Spar pattern
	Motor Box	Mahogany
	Motor Bed	Yellow deal
	Fastenings	Copper throughout

Rudder — Steel plate on steel post hung on ball bearings

Rudder trunk — Steel tube bushed brass

Steering Gear — Gunmetal Eccentric & lever pultern with wood rimmed & aluminium centred wheel

Wrot iron connecting rod & G M lever

Stern Tube — Steel tube bushed with G-M Stuffing box & Gland inboard

Propeller — G metal 3 bladed

Propeller Shaft — Steel tapered for propeller & fitted C J coupling

Thrust Block

Stem & Stern

Bands — ½ Round. Brass to be carried well below waterline & over nose finished ornamentally on brestworks

Deck Fittings — Brass band round covering board. 2 Brass cleats. 4 Brass Fairleads

Electrical Gear — Cells [Probably thirty cells Exide AXE8 cells of 120 ampere-hours and weighing 24 lb.]

Motor 2½ hp series wound. Weight 112 lb.

	Controller	Two speeds ahead & astern. Cased in mahogany with G M lever & index plate
	Charging Board	Slate fitted with brass terminals & D P Fuses
	Cutout Switch	D.P. on slate Bases in Armature & Field circuits

Navigation Lamp — 3 Electric Copper lamps with 15 C P. lamps wired with switch & fuse & plugs

Boat Hooks — Two pine staffs & G M heads

Cushions — 8 Fitted to floor & backs

The specification for the Short Bros canoe built in 1919 gives the following data: Length 24 ft 10 in, beam 4 ft, draught 1 ft. Single skin, carvel built in mahogany. Fitted with a 2½ hp series wound 70 volt, 33 amp, 650 rpm motor and thirty-four two volt Exide cells with a capacity of 122 ampere-hours.

Chapter 14

RESURGENCE: POST-1945

After the Second World War the need once again to switch from munitions to peacetime manufacture tempted a few individuals and businesses to build electric boats. In the UK in 1947 the Silvery Ouse business in Bedford revived its regular tripping service of three electric launches, and Warwick Productions of Kenilworth produced a fleet of hireboats for use on public boating lakes. During the following year Captain Hirst of Leroys Boathouses in Guildford built a 30 ft twenty-passenger craft as a tripping boat on the River Wey. In 1952 Townsend Bros of Bourne End built the 17 ft *Ave* as a private ferry boat for the Spencers to go the mile and a quarter downstream across the river between their house and their garage at Bourne End, and a few private electric canoes were still to be seen.[1] In Sweden an electric passenger boat plied between the mainland and the island of Marstrand, and during the 1960s several American companies began to make electric outboard motors for trolling while fishing on the lakes.[2] Thus were laid the foundations for several strands of development in the resurgence of interest in electric boating.

During the 1970s Rear-Admiral Percy Gick of Emsworth Shipyard became interested in electric boats, and in 1978 he fitted out a 25 ft cruiser *Electra of Emsworth*, which was taken on a 600 mile promotional trip around the UK canals and down the Thames. Other canal boatbuilders became interested and an important step was taken when the Midlands Electricity Board set up a chain of charging points around the central Midlands canals and rivers, giving access to 140 miles of cruising for electric boats.

The year 1982 was another important landmark. Rupert Latham set up the Steam and Electric Launch Co. in Norfolk and began to build a very successful range of electric launches of traditional Thames design, using the new technologies of glass reinforced plastic hulls, transistorized controllers and semi-traction batteries. In the same year Viscount St Davids, supported by the Lead Development Association, set up the Electric Boat Association.

Gradually, the revival of electric boating seeped into the public consciousness. The technology improved and new types of boat were built; new records were established, including the world speed record for electric boats of 50.825 mph captured by Fiona, Countess of Arran in *An Stradag*, and subsequently passed back to America in 1994 when Norm Body in *Hardly Normal* achieved a speed of 55.913 mph.[3] Rupert Latham's launches became very popular and the Thames once again became the centre of electric boating.

Many boatbuilders are building electric boats to traditional designs; others are fitting electrics into existing GRP low maintenance hulls; canal boatbuilders are developing

140. *ELECTRA OF EMSWORTH*, **1978**. This cruiser was the harbinger of the resurgence in electric boating in the UK. Rear Admiral Percy Gick (on board) of the Emsworth Shipyard Group, backed by the Electricity Council and the Lead Development Association, fitted an electric propulsion system into an existing 23 ft Trentcraft cruiser. The boat made a 600 mile cruise from Chertsey along the Thames and canals to Manchester and back. The cruise is now commemorated by the Emsworth Trophy awarded annually to the member of the Electric Boat Association who carries out the longest cruise of the year by a boat propelled by battery-electric power. Admiral Gick was one of the founders of the Electric Boat Association and has been its President since 1991.

Canal & Riverboat, *December 1978*

designs to make use of the environmental advantages of electric propulsion, sometimes as hybrid diesel/electric systems; and boathirers are discovering the commercial merits of reduced noise, less vibration, and lower running costs of electrical equipment. The components of electric propulsion systems tend to be adapted from the electric vehicle field, but there are new developments, such as the high efficiency Lynch motor, which are being fitted in some boats, and complete electric propulsion systems which are being offered as kits, such as those supplied by the Thames Electric Launch Company at Goring. Improved and more powerful electric outboard motors have been developed and have opened up the market for electric dinghies and easily trailable boats.

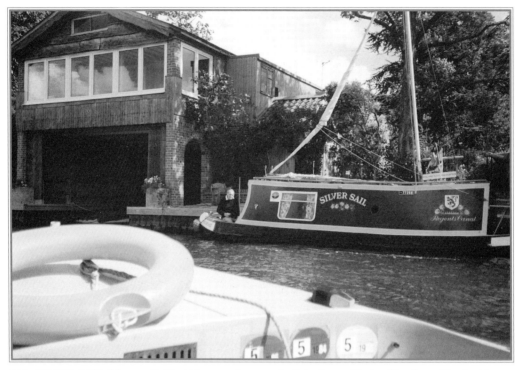

141. **SILVER SAIL**. Viscount St Davids' narrow boat was built by Roger Davis of Evesham. Fitted with two Lynch motors, she was cruised up the Thames every summer and over the years covered more than 4,000 miles of the Inland Waterways. He was the founder, Chairman of the Users Group and President of the Electric Boat Association, 1981–1991.

E.P. Hawthorne

142. **DYNIA, THE SHOPPING BOAT**. Fitted in 1976 with a Johnson electric outboard and subsequently changed to an Acumot underwater pod-mounted motor, this 15 ft GRP boat was used by Dinnie Hawthorne to cross the Thames at Cookham to do the family shopping. Its four 175 ampere-hours batteries were replaced in 1991 after seven years use. Left outside summer and winter, she has required virtually no maintenance and is still in use.

143. *BACK-TO-THE-FUTURE,* **1990.** Conceived by Chris Dowling and Brynn Thomas of Classic Marine Technology, this 'Henley Slipper Launch' was specially developed as an electric version of the well-established slipper launches built since 1920. Designed by John Sharp of Chichester, the special hull was developed from extensive tank-testing to give low drag. Built by Dredge Boatbuilders of Emsworth in GRP, with varnished mahogany sides and traditional pine planking decks, she was equipped with a 2 kw 48 volt Nelco motor supplied from sixteen 6-volt 400 ampere-hour Oldham-Crompton batteries, achieving a speed of 8 knots. Length 26 ft 6 in, beam 6 ft 7 in, draft 1 ft 4 in.

Electric Boat Association News, September 1990

144. **THE STEAM AND ELECTRIC LAUNCH COMPANY BOATS.** The founder of the company, Rupert Latham, is the pioneer of the resurgence of electric boatbuilding in the UK. These are three of his boats at Cookham Regatta in 1993. The traditional Frolic 21 ft open and the Frolic 30 ft saloon launches and, in the foreground, the Deltic 24 ft weekend cruiser. *EB News,* January 1993.

E. Barrell

145. **WAGTAIL V, 1991**. This launch is a characteristic example of the combination of traditional design with modern materials. The hull was made in GRP by Steam and Electric Launch Co., which also supplied the electrical system. The decks and superstructure were constructed of teak. Electrics comprise a 3 kw 72 volt Nelco motor supplied by two banks of twelve 175 ampere-hour Crompton batteries. These give a range of 39 miles on one bank at the long-distance cruising speed of 4 mph. She was fitted out for the owners, Pat and Paul Wagstaffe, by the apprentices at the International Boatbuilding Training Centre at Lowestoft. Length 31 ft, beam, 6 ft 9 in.

Motor Boats Monthly

146. **LUELLA, 1991** (opposite top). Peter Freebody's yard at Hurley has an enviable reputation for superb craftsmanship in building wooden craft to traditional designs and *Luella* is a classic example of these skills. Based on the 1890s design of electric boat, she is constructed of teak and incorporates two complete propulsion systems, including twin propellers, based on 48 volt 1¼ kw Nelco motors which give the launch a speed of up to 9 knots. Built for an American customer, she is now in use on a lake in up-state New York. Length 33 ft, beam 6 ft 8 in, draught 2 ft.

Dean Rhoads

147. **TADPOLE, 1994** (opposite bottom). Another of Peter Freebody's traditional electric launches, this *Tadpole* derives its design from a launch which was too far gone to restore. It may well have been the *Tadpole* built in 1893 and looked after by Carr at the Ray Motor Co. between 1904 and 1912.

Peter Freebody

148. **THE WARGRAVE ELECTRIC BOAT RALLY, 1993.** Electric Boat Association members picnicking on the famous Temple Island at the start of the Henley Regatta Course. Thirty electric boats took part in the seventh of these annual rallies.

E.P. Hawthorne

In America, during this same period, the Duffield Company has built several hundred boats and the famous ELCO Company has come back into the launch market with its range of traditional hull designs. Electric boating is also expanding throughout Europe; Austria and Holland ban non-electric power boats on some lakes and waterways; large passenger waterbuses are running in Venice; there have been races in Switzerland for boats driven only by solar power. Electric Boat Associations are now established in a number of countries such as America, Holland and France.

The social activities of the Thames are still very popular but have changed with the growth and altered characteristics of the river population and visitors. The rowing regattas are more popular than ever but skiffs, punts and houseboats have given way to motor boats, cruisers and large hospitality boats. Many of the old regattas are being revived; Cookham Regatta, for example, is in its fourth year and has proved to be an increasingly popular event, not least for the eighteen or so electric launches and canoes which take part in the parade of boats. The older electric boats still in commission are to be seen at the traditional boat rallies.

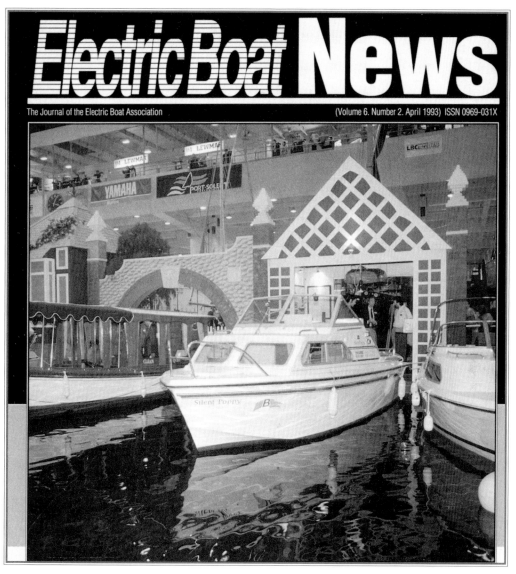

Electric Boat News

The Journal of the Electric Boat Association

(Volume 6. Number 2. April 1993) ISSN 0969-031X

149. **LONDON BOAT SHOW, 1993**. Three of the four electric boats on the pool beside the Electric Boat Association stand sponsored by the Electricity Council. Left: Eastern Electric's Frolic 31 ft. Centre: Facey's 26 ft hire cruiser. Right: Steam & Electric Company's 24 ft Deltic weekend cruiser.

E. Barrell

150. *LAMBOURN, 1994* (opposite top). She was the first Thames patrol boat of the National Rivers Authority to have an electric propulsion system added to its existing Thornycroft 60 hp diesel drive. The electric system, installed by the Thames Electric Launch Co., is used for normal cruising, quiet and virtually vibrationless, which constitutes the bulk of the day's running, and the diesel provides high power in emergencies or for driving fire pumps. Switching over is almost instantaneous.

E. Barrell

151. **DIESEL AND ELECTRIC IN THE NRA LAUNCH** *COLNE* (opposite bottom). The installation in the second NRA patrol boat to be converted to this system. The radial armature Lynch motor, 200 mm diameter and 80 mm long (white band with ventilation holes), drives through clutches and a toothed rubber belt on to the existing drive shaft from the 60 hp diesel engine. Two banks of six Chloride Trekker batteries 3ET 175 ampere-hour batteries provide enough power for six hours continuous running at about 5 mph.

E. Barrell

152. **THE 21 FT ELECTRIC LAUNCH** *MYSTERE*. The traditions of Thames electric boating live on in Edward Hawthorne's day launch. The hull is a standard 21 ft Frolic from Steam and Electric Co. and the traditional mahogany interior and decking were fitted out by David Smith of Maidenhead.

E. Barrell

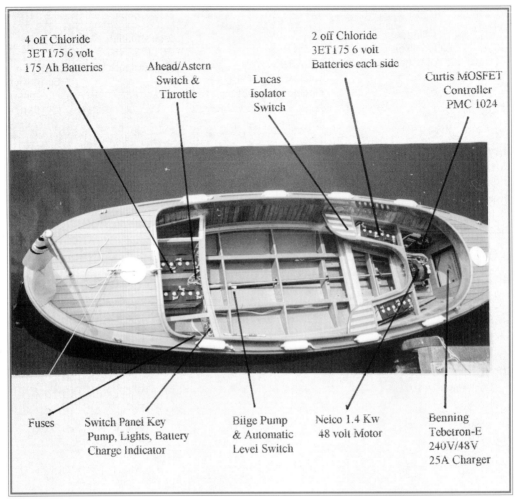

4 off Chloride
3ET175 6 volt
175 Ah Batteries

Ahead/Astern
Switch &
Throttle

Lucas
Isolator
Switch

2 off Chloride
3ET175 6 volt
Batteries each side

Curtis MOSFET
Controller
PMC 1024

Fuses

Switch Panel Key
Pump, Lights, Battery
Charge Indicator

Bilge Pump
& Automatic
Level Switch

Nelco 1.4 Kw
48 volt Motor

Benning
Tebetron-E
240V/48V
25A Charger

153. **THE ELECTRICAL SYSTEM OF THE** *MYSTERE* **21 FT OPEN LAUNCH**, showing the layout of the components of the electrical propulsion system. In order to leave clear space in the centre of the launch for occasional wicker chairs, only eight batteries are fitted. The standard Frolic 21 is usually fitted with sixteen similar batteries.

E.P. Hawthorne

A new scene is provided by the rallies for electric boats only, foremost of which is the Wargrave Electric Boat Rally, often attracting more than thirty members from the locality in their decorated boats and launches. Other electric boat rallies are taking place elsewhere, such as on the Broads.

The Electric Boat Association has become a powerful force in publicizing and promoting the benefits and pleasures of electric boating. Comprising trade and private owner members, it has drawn together sponsors, particularly the electricity companies,

154. ***OHMEGA* CANAL BOAT, 1990**. During the early 1980s the Midland Electricity Board set up a chain of charging points across the central midland canals and rivers giving 140 miles of cruising for electric boats. At the same time Castle Narrow Boats and Anglo-Welsh Boats operated a number of hireboats on the system. With a length of 45 ft and carrying forty passengers *Ohmega* has been operated as a tripping boat by Castle Narrow Boats of Gwent.

EBA News, September 1990

155. **ELECTRIC RANGER 13, 1992**. She is typical of the electric outboard small boat. Length 12 ft 8 in, beam 5 ft 6 in, weight complete 500 lb (227 kg). Hull in GRP built by Thames Electric Launch Co. Combi outboard, 700 watt, 24 volt. Batteries: four 170 ampere-hours. Range up to nine hours on one charge.

E. Barrell

156. **TOM TOM ELECTRIC, 1993**. Designed and built by Bossom's Boatyard, this boat has become very popular with hire operators at boating pools and lakes because of its quietness, reliability under continuous daily use and ease of maintenance. Length 9 ft, beam 4 ft 10 in, draught 10 in, weight, including batteries, 600 lb. Constructed in heavy duty GRP she is fitted with a 400 watt submerged electric motor and four 6 volt 175 ampere-hour traction batteries with an endurance of ten hours.

Bossom's Boatyard Ltd

157. **ELECTRIC YACHT *EXCALIBUR*, 1992.** This is operated as one of two sail/electric hireboats on the Broads by Camelot Craft, Norfolk. This fast cruiser/racer is a Pegasus 800 type with an electric drive fitted by London Innovation using a 12 volt Lynch motor supplied by six 2 volt cells giving 12–15 hours running. Length 25 ft 9 in, beam 8 ft 9 in, displacement 2 tons. Sleeps four.

Peter Howe

158. **ELEKTRA SYSTEM CRUISER, 1994**. Designed and installed by HFL Industrial and Marine Power Ltd in a Shadow 26 ft cruiser, this system comprises an HFL Gemini three-phase diesel generator supplying a small AC electric motor driving the propeller. The generator can also supply domestic power for the cruiser's cookers, fridges and air conditioning etc. *EB News*, Autumn 1994

R. Devereux

159. **ECO 22, 1994**. Designed by John Moxham and built by the Steam & Electric Launch Co, this 22 ft cruiser has a specially designed 'Hydraflow' low wash hull. The first boat of this type has been put into service by Broads Tours. *EB News*, Spring and Winter 1994.

P. Wagstaffe

160. **BLENDING TRADITIONAL AND MODERN, 1995**. Designed by her owner, Tony Mayes, the
31 ft *Lillie Langtry* combines the best of traditional saloon electric launch design with modern GRP hull,
propulsion equipment and woodworking methods.

E.P. Hawthorne

who have liberally supported stands at many of the inland waterways rallies and the more
important exhibitions, such as the London Boat Show. It organizes record-breaking
events and challenges, and awards the Emsworth Trophy for the longest cruise in the year
by an electric boat and the St David's Trophy for a significant advance in the field of
electric boating. It publishes the *Electric Boat News*, giving news of electric boating
activities worldwide, and a series of information sheets written by technical experts.

New and upgraded technologies in motors, hybrid systems, controllers, batteries and
solar power hold out the promise of an ever-widening and exciting future. Boathirers,
builders and private owners are rediscovering the attractions of electric boating.
Environmentally acceptable, in some places legally enforced; easy to use and simple to
maintain; ranging in size from dinghies to cruisers, canal and large passenger-carrying
vessels, electric boats are once again becoming a familiar sight on inland waterways and
lakes.

APPENDIX 1

THE IMMISCH FLEET

Many of the launches in the Immisch fleet were characterized by being named after the letters of the Greek alphabet. The dates given are when the first report of the boat has been noted and some may therefore have been built earlier.

Key to sources:

MA	*Maidenhead Advertiser*
Dix	*Royal River Highway*, Frank L. Dix, David & Charles, Newton Abbot, 1985
Brochure	Brochure by the Immisch Launch & Boat Co. Ltd, 1904

The journals *Electrical Review*, *The Electrician* and *Engineering*.

BOAT NAME	DATE	EVENT	SOURCE
CHARGING STATIONS	1888	A 'hulk' is fitted out with a 20 hp Fowler steam engine (under-type with loco-boiler) driving an Immisch dynamo. Used to watch Cambridge win the Boat race.	*Electrician*. 30 March 1888
	1889	Electric Charging Station No. 1 is now stationed above Boulter's weir.	*El. Review*, April 1889
	1889	Advertisement lists charging stations at Platt's Eyot, Staines, Maidenhead, Henley and Reading.	MA, 12 June 1889
	1891	'Sunday, nine electric launches charged at Immisch's station above Boulter's Lock'.	MA, 8 July 1891
	1898	The Platt's Eyot stationary charging station has a 25 hp Fowler steam engine with belt connection to two Immisch dynamos of 50 amps at 250 and 365 volts. The two floating stations *Ohm* and *Watt* are equipped with steam plant geared to 160 volt 60 amp Immisch dynamo. The station at Bray has a 25 hp Marshall engine connected by belt to three Immisch dynamos giving 50 amps at 350, 250 and 160 volts; also a 10 hp marine engine direct coupled to a Paterson & Cooper dynamo giving 35 amps at 160 volts.	*Electrician*, 17 June 1898
Malden	1888	Built by W. Sargeant of Strand-on-the-Green.	*Electrician*, 22 June 1888
A Skiff	1888	An electric skiff was used as a tender for the floating charging station which had been towed up to Henley for the Regatta.	*Electrician*, 6 July 1888
Viscountess Bury	1888	Designed and built by W. Sargeant and launched on 8 October 1888 from the builder's yard at Strand-on-the-Green. For details and subsequent history see Chapter 11.	*Electrician*, 12 October 1888
Alpha	1889	Built by Tagg & Son, Island Works, East Molesey. Licensed for 27 passengers. Possibly 35 ft length.	*Electrician*, December 1888, & Dix
	1892	Seen afloat at Maidenhead.	MA, 8 June 1892

BOAT NAME	DATE	EVENT	SOURCE
	1904	8 passengers. Has awning.	Brochure
Beta	1889	Built by Tagg & Son, Island Works, East Molesey. Licensed for 27 passengers. Possibly 35 ft length.	*Electrician*, December 1888, & Dix
	1904	Not listed in brochure	
Gamma	1889	Built by Tagg & Son, Island Works, East Molesey. Licensed for 20 passengers.	*Electrician*, December 1888, & Dix
	1893	Seen afloat at Maidenhead.	MA, 31 May 1893
	1904	8 passengers. Has awning.	Brochure
	1908	Maidenhead depot hired *Gamma* to the Ray Motor Co. at Boulter's Lock.	Invoice to Ray Motor Co.
Delta	1889	Built by Tagg & Son, Island Works, East Molesey. Licensed for 22 passengers. Length 33 ft, beam 6 ft, draught (forward) 15 in, (aft) 18 in. 44 cells weighing 2,520 lb, placed under seats on each side of the boat.	*Electrician*, December 1888, & Dix
	1904	8 passengers. Has awning	Brochure.
Epsilon	1890	One of the second batch of launches ordered from Tagg & Son for the 1890 season. Open launch. Length 42 ft. 25 passengers.	Immisch prospectus. *Lock to Lock Times*, 8 July 1890
	1893	Licensed to carry 25 passengers.	Dix
	1904	Name appears to have been transferred to a Cabin Launch. 11 passengers. Licensed for hire until 1910.	Brochure
Zeta	1904	4 passengers. Open launch with awning.	Brochure
Eta	1889	Built by Tagg & Son, Island Works, East Molesey.	
	1889	Report of excursion from Hampton to Oxford and back to Maidenhead over 5 days. 60 miles from Goring to Oxford and back on one charge.	*Electrical Review*, Sept. 1889
	1891	Licensed for 34 passengers.	Dix
	1904	16 Passengers. Has cabin. Licensed and sighted until 1910.	Brochure, Dix, and MA
Theta	1891	Licensed for 20 passengers.	Dix
	1893	Sighted at Maidenhead.	MA, 7 June 1893
	1904	8 passengers. Open launch with awning.	Brochure
Iota	1904	10 passengers. Cabin launch.	Brochure
Kappa	1889	Licensed for hire from 1889.	Dix
	1892	*Koppa* (misprint for *Kappa*?) sighted at Maidenhead.	MA, 22 June 1892
	1904	8 passengers. Open launch with awning.	Brochure
Lambda	1893	Licensed for 30 passengers.	Dix
	1904	16 passengers. Cabin launch.	Brochure
Mu	1893	Sighted at Maidenhead.	MA, 31 May 1893
		'Lawson was in the pretty little electric *Mu*.'	MA, 28 June 1893
Nu	1904	6 passengers. Open launch with awning.	Brochure
Omicron	1889	Licensed.	Dix
Eksei	1904	10 passengers. Cabin launch.	Brochure
Rho	1904	4 passengers. Open launch with awning.	Brochure
Sigma	1904	6 passengers. Open launch with awning.	Brochure
Tau	1904	8 passengers. Open launch with awning.	Brochure
Phi	1904	6 passengers. Open launch with awning.	Brochure
Omega	1889	Licensed 1889.	Dix
Aloha	1904	8 passengers. Open launch with awning.	Brochure
Celia	1898	Reported that *Celia* is smallest of Immisch fleet. Length 22 ft, beam 5 ft 6 in; 4 passengers. 22 B-15 Electric Power Storage cells.	*Electrician*, 17 June 1898

BOAT NAME	DATE	EVENT	SOURCE
Emerald Isle	1904	10 passengers. Cabin launch.	Brochure
Flosshilde	1894	Licensed to carry 38 passengers.	Dix
	1904	25 passengers. Cabin launch. Licensed until 1914.	Brochure, & Dix
	1918	Operated by Bond of Maidenhead until 1939. Initially steam and converted to petrol.	
	1939	Used by Army during the Second World War carrying ballast for building blockhouses up river. After war, converted at Putney to a houseboat and moored in Staines area. Length 60 ft or more. Beamy boat with cabin and sundeck over.	G. Banham
Lady Lena	1890	Licensed to carry 28 passengers.	Dix
	1892	Sighted afloat at Maidenhead.	MA, 8 and 22 June 1892
	1893	Sighted afloat at Maidenhead.	MA, 31 May, 7 June 1893
	1904	10 passengers. Cabin launch.	Brochure
Lady Suzan	1889	Licensed for 24 passengers.	Dix
Rosalind	1898	Reported fitted with 'Taunton' motor (i.e. Newton Electrical Works Ltd).	*Electrician*, 17 June 1898
	1904	10 passengers. Cabin launch.	Brochure

Other launches listed in the 1904 brochure were *Viola*, a ten-passenger steam open launch with awning; *Spy*, *B.E.T.* and *Portia*, petrol-engined open launches carrying eight, six and four passengers respectively.

APPENDIX 2

UK ELECTRIC BOATBUILDERS, 1882–1914

Many boatbuilders throughout the UK, with experience of steam launches, were prepared to build electric boats, and the following table gives such information as has emerged during the main research for this book. The list, of course, is not exhaustive but gives some idea of the extensive interest in electric boating. The column headed 'First Date' gives the earliest date when a reference to activity in electric boats has been found, but does not represent the date when the business first entered the field.

BUILDER	TYPES OF BOAT	FIRST DATE	REFERENCES
Acme Motor & Traction Co. The Ham, Brentford, Middx		1904	Blue Book 1904
Andrews, E. & Son, Maidenhead	Built & operated fleet of 12 launches up to 45 ft length	1900	see Chap. 8.
Bond J., Maidenhead	Electric and Steam Launch Builder	1904	RMC records 1904
Bowen, Kerbey. Ray Mead Hotel, Maidenhead, Henley & London	Operated *Ray Mead* until 1896	1889	*Electrician* 1889, Kelly's Directory 1891, Blue Book 1896
British Electric Traction Co.	Took over Immisch Electric Launch Co. in 1898	1898	*Electrical Review* 1898
Burgoine, Alfred, Kingston-on-Thames	Launch Builder	1892	*Lock to Lock Times* 1892. Blue Book 1904
Cheshire Electric & Steam Launch Co. Liverpool		1896	Blue Book 1896
Clark, E. & Sons, Sunbury & Walton	Advertised electric launches for hire	1892	*Lock to Lock Times* 1892
Drake & Gorham, London	Involved in first launches. Operated two more in 1893	1893	*Electrician* 1893
East, A.H., Caversham Lock, Reading	Advertised as builder of electric launches	1895	Kelly's Directory 1895
Edwards & Co., Millwall		1904	Blue Book 1904
Electrical Power Storage Co., Millwall	Fitted out early electric boats, 1883–8	1883	*Electrician*, Oct. 1883
Elieson Electric Co.	Built largest electric launch, the 90 ft *Countess*	1887	*Electrician*, Oct. 1887
Ellis, G.A., Goring-on-Thames	Specialist equipment for electric launches	1904	Salter's Guide 1904
Fellows, H. & Son, Great Yarmouth		1896	Blue Book 1896
Forrest & Son, London	Built hull of *Australia*	1884	*Electrician* 1884. Blue Book 1904

BUILDER	TYPES OF BOAT	FIRST DATE	REFERENCES
Hart & Harden, Hampton Wick	Hart designed 32 ft electric launch for Meakes in 1900	1905	H.Tough 1991 Neil Garside 1993
Hobbs, Henley-on-Thames	Installed electric charging station at Thames Meadow	1898	J. Hobbs 1994
Immisch Electric Launch Co., Platt's Eyot, Hampton	Builder and hirer of launches. Taken over by British Electric Traction Co. in 1897. Reformed as Immisch Launch & Boat Co. in 1904	1888	*Electrician* 1888
Jones, Paul & Son		1896	Blue Book 1896
Maidenhead & District Boating Co., Maidenhead	Owned by H. Woodhouse of Thames Hotel, Maidenhead	1898	RMC records
Martin, Tom, Strand-on-the-Green, London		1896	Blue Book 1896
Meakes & Redknap, Marlow	Reported to have built electric canoes in 1890s and 1907	189?	Steam Boat Association Register 1986
Morton & Williamson	Designed the four launches used at the Edinburgh International Exhibition	1890	Official Catalogue
Orr, Thomas, Gourock		1896	Blue Book 1896
Paterson & Cooper, London & Glasgow		1896	Blue Book 1896
Pullen, C.T., Henley	Hirer. *Glow Worm*	1900	Dix 1985
Ray Motor Co., Maidenhead	Ran TVL depot from 1896 to 1904, then as Ray Motor Co. until 1934	1896	RMC records
Redpath & Paris, Limehouse	*Lady Cooper*, 1888	1888	*Electrician* 1888
Sargeant, William, Strand-on-the-Green.	Built Immisch's floating charging stations, *Viscountess Bury* and others. Taken over in 1890 by Woodhouse & Rawson. In 1894 became Thames Electric & Steam Launch Co.	1888	*Electrical Review* 1888
Saunders Patent Launch Building Syndicate, Goring-on-Thames	Builder and hirer of launches. First launch built was *Avalon* in 1895	1895	Wheeler 1993
Seath, T.B., Rutherglen	Built four launches used at Edinburgh International Exhibition	1890	Official Catalogue
Shaw, Robert, Marlow & Bourne End	Advertised as builder of electric launches	1897	Postal Directory 1897
Skelton, Millwall	Built *Volta*, 1885. See Stephens, Smith & Co.		
Smith, F.H. & Co., Liverpool	Designed & supplied electric launch to Liverpool Corporation for towing & inspection use on Lake Vyrnwy	1906	*Motor Boat* 1906
Stephens, Smith & Co., Millwall	*Australia* and *Volta*, 1885		
Tagg & Son, East Molesey	Built Immisch's first five launches, 1889	1889	*Electrician* 1888
Tagg, T.C. & Son, Gourock		1896	Blue Book 1896
Tagg, T.G. & Son, East Molesey	Advertised electric launches for sale & hire	1892	*Lock to Lock Times* 1892
Taylor, James, Chertsey	Hired out small electric launch *La Reine*	1898	Dix
Taylor, T. & Sons, Staines	Advertised as builder of electric launches.	1892	*Lock to Lock Times* 1892
	Acquired *Ray Mead*	1896	Dix 1985

BUILDER	TYPES OF BOAT	FIRST DATE	REFERENCES
T.G. Electric Power & Traction Co., London and Platt's Eyot, Hampton	Advertised Elegant Electric Launches (fourteen in number) for hire. Holding company for Immisch's interests	1891	*Lock to Lock Times* 6 June 1891
Thames Electric & Steam Launch Co., Eel Pie Island, Twickenham	Launches up to 70 ft. Became Thames Electric & Motor Boat Co. in 1906	1896	Blue Book 1896
Thames Valley Launch Co., Weybridge	Open and saloon launches up to 45 ft	1896	Blue Book 1896
Thames Iron Works & Ship-building Co., Blackwall, London		1896	Blue Book 1896
Tims, J. & Sons, Staines	Charging station for Electric Launches at Staines	1904	Salter's Guide 1904
Tolch & Co., Fulham, London		1904	Blue Book 1904
Tooley, H., East Molesey	Steam & Electric Launch Builder	1892	*Lock to Lock Times* 10 Sept. 1892
Upper Thames Electric Launch Co., Henley-on-Thames	Owned about five launches named after Scottish lochs. Taken over by TVL Co. in 1899	1896	Blue Book 1896
Watkins & Co., Blackwall		1904	Blue Book 1904
Westmacott, Stewart & Co., St Helen's, Isle of Wight	24 ft electric launches	1900	*The Yachtsman* 1900
Whatford R. & Sons, Thames Ditton	Builder of Yacht, Electric & Steam Launches	1892	*Lock to Lock Times* 10 Sept. 1892
Wilder, H., & Son, Maidenhead	Hire Launches. During 1912 was hiring *Avondale*, still in use as *Hero*	1912	RMC records 1912
Woodhouse & Rawson United	Bought Sargeant's business. Liquidated in 1893	1890	*Electrician* 11 July 1890
Woodhouse, H., Maidenhead	Builder and hirer. Became Maidenhead & District Boating Co.	1898	RMC records
Yarrow & Co., Poplar	Built second electric launch on the Thames	1883	*Electrician* July 1883

References:

Blue Book	The Electrical Directory
Electrician	The journal
Electrical Review	The journal
Kelly's Directory	Berkshire, Bucks. & Oxon. Courtesy Maidenhead Library
Lock to Lock Times	
H. Tough	'Geographical Factors determining distribution of Boatbuilders on the Thames from Chiswick to Chertsey 1850–1950'. Thesis by Helen Tough
J. Hobbs	Hobbs of Henley. Private communication
Steam Boat Association	Register of boats
Dix	*Royal River Highway*, Frank L. Dix. David & Charles 1985
Wheeler	*From River to Sea*, Raymond L. Wheeler. Cross Publishing, Isle of Wight, 1993
Official Catalogue	of the International Exhibition of Electrical Engineering, General Inventions and Industries at Edinburgh, 1890. Courtesy Central Library, Edinburgh
RMC records	Ray Motor Co. records. Courtesy G. Banham
Postal Directory	'The Postal Directory of Maidenhead, Marlow and District'. G.R. Smith, County Directory Office, Reading. Courtesy Maidenhead Library
Motor Boat	The journal
The Yachtsman	The journal
Neil Garside	Private communication
Steam Boat Association	Register 1986
Salter's Guide	Salter Bros., Oxford

NOTES

Chapter 1

1 · *The Guinness Book of Motor Boating*, Kevin Desmond (ed.), Guiness Superlatives Ltd, London. Also see *An Electric Launch*. Letter to *The Times*, from Professor Sylvanus Thompson. Reported in *The Electrician*, 7 October 1882.

2 Reckenzaun became engineer to the EPS Co. in 1883 and was responsible for many of the developments in battery-operated trams. He died at the age of only forty-three from pleurisy in 1893. The author is indebted to Nick Kelly for information on the early electric tramways developers, including Reckenzaun and Immisch.

3 Described in detail in a paper read before the Mechanical Section, British Association, September 1883 and reported in the article 'On Electric Launches', M.A. Reckenzaun. *The Electrician*, 20 October 1883.

4 Since 1832, when Professor Jacobi was nearly asphyxiated by the fumes of the motor and batteries in the boat which he was demonstrating to the Emperor Czar Nicholas I of Russia, there had been sporadic attempts to put together an electrical propulsion system which worked satisfactorily. One such attempt was made in 1856 by Mr G.E. Dering who built a boat at Messrs Searle's yard on the Thames. This used a motor in which the rotation was produced by magnets arranged within coils, like galvanometer needles, and acted on successively by currents from a battery. There is no record of how this boat performed but presumably she was the first electric boat running on the Thames. For information on these earlier developments, see A. Reckenzaun, 'Electric Launches', *The Electrician*, 19 January 1884.

5 'An Electrical Steam Launch', *The Electrician*, 21 July 1883. (This editor was not the only person to have a problem in deciding how this new-fangled boat should be described.)

6 A.F. Yarrow himself gave a detailed description of the launch and the trials in a paper presented to the Institution of Naval Architects on 2 April 1884. This was reproduced in *The Electrician*, 5 April 1884.

7 'Race between Two Electrical Launches', *The Electrician*, 20 September 1884.

8 'Competitive Trial of Electric launches', *The Electrician*, 27 September 1884.

9 'The *Volta*', *The Electrician*, 17 September 1886.

10 'Reckenzaun's Electric Launches', *The Electrician*, 11 December 1885.

11 Kevin Desmond, 'For the Pleasure of a Duke'. *Electric Boat News*, June 1990, September 1990, Winter 1990/91. (A very detailed record of the *Northumbria* and some of its voyages culled from the archives of the Duke of Bedford.)

12 'Reckenzaun's Electric Launches', *The Electrician*, 11 December 1885.

13 'Trial of the Elieson Electric Boat', *The Electrician*, 14 October 1887.

14 'Elieson's Electric Locomotive', *Engineering*, 14 October 1887. Elieson had been very active in developing special designs of accumulators, motors and controllers for use in battery-operated electric trams. For example, during 1887 six of his locomotives were in constant use for the North Metropolitan Tramways Co. on their line running between Stratford Church and Manor Park, chalking up an average of 500 miles and 5,000 passengers per week. These locomotives were also remarkable for the ingenious design of the transmission and gearing system between the motor and the axles, described as like a 'cockchafer buzzing round on the point of a pin'. (A cockchafer is a large greyish brown beetle with a voracious appetite for vegetation.)

15 See Chapters 2 and 11 for description of *Viscountess Bury*.

16 'The Electric Launch *Lady Cooper*', *The Electrician*, 13 April 1888. (Named after the wife of Sir Daniel Cooper, chairman of the Electrical Power Storage Co.)

Chapter 2

1 *Watchmakers and Clockmakers of the World*, G.H. Baillie. N.A.G. Press Ltd, London, 1972. Also see *Old Clocks & Watches and Their Makers*, F.J. Britten. Methuen, London, 1982.

2 *British Electric Traction Co. Monthly Gazette*, November 1903, p. 284.

3 *Magnus Volk of Brighton*. Conrad Volk. Phillimore & Co., Chichester, Sussex, 1971.

4 'Electric Dog Cart', *The Engineer*, 14 September 1888.

5 The author is indebted to Keith Langridge for searching the Patent Office records for Immisch patents.

6 See Immisch Advertisement, page 150, chapter 12.

7 *Five Decades of B.E.T.* The story of the British Electric Traction Company Ltd, 1896–1946, Roger Fulford. Published by B.E.T., October 1946.

8 The author is indebted to Nick Kelly for information on the activities of Anthony Reckenzaun, Viscount Bury and Immisch in developing battery trams.

9 A sketch of the life of Viscount Bury was written by Jonathan Mardle (alias Eric Fowler) in the *Eastern Daily Express* of Norwich and reprinted in *Norfolk Characters* published by George Nobbs Publishing of Norwich, 1976. The picture of the Viscount on a bicycle is reproduced from that publication.

10 'Viscountess for Sale', Kevin Desmond. *Electric Boat News*, Spring 1991.

11 Ibid. Also communication from G. Tough.

12 'Messrs. Immisch & Co.', *Electrical Review*, 1 January 1890.

13 'Electric Launches at the Boat Race', *The Electrician* 30 March 1888.

14 See Chapter 1.

15 'Electric Launches at the Boat Race', *The Electrician* 30 March 1888.

16   'Electric Launches on the Thames', *The Electrician*, 22 June 1888.

17   'The Electric Launch *Viscountess Bury'*, *Electrical Review*, 19 October 1888.

18   'Electric Launches at Henley', *The Electrician*, 6 July 1888.

19   'Messrs Immisch & Co's Electric Launches', *The Electrician*, 12 October 1888. Also 'Electric Launches', *The Electrician*, 28 December 1888. See Chapter 11 for a detailed history.

20   'Messrs Immisch & Co's Electric Launches.' *The Electrician*, 12 October 1888.

21   Extract from *Victorians on the Thames*, R.R. Bolland. Midas Books, Kent, 1974.

22   Reprinted in *The Electrician*, 14 June 1889.

23   'The Electric Launches on the Thames', *The Electrician*, 9 August 1889.

24   *Maidenhead Advertiser*, 10 July 1889.

25   'Electric launches on the River', *The Electrician*, 14 June 1889.

26   'Messrs Immisch & Co.', *Electrical Review*, 10 January 1890.

27   'Electric Launches on the Thames', Professor G. Forbes. *The Electrician*, 20 September 1889. (From a paper read before the British Association in Section G, Newcastle-on-Tyne, September 1889.) During the discussion, Mr Anderson described how at the Waltham Abbey Ordnance factory, an electric launch was used to get about on the canals which intersected the factory. She was ideal because the fire risk of a steam launch was eliminated.

28   Ibid.

29   'Electric Launches on the Thames', *Electrical Review*, 20 September 1889.

30   'Messrs Immisch & Co.', *Electrical Review*, 10 January 1890.

31   No connection with the General Electric Co. The electric launch activities of the new company were illustrated in the four-page advertisement placed in the *Lock to Lock Times* of 8 July 1890. The author is indebted to Jim Cowan of Shiplake for allowing this and other pictures from his original copies of the *Lock to Lock Times* to be copied. Reproduction was by K.H. Photographics of Henley.

32   'The Thames Electric Launch Fleet', *The Electrician*, 30 May 1890.

33   Ibid.

34   *Maidenhead Advertiser*, 25 June 1890.

35   Ibid. 30 July 1890.

36   Ibid. 8 April 1891.

37   Ibid. 3 June 1891. (This is the first mention that Mr Bowen of the Ray Mead Hotel had a small fleet of electric launches in addition to the large *Ray Mead*.)

38   Ibid. 6 June 1890.

39   Ibid. 8 July 1891.

40   *Electrical Review*, 11 April 1890. Fig. 12 shows a picture by courtesy of Edinburgh Central Library from A. Scott Rankin, *Edinburgh Exhibition Sketches*, published by Geo. Stewart & Co., Edinburgh. The official catalogue listed eight other Immisch exhibits as follows: Tramcar motor as used by the North Metropolitan Tramway Co. at Barking, of 10 hp at 1,000 rpm and weighing 5 cwt; launch motor used in the launches at the exhibition and on the Thames; motor with rotating field for launch work; mining motor used for pumping, hauling, fan-driving, working stamps, etc.; 'Ingersoll'

percussion rock drill worked by an Immisch electric motor, can be used for 'Heading'; magnetic grip pulley for transmitting power by iron or steel ropes; model showing application of electric motor to tramcar, Immisch's patent; and motor for running on constant current circuit, with mechanical governor.

41 *Maidenhead Advertiser*, 19 August 1891.

42 Ibid. 26 August 1891.

43 Ibid. 8 and 15 July 1891.

44 Ibid. 27 May 1891.

45 Ibid. 2 September 1891.

46 A detailed estimate for an electric launch hire business in 1892 was given in Kempe's *Electrical Engineer's Pocket-Book*.

Chapter 3

1 Conrad Volk, *Magnus Volk of Brighton*. Phillimore & Co., Sussex, 1971.

2 List from *The Oarsman's and Angler's Map of the Thames* compiled by E.G. Ravenstein, published in 1893 by James Reynolds & Sons, 174 Strand, London, and reprinted in 1991 by Old House Books, Sutton Mead, Moreton-hampstead, Devon TP13 8PW.

3 *Maidenhead Advertiser*. 30 March 1892.

4 Ibid. 13 April 1892.

5 Ibid. 11 May 1892.

6 Ibid. 4 May 1892.

7 Ibid. 22 June 1892.

8 Ibid. 8 June 1892.

9 Ibid. 22 June 1892.

10 Ibid. 5 and 12 April 1893.

11 Ibid. 17, 31 May; 7, 28 June; 24 July 1893. See Chapter 6 for details of *Loosestrife*.

12 The author is indebted to Jim Cowan of Shiplake for allowing the photograph on page 34 to be copied from his original of the *Lock to Lock Times*. Reproduction by K.H. Photographics of Henley. This photograph was originally taken by Marsh of Henley and is numbered 20. A photograph taken from an identical position, numbered 19, was reproduced in R.R. Bolland's book *Victorians on the Thames*, published in 1974 by Midas Books, Tunbridge Wells. One of the differences between the two pictures is that this photograph shows a race in progress.

13 Ibid. *Maidenhead Advertiser* 30 March 1893.

14 T.C. Barker & Michael Robbins, *A History of London Transport*, vol. 1, The Nineteenth Century. George Allen & Unwin, London, 1963.

15 Garcke, *Manual of Electrical Undertakings*, 1897.

16 Tom Middleton, *The Book of Maidenhead*, Barracuda Books Ltd. The Directory became known as the 'Blue Book'.

17 *Maidenhead Advertiser*, 6 July 1898.

18 Roger Fulford, *Five Decades of B.E.T.*, B.E.T., October 1946.

19 Ibid. Garcke, 1898–9.

20 *Maidenhead Advertiser*, 20 May 1903.

21 Ibid. 24 June 1903.

22 Ibid. 13 January 1904.

23 Ibid. 18 May 1904.

24 Ibid. Garcke 1903.

25 The naval architect, Linton Hope, was commissioned to design these launches, *B.E.T. Gazette*, 15 April 1905.

26 Possibly published in 1904. The brochure comprised 32 pages (three of which are reproduced here full size, see pages 35–6) with pictures of the launches *Delta, Eta, Lady Lena,*

Viscountess Bury and the company's yard at Platt's Eyot. There were descriptions of the chief places of interest, maps of the river between Oxford and Richmond and a list of recommended hotels.

27   A list of Immisch's electric boats reported in the press between 1889 and 1914 is given in Appendix 1.

28   *B.E.T. Gazette*, 15 April 1905.

29   *B.E.T. Gazette*, 15 December 1905.

30   *Maidenhead Advertiser*, 25 June 1913. The author is indebted to Patricia Burstall, author of *Golden Years of the Thames* for making information available from her research notes.

31   Garcke, *Manual of Electrical Undertakings*, 1915/16.

32   'An Electric Launch for the East', *The Motor Ship and Motor Boat*, 31 October 1912. Courtesy the National Motor Boat Museum, Basildon. She was built of teak throughout and finished off in bright blue enamel, the bottom being covered with 14 oz copper sheathing. The seating included 'five revolving lounge chairs, upholstered in royal blue morocco leather, especially made to suit people of small stature, such as the Siamese'. The fore and aft seats were upholstered in the same manner and the floor was covered with linoleum to match. The motor was controlled by a switch located on the floor beside the steersman and giving two speeds ahead and two astern. Fittings were in polished gunmetal, a motor-car steering wheel was provided and a small searchlight fitted on the fore deck. Beam 4 ft 6 in, draught 1 ft, motor: Immisch 3½ hp, 750 rpm, 34 cells, speed 6.3–7 mph for 5 hours.

33   Peter H. Chaplin. *The Thames – from source to tideway*, Whittet Books Ltd, 1982.

34   *B.E.T. Gazette*, November 1903, p. 284. By courtesy of the National Tramways Museum.

Chapter 4

1   The Thames Valley Launch Co. produced a 44-page brochure *c.* 1900. The illustrations in this chapter show the range of sizes and types of the launches in the hire fleet and reproduce some of the information provided. The author is indebted to George Banham for permission to reproduce pages from his copy of the brochure.

2   'Electric Launches', *Electrical Review*, 16 April 1897.

3   Ibid. Sept 1897.

4   'Electric Launches at Colombo', *Electrical Review*, 18 August 1899 and TVL Brochure.

5   'Electric Launches on the Thames', *Electrician*, 22 June 1900. 'Electric Launches', 24 January 1902.

6   E.P. Hawthorne, 'Electric Launches on the Thames in 1900', *Classic Boat*, October 1989.

7   Septimus Felix Beevor was a Cambridge graduate who had 'gone through an electrical practical course and work' and had been admitted as an Associate of the Institution of Electrical Engineers on 13 December 1889. At that time he lived at 129 Harley Street, London, and was working as Installation Engineer and Inspector of mains pipe laying (presumably electric), taking charge during the Manager's absence. There is no record that he worked full-time with Edwards and it is probable that

he undertook various design and development jobs from time to time. Source: Institution of Electrical Engineers, membership records.

8 'Electric Launch', *Electrical Review*, 25 July 1902 and TVL Brochure.

9 RMC record books, TVL99:162. These record books are in the possession of G. Banham. The reference, e.g. TVL 99:162, is the year and the number of the page from a record book. 99:162 is year 1899, page 162.

10 E.P. Hawthorne, 'Electric launches on the Thames in 1900', *Classic Boat*, No. 17, October 1989.

11 *Maidenhead Advertiser*, 31 May 1899.

12 RMC record books, TVL 99:69.

13 Ibid. TVL99:99.

14 Ibid. TVL99:107.

15 Ibid. TVL99:100, 110.

16 These were the Immisch Launch Co., Ray Motor Co., Kerbey Bowen, H. Woodhouse (running the Maidenhead Court Boatyard), Harry Wilder & Son, E. Andrews & Son, J. Bond.

17 *Maidenhead Advertiser*, 3 June 1903.

18 Ibid. 10 June 1903.

19 RMC record books, TVL99:136, 143.

20 'Electric Launch', *Electrical Review*, 25 July 1902.

21 Letter from L.S. Carr to W. Rowland Edwards Esq., 26 July 1904. Courtesy G. Banham.

Chapter 5

1 The author is indebted to G. Banham for the loan of Carr's record and account books from which much of the information concerning the Ray Motor Co. in this chapter has been gleaned.

2 Carr's record book TVL99: 223.

3 Ibid. TVL99: 181, 187, 199, 206.

4 The weekly time sheets for the period from 8 June 1909 until 17 September 1909 are in the possession of G. Banham. They are summarized in Tables 1 and 2 at the end of this chapter, and the entries for two weeks are reproduced on page 56. These show that the electric boats worked on were Mr Fitch's *Frou Frou* (cells and charging), Mr Kessler's *Charlotte* (fitting out) and Col. Somerville's *Mina* (repairs to control switch). Building of Col. Ricardo's sailing yawl continued and four punts were repaired and got ready for the season but only a few hours were spent on petrol boats apart from the general work about the yard. Electrical contracting work included attending to the lights at Fitch's and Leonard's houses and the house-boat *Romani*. Other jobs included repairing the bells at Rose's house and the Ray Mead Hotel. Mr Carr himself spent two hours during each of these weeks repairing the petrol engine of the launch *Mayada*.

5 See later in this chapter for more about *Mina*, *Tadpole* and *Charlotte* and in Chapter 11 for *Esperanza*.

6 Carr's record book RMC13–24:159.

7 *Maidenhead Advertiser*, 21 December 1910.

8 It may well have been this experience which eventually resulted in the phrase 'We do not accept responsibility for any loss through fire' being printed on the Ray Motor Co. invoices.

9 See Chapter 11 for a history of the *Esperanza*, which is still in use

although now fitted with a steam engine.

10 Reported in the *Maidenhead Advertiser*, 29 May 1912.

11 *Maidenhead Advertiser*, 26 June 1907. This number included 158 launches and 938 small craft. It was estimated that about another 300 craft didn't get through the lock.

12 *Maidenhead Advertiser*, 26 June 1912.

13 See description of *Mina* later in this chapter.

14 Anagnos sold her on to Mr J. Richardson who was evidently a slow payer because Carr was writing to him in September 1921 that it is 'nearly time you gave us settlement as promised so often. . .'. By 1922 the canoe had passed to Mr F. Bellamy Courtney who renamed her *Bunting*. However, by August that year Courtney put it on the market again. Carr was not very encouraging, writing that 'hardly any need to tell you that there is not much hope of finding a buyer this end of the season and especially after such a wet one'. There wasn't much hope either during the following season, and in June 1924 Carr told the Thames Conservancy that his company had purchased *Bunting* and wanted the name changed to *Genella*.

15 See Chapters 12 and 13.

16 The yard had been leased from Oxford University in 1896 and Carr managed to acquire the freehold in 1909.

17 Robin Newlands recollection.

18 Bleriot, the first aviator to cross the Channel, lived at Riversdale House for a time and the rose garden still retains the shape of a propeller in which it was laid out to commemorate his flight. The house was burnt down and replaced by a smaller house named Merlin's Mead.

19 Brian B. Wheals, *Theirs were but Human Hearts*, H.S. Publishing, Bourne End, 1983.

20 *Maidenhead Advertiser*, 15 May 1907.

21 L.S. Carr's Ray Motor Co. invoice book. Courtesy George Banham.

22 C.A. Lee's recollections. For further history of *Lady Frainy* see the section on *Esperanza* in Chapter 11.

23 *Maidenhead Advertiser*, 17 August 1910.

24 Dix, Frank L., *Royal River Highway*, David & Charles, Newton Abbot, 1985.

25 Invoice from Ray Motor Co. to Major Fenner, 13 September 1909. To 1 Battery charge (*Pearl*) 1s 6d. At that time the cost of a charge was 1s per unit.

26 The extracts from the Ray Motor Co. (RMC) account books are courtesy of George Banham. From Ray Motor Co. invoice book page 182. Letter to Thames Conservancy, 21 April 1920, registering change of name to *Madeleine*.

27 See page 47.

28 Carr's record book, pp. 27 and 33, 25 June 1909.

29 Ibid. p. 448, 26 June 1913.

30 Ibid. p. 150, 5 January 1920.

31 Ibid. p. 340, 21 April 1920.

32 Ibid. p. 352, 12 July 1920.

33 Ibid. p. 208, 1 October 1920.

34 Ibid. p. 261, 20 June 1921. Letter sent to J.H. Woodward Esq.

35 Ibid. p. 267, 27 July 1921. Letter to J.H. Woodward.

36 Ibid. p. 388, 8 February 1923.

37 Ibid. p. 100, 20 July 1926.

Chapter 6

1 Sargeant lived at Zachary House, Strand-on-the-Green.

2 Private communications from T.C. Sargeant, to whom the author is especially indebted for much research on the history of his great-grand-uncle William.

3 For details of the *Viscountess Bury*, see Chapter 11.

4 'The Electric Launch Viscountess Bury', *Electrical Review*, 19 October 1888.

5 The other brother in the famous A & F Pears soap company was Frank, who lived downstream at Hampton and with Emile Garcke rescued the Immisch launch business in 1894. See Chapter 3.

6 'Electric Launches on the Thames', *Electrical Review*, 7 June 1889.

7 'Electric Launches on the River', *The Electrician*, 14 June 1889. These quotations and others mentioned in the section on Kerbey Bowen in Chapter 10 were said to be taken from an article in the *Daily News*.

8 *Maidenhead Advertiser*, 27 May 1896.

9 Ibid. 2 May 1900.

10 Advertisement in *Engineering*, 23 January 1891.

11 'Electric Launches', *The Electrician* 11 July 1890.

12 'Launch of the "Electric",' *The Electrician*, 13 March 1891.

13 'Charging Station for Electric Launches', *Electrical Review*, 10 April 1891.

14 'Electric Launches on the Thames', *Electrical Review* and *The Electrician* both 12 June 1891. *Electrical Review* 13 May 1892. These journals quote the name as *Myiomi* but it is spelt *Myionu* on the launch depicted in the advertisement in the *Lock to Lock Times* on 27 August 1892. The author is indebted to Jim Cowan of Shiplake for allowing the pictures in this advertisement from his original of the *Lock to Lock Times* to be copied. Photograph by K.H. Photographics of Henley.

15 *Lock to Lock Times*, 5 July 1892.

16 *Lock to Lock Times*, 5 July 1892.

17 *Henley & South Oxfordshire Standard*, 2 July 1897.

18 The author is indebted to Robert Field for the loan of a copy of the advertisement which was given to his father by a previous owner of the Red Lion Hotel, and to Mr Miller, the present owner, for permission to reproduce the picture of *Glow Worm*. The original still hangs in the hotel. Photograph by E.P. Hawthorne.

19 'A New Launch Charging Station', *The Electrician* 5 February 1892.

20 'Electric Launches', *Electrical Review*, 29 April 1892.

21 'Electric Launches', *Electrical Review*, 22 April 1892.

22 Ibid.

23 'Electric Launch Building', *Electrical Review*, 13 May 1892.

24 Ibid.

25 'Launches and Yachts, The 1902 Elco Catalog'. With introduction and notes by William C. Swanson. Published in 1984 by Swanson Marine Enterprises, 829 Copley Ave., Waldorf, Maryland, 20602, USA.

26 'Electric Launches', *The Electrician*, 20 January 1893.

27 Frank L. Dix, *Royal River Highway*, David & Charles, Newton Abbot, 1985.

28 'An Electric Launch in Trouble', *Electrical Review*, October 1896.

29 Dix, op. cit.

Chapter 7

1 Raymond L. Wheeler, *From River to Sea*, Cross Publishing, Isle of Wight, 1993. (The author is indebted to Ray Wheeler for permission to use information and pictures from his books.)
2 R.L. Wheeler and A.E. Tagg, *From Sea to Air*, Crossprint, Isle of Wight, 1991.
3 *Electrical Review*, 20 September 1889, p. 329.
4 Peter H. Chaplin, *The Thames from Source to Tideway*, Whittet Books Ltd, London, 1982.
5 'From Electricity to Petrol', *The Motor Boat*, 28 February 1907.
6 'Patricia', *Classic Boat*, July 1990.

Chapter 8

1 'Ned Andrews', *Maidenhead Advertiser*, 22 June 1898. This is an extract of a portrait of Ned Andrews published in the 'Rod and Gun and Thames Life', 15 June 1898, summarizing his life as a fisherman and champion punter.
2 *The Thames of Henry Taunt*, Susan Read (ed.), Alan Sutton Publishing Ltd, 1989.
3 *The Golden Age of the Thames*, Patricia Burstall, David & Charles, Newton Abbot, 1981.
4 *Maidenhead Advertiser*, 15 and 22 June 1898.
5 Ibid. 14 September 1910.

Chapter 9

1 The author is indebted to S.S. Smith, the owner and Managing Director of Bond's from January 1937 to March 1956, and John Fenn for many details of this history.
2 Peter H. Chaplin, *The Thames from Source to Tideway*, Whittet Books, London, 1982.
3 *Maidenhead and District, Illustrated*, published by Tyer & Abbott, London, 1895. Courtesy Maidenhead Library.
4 *Financial Times*, 10 February 1891.
5 From S.S. Smith's recollections.
6 *Maidenhead Advertiser*, 26 June 1889.
7 The Postal Directory of Maidenhead, Marlow and District, 1897.
8 *Maidenhead Advertiser*, 22 September 1897.
9 See Chapter 11.
10 Raymond L. Wheeler, *From River to Sea*, Cross Publishing, Isle of Wight, 1993.
11 Salter's Guide to the River Thames, tenth edition, April 1904, and thirty-eighth edition, 1936. Courtesy H. Horsham. The 1904 advertisement carries a picture of what must be an electric launch with clipper bow, counter stern and saloon. It bears a close similarity to the launch *Charlotte* owned in 1908 by Kessler. The *Kerlew* was a saloon launch seating 12 and 8 to dine; The *Colonial* had an awning and seated 10.
12 The *Flosshilde* was reconverted to electric drive during the 1939–45 war when petrol rationing was imposed.
13 At one time, Bond's advertised eight canoes for hire (all with a comfortable carrying capacity of 6 passengers): *Clarijim, Nelson, Maruchita, Neil, B, Hermit, Gee, Woggs*. The hire rates were 3, 4 and 5 guineas per day for weekdays, Saturday and Sunday respectively.
14 See 'Silent Transport', *The Motor Boat*, 16 July 1937.

Chapter 10

1   *Maidenhead Advertiser*, 21 June 1899.

2   Ibid. 26 June 1901.

3   Ibid. 24 July 1901.

4   'Electric Launch for Lake Vyrnwy', *The Motor Boat*, 11 October 1906. Courtesy: National Motor Boat Museum, Basildon.

5   *Lock to Lock Times*, 2 July 1892.

6   Advertisement, Kelly's Directory, 1895.

7   Kelly's Directory of Berkshire, Bucks. & Oxon, 1891 (Maidenhead section).

8   'An Electric Launch', *Electrical Review*, 26 April 1889. Length 60 ft, beam 11 ft, draught 2 ft 9 in. Licensed to carry 85 passengers. Range 50 miles.

9   *The Thames; Waterway of the World*, Stratten & Stratten, London, 1893.

10 *Maidenhead Advertiser*, 29 April 1891.

11 Ibid. 3 June 1891.

12 *Maidenhead Advertiser*, 21 May 1890.

13 Frank L. Dix, *Royal River Highway*, David & Charles, 1985.

14 *Maidenhead Advertiser*, 10 May 1893.

15 William C. Swanson, 'Launches and Yachts, The 1902 Elco Catalog', Swanson Marine Enterprises, Waldorf, Maryland, USA.

16 Emily J. Climenson, 'A Guide to Henley-on-Thames', Sidney H. Higgins, Henley-on-Thames, 1896.

17 The author is indebted to John Hobbs, the present owner of Hobbs & Sons for information on the family business.

18 The Red Lion Boathouse had operated the electric launch *Glow Worm* at the turn of the century.

19 I am indebted to Mrs Aust, J.G. Meakes' granddaughter, for the history of this well-known Marlow family.

20 *The Thames of Henry Taunt*, Susan Read (ed.), Alan Sutton Publishing. Originally published in 1886, this edition 1989. Taunt mentions boats are housed or let by Shaw & Sons, Meakes & Redknap, on the Berkshire side, J. Cannon, at the bridge.

21 See Boat History of *Princess Beatrice*, Chapter 11. Communication from Neil Garside.

22 Among Carr's Ray Motor Co. papers are two letters from Brooke-Hitching instructing Carr to send *Esperanza* up to Riversleigh. See Chapter 11 for the history of *Esperanza*.

23 Salter's Guide to the Thames. Tenth Edition, 1904.

24 'The Postal Directory of Maidenhead, Marlow and District', 1897.

25 *Lock to Lock Times*, 10 September 1892.

26 *A Guide to Henley-on-Thames*, op. cit.

27 *Lock to Lock Times*, 10 September 1892.

28 Extracts from a biographical sketch in the July 1898 issue of Rod and Gun and River Life were published in the *Maidenhead Advertiser*, 20 July 1898.

29 Ibid.

30 *Maidenhead Advertiser*, 20 July 1898 and 1 March 1911.

31 The Postal Directory of Maidenhead, Marlow and District, 1897. (For a period the hotel was called the New Thames Hotel, but by 1900 the Woodhouses dropped the *New*.)

32 During the first year over 12,000 telegrams were dealt with.

33 Patricia Burstall, *The Golden Age of the Thames*, David & Charles, Newton Abbot, 1981.

34 *Maidenhead Advertiser*, 3 July 1889.

35 Ibid. 20 July 1898.

36   Ibid. 7 June 1899.

37   Ibid. 1 May 1901.

38   Ibid. 17 July 1901.

39   *Maidenhead Advertiser*, 26 October 1910.

40   *Dace* was built by Ned Andrews of Maidenhead in 1899.

41   Salter's Guide to the River Thames. Tenth Edition, 1904.

42   Patricia Burstall, *The Golden Age of the Thames*, David & Charles, Newton Abbot, 1981.

43   'The Thames Electric Launch Fleet', *The Electrician*, 30 May 1890.

44   Roger Fulford, *Five Decades of B.E.T.*, B.E.T., October 1946.

45   'New Electric Launch for the Czar', *Electrical Review*, 2 August 1895.

46   'Electric Launch', *Electrical Review*, 25 July 1902.

Chapter 11

1   As the eldest son of the Earl of Albemarle, William Coutts Keppel held the title of Viscount Bury. He was elected as Liberal MP for Norwich in 1857, Wick in 1860 and Berwick in 1868. He was Treasurer of Queen Victoria's Household in 1859 and Under-Secretary of State for War between 1878 and 1880 and again from 1885 to 1886. He succeeded to the earldom in 1891. Unfortunately he died in 1894 and so did not see the full flowering of the development of commercial electric launches which he and Immisch pioneered. His wife, Sophia, whom he had married in 1855, lived through the whole period of the growth and decline of the Edwardian electric boating scene, dying in 1917. Marina, the present Viscountess Bury and mother of the tenth Earl of Albemarle, lives in Florence.

2   'Viscountess for Sale', Kevin Desmond, *Electric Boat Association News*, Spring 1991.

3   'The Electric Launch Viscountess Bury', *Electrical Review*, 19 October 1888.

4   This was the *Countess* which had a length of 90 ft and beam of 11 ft 6 in. Launched in May 1887, it apparently was not a success as an electric boat. See Elieson Electric Co., Chapter 1.

5   The General Electric Power & Traction Co., the company promoted by Viscount Bury and Moritz Immisch to develop battery electric trams, trains and boats. See Chapter 2. For Sargeant, see Chapter 6.

6   This statement that the hull had three skins is not consistent with the fact that she actually has two skins.

7   It seems that there is a misprint. Surely, acid would not slop over if lids were fitted?

8   *Maidenhead Advertiser*, 10 July 1889.

9   'The Thames Electric Launch Fleet', *The Electrician*, 30 May 1890.

10   *Maidenhead Advertiser*, 19 August 1891.

11   Ibid. July 1897.

12   Ibid. 19 June 1901.

13   *Royal River Highway*, Frank L. Dix, David & Charles, Newton Abbot, 1985.

14   This information is taken from an unpublished paper on the history of the *Viscountess Bury* written in 1973 by A.F. Leach of Cambridge. Courtesy Linda Ashton.

15   'Ely, Cathedral City and Market Town', The Ely Society, 1972. The photograph published by the Ely Society was from the collection of Mrs D. Rogers.

16 See Chapter 5.

17 *From River to Sea*, Raymond L. Wheeler, Cross Publishing, Newport, Isle of Wight, 1993.

18 See Chapter 12, Batteries. Three estimates were obtained: renewal of positive sections only; renewal of positive and negative sections; completely new battery of 'Fors' type which would have had half the weight of the existing batteries and improved performance.

19 See Chapter 10, Other Electric Boatbuilders, for details of Meakes & Redknap.

20 Letter to Carr, 9 April 1913.

21 The author is indebted to Lawrence Weaver for permission to publish details and photographs of *Esperanza*. Also David Roberts, who jointly with Roger Angold now owns *Thames Esperanza*, very kindly allowed the author to examine his files which contain the papers kept by the previous owner, Lawrence Weaver, since 1968.

22 *Maidenhead Advertiser*, 15 May 1912. Locally, he was known as Maharajah Dhunjibhoy.

23 Some of these details were given in a letter from Lady Frainy Dhunjibhoy to Lawrence Weaver in 1968.

24 *The Book of Maidenhead*, Tom Middleton, Barracuda Books Ltd, 1975.

25 Mr C.A. Lee's recollections.

26 *Royal River Highway*, Frank L. Dix, David & Charles, Newton Abbot, 1985.

27 *Maidenhead Advertiser*, 8 June 1892; 31 May and 7 June 1893.

28 For further details of the operations of these two companies see Chapter 13.

29 Smith may well have been the only hire business in the country which continued to operate an old electric tripping boat after 1945. In 1956 these three electric boats ran a service every 20 minutes from the Town Bridge.

30 The author is indebted to Jenkyn Knill for providing this history of *Lady Lena*.

31 The information on the 'Goldings period' is from George Banham's recollections.

32 Ibid.

33 *Maidenhead Advertiser*, 22 June 1904.

34 W. Emony joined Carr at the Ray Motor Co. boatyard on Boulter's Island in 1919.

35 Communication Brian Bidston: *Maidenhead Advertiser*, 24 June 1908. H. Andrews was Ned Andrews son.

36 Communication Brian Bidston.

37 George Banham recollections.

38 *Maidenhead Advertiser*, 14 August 1901.

39 See letter from Wilder to Carr of Ray Motor Co. Source: Carr records in G. Banham collection.

40 I am indebted to Christopher Stirling and Terence Casey for much of the following information.

41 George Banham recollections. He remembers driving *Pike* and because of her shallow draught he considers that, if there is no positive proof otherwise, it is quite possible that the launch being restored at Wargrave and which is believed to be *Tench* may in fact be the *Pike*.

42 Goldings ran her initially with 44 passengers, but they had to reduce to 36 passengers to meet new Board of Trade regulations.

43 Ray Wheeler, *From River to Sea*, Cross Publishing, Isle of Wight,

1993. Also 'Partners at Putney', *Thames User*, May 1992.

44 This history draws on material kindly supplied by Graham Mackereth and the Director of Library Services, Leeds Central Library; from the Roundhay Park Centenary booklet; and the *Yorkshire Evening Post* articles of 10 April 1957, 7 and 16 July 1966, and 11 November and 2 December 1972.

45 *Lock to Lock Times*, 27 August 1892. Advertisement for Woodhouse & Rawson. See Chapter 6.

46 *Maidenhead Advertiser*, 18 June 1913.

47 The author is indebted to Patricia Burstall, author of *The Golden Age of the Thames*, for drawing his attention to this item in the *Maidenhead Advertiser*, 17 June 1914.

48 *Maidenhead Advertiser*, 19 August 1914.

49 The author is indebted to William and Penny Rose for their recollections on the history of canoes. See also Chapter 13.

50 *Beazie*, Kevin Desmond, *Electric Boat News*, Winter 1990/1. Electric Boat Association.

51 Communication, Rupert Latham.

52 For further details, see auction particulars, Traditional River Craft and Ephemera, Phillips, Son & Neale, July 1994.

Chapter 12

1 'An Electric Launch'. Report of letter to *The Times* by Professor Silvanus P. Thompson. *The Electrician* 7 October 1882.

2 'On Electric Launches', M.A. Reckenzaun. Paper read before the Mechanical Section, British Association Meeting, September

1883. Reported in *The Electrician*, 20 October 1883.

3 'An Electrical Steam Launch', *The Electrician*, 21 July 1883.

4 'Description of the Electrical Launch Built Last Year', A.F. Yarrow. A paper read before the Institution of Naval Architects, 2 April 1884. (Also reported in *The Electrician*, 5 April 1884.)

5 'Electric Launches', A. Reckenzaun. Paper read at the Society of Arts 16 January 1884 and reported in *The Electrician*, 9 February 1884. A modern electric boat motor has a specific power-weight ratio of about 30 watts/kg.

6 'Competitive Trial of Electric Launches', *The Electrician*, 27 September 1884.

7 'The Electric Launch *Volta*', *The Electrician*, 4 September 1885.

8 'The *Volta*', *The Electrician*, 17 September 1886.

9 'Trial of the Elieson Electric Boat', *The Electrician*, October 1887.

10 'Electric Launches', *Electrical Review*, 22 April 1892.

11 'Electric Launches', *Electrical Review*, 29 April 1892.

12 From a draft of a Saunders brochure produced about 1905. This information and picture is published by kind permission of Raymond L. Wheeler, author of *From River to Sea*, Cross Publishing, Isle of Wight, 1993. For information about Sam Saunders see Chapter 7, Wheeler's book *From River to Sea* and *From Sea to Air*, R.L. Wheeler and A.E. Tagg. Crossprint, Isle of Wight, 1990.

13 This is equivalent to a specific power of about 15 watts/kg.

14 The blueprint is in Neil Garside's collection.

ELECTRIC BOATS ON THE THAMES

15 'An Electric Launch', *Engineering*, 6
October 1882.

16 'An Electrical Steam Launch', *The
Electrician*, 21 July 1883.

17 'Description of the Electrical Launch
built last year', A.F. Yarrow, *The
Electrician*, 5 April 1884.

18 'The Electric Launch *Volta*', *The
Electrician*, 4 September 1885.

19 'The *Volta*', *The Electrician*, 17
September 1886.

20 'The Electric Launch *Lady Cooper*',
The Electrician, 13 April 1888.

21 'Electric Launches on the Thames',
Professor G. Forbes, *The Electrician*,
20 September 1889.

22 'Electric Launches', *Electrical Review*,
29 April 1892.

23 'Thames Electric Launches', *The
Electrician*, 17 June 1898.

24 Thames Valley Launch Co. Brochure,
1900. Courtesy G. Banham (see
Chapter 4).

25 *Magneto- and Dynamo-electric Machines*,
Glacer de Cew, trans by F. Krohn,
edited by Paget Higgs, Whitakker
and Co., London, 1885.

26 Ibid; wh/kg is watthours per kg
weight of cell or battery complete
with acid, lugs and connectors.

27 'The Origins of MotorBoating',
Kevin Desmond, *The Guinness Book
of Motorboating Facts and Feats*.

28 'An Electric Launch', *The Electrician*,
7 October 1882.

29 'On Electric Launches', M.A.
Reckenzaun, *The Electrician*, 20
October 1883 (based on a paper
presented to the British Association
Meeting, September 1883) 19
January, 9 February and 1 March
1884 (based on paper read at the
Society of Arts, 16 January 1884).

30 'Description of the Electric Launch

Built Last Year', A.F. Yarrow. A paper
read before the Institution of Naval
Architects, 2 April 1884. (Also
reported in *The Electrician*, 5 April
1884.)

31 Lead monoxide.

32 'Electric Launches', A. Reckenzaun,
The Electrician, 1 March 1884.
(Report of a paper read at the
Society of Arts on 16 January 1884.)

33 'The Electric Launch *Lady Cooper*',
The Electrician, 13 April 1888.

34 *A History of London Transport*, T.C.
Barker & Michael Robbins. Vol. 1,
The Nineteenth Century. George
Allen & Unwin, London, 1963.

35 'Messrs Immisch & Co.', *Electrical
Review*, 10 October 1890. The cost
of electric traction was estimated to
be less than 4½d per car mile.

36 Chloride Brochure, 1982.

37 'Electric Launch', *The Electrical
Review*, 25 July 1902.

38 'Thames Electric Launches' (a
reference to the Immisch fleet), *The
Electrician*, 17 June 1898.

39 Catalogue of the Electric Power
Storage Co. Ltd, July 1905.
Presumably, these batteries were
mainly intended for uses such as ferry
boats where many journeys of short
duration at full power were required.
However, they were fitted on the
Viscountess Bury in 1898.

40 *The Electrical Engineer's Pocket Book*,
H.R. Kempe. Crosby Lockwood and
Son, London, 1892. The launch was
fitted with a 10 hp motor supplied
from 56 cells, presumably EPS Co.,
weighing 2,400 lb and having a
capacity of 16,240 watt hrs. per ton
(15.95 wh/kg). Connected in
parallel, the launch had a speed of
6 mph and completed 60 miles in 10

216

hours on a single charge. The speed could be increased to 10 mph by connecting the cells in series.

41 EPS Co. catalogue 1905; Carr's Ray Motor Co. letterbook, 1919 (E.L. *Mina*).

42 The boxes measured internally 4.75 in x 7.375 in x 11.75 in high. It was also specified that the complete cell must not exceed 13.5 in in height. The cells had a discharge rate of 36 amps.

43 Private communication, Rupert Latham, Steam & Electric Launch Co. Ltd.

44 'Electric Launches'. A paper read by A. Reckenzaun before the Society of Arts and reported in *The Electrician*, 19 January 1884.

45 'An Electric Launch', *Electrical Review*, 26 April 1889.

46 'Electric River Navigation', *Electrical Review*, 7 June 1889.

47 Ibid.

48 *From River to Sea*, R.L. Wheeler. Cross Publishing, Isle of Wight, 1993.

49 'Electric Launches on the Thames', *Electrical Review*, 20 September 1889.

50 'Electric Launches on the Thames', Professor G. Forbes, *The Electrician*, 20 September 1889. A paper read before the British Association for Science, September 1889.

51 *The Electrician*, 1 June 1900.

52 'Electric Launches on the Thames', *The Electrician*, 22 June 1888.

53 'Electric Launches at Henley', *The Electrician*, 6 July 1888.

54 'Electric Launches on the River', *The Electrician*, 14 June 1889.

55 *Electrician*, 30 May 1890.

56 *Electrical Review*, 10 April 1891 and 12 June 1891.

57 *Electrician*, 5 February 1892, and *Electrical Review*, 29 April 1892.

58 *Electrician,* 17 June 1898.

59 Ibid.

60 TVL Co. Brochure, 1900. Courtesy G. Banham.

61 TVL Co. Brochure. Also *A Guide to Henley-on-Thames*, E.J. Climenson, S.H. Higgins, Henley, 1896.

62 *Electrician*, 24 January and 16 May 1902.

63 *Modern Engines and Power Generators*, vol. 1. Rankin Kennedy, C.E. The Caxton Publishing Co., London. Probably published in 1903. This installation had a fall of 300 ft to a 15 hp Girard turbine coupled to a multipolar dynamo of 75 amps at 130 volts. No accumulator cells were used, the lights being coupled direct from the dynamo and also cables ran down to the pier and charged direct into the cells on board the launch as required. Steady illumination was achieved by using a Gunther governor on the water turbine.

64 *Electrician*, 24 January 1902.

Chapter 13

1 Record and invoice books of Ray Motor Co. Ltd. Courtesy G. Banham.

2 His first choice of name had been *Adele*. For further details of *Aris* see Chapter 5.

3 This information and photograph kindly supplied by George Banham, Harry Horsham and Robin Newlands.

4 Letter from Short Brothers (Rochester & Bedford) Ltd to H. Wright Esq, Frinton-on-Sea, dated 17 March 1921. Courtesy G. Banham.

5   Illustrated brochure of Hobbs & Sons Ltd.

6   'Silent Transport', *The Motor Boat*, 16 July 1937.

7   These records are extracted from the Ray Motor Co. ledgers held in the G. Banham collection.

8   The history of *San Martin* has been provided by W.D. Davies, John Murch and Peter Freebody. Photos: courtesy G. Banham and J. Murch.

9   S.S. Smith recollections. See Chapter 9.

10 The author is indebted to Alan Faulkner and Jenkyn Knill for this history and pictures. Further details can be found in Faulkner's two papers published in *Lock Gate*, vol. 4, No. 8, July 1975 and No. 10, January 1976. *Lock Gate* was the journal of the Great Ouse Restoration Society, since disbanded. The history of *Lady Lena*, which is still in use, is detailed in Chapter 11.

11 Courtesy G. Banham.

Chapter 14

1   'Electric Launch as a Private Ferry', *The Motor Boat and Yachting*, March 1952.

2   'A Chronology of Electric Boat Development'. Privately produced for the Electric Boat Association by Kevin Desmond, 1991. Also see 'Electric Boats – Whence and Whereto Now?'. Kevin Desmond. *Ship & Boat International*, November 1990.

3   'Silent Triumph', *Motorboats Monthly*, January 1980.

ILLUSTRATION NOTES

Additional acknowledgements, information on sources and notes for some of the pictures are as follows:

Frontispiece   First drawn to the author's attention by Peter Turner of Ferry Antiques, Wargrave. Believed original taken 1913.

Fig 1   From an advertisement held in the Bedford Estate archives.

5   See *Magnus Volk of Brighton*, Conrad Volk. Phillimore & Co., Chichester, Sussex. 1971.

6   See also *Norfolk Characters*, Jonathan Mardle. Published by George Nobbs Publishing of Norwich, 1976.

8, 9, 10, 11, 15   From the collection of Jim Cowan of Shiplake. Reproduction by KH Photographics of Henley. Fig 15, original photograph by Marsh of Henley.

12   From A. Scott Rankin, *Edinburgh Exhibition Sketches*. Published by Geo. Stewart & Co., Edinburgh.

20   From *Official Guide and Invitation to Maidenhead on Thames*, published in 1906 and kindly loaned to the author by Mr J. Hazelton of Boulter's Lock Hotel.

23 to 35   From a copy of the Thames Valley Launch Co. brochure, published 1900, in the G. Banham collection.

42   Original in H. Horsham collection and reproduced in Brian B. Wheals, *Theirs were but Human Hearts*. H.S. Publishing, Bourne End, 1983.

48, 78   *Lock to Lock Times,* 9 July 1892.

51, 52   *Lock to Lock Times,* 5 July 1892.

53   *Lock to Lock Times,* 30 July 1892.

58–62, 109, 116, 122   Reproduced by kind permission of R.L. Wheeler, *From River to Sea. The Maritime Heritage of Sam Saunders.* Cross Publishing, Newport, Isle of Wight, 1993.

64   Original photograph by A. Plummer, Maidenhead.

65–68   The author is indebted to S. Arthur for the loan of original photographs by H. Gude of Maidenhead.

71   Reference to Major Bateman from the *Maidenhead Advertiser*, 14 June 1899. Photograph from the G. Banham collection and believed taken in 1912 at Boulter's Lock.

79   *Lock to Lock Times,* 2 July 1892.

87   Photograph from Mrs D. Rogers collection and first published in *Ely, Cathedral City and Market Town,* 1972 and reproduced by permission of the Ely Society.

102   Source of this postcard is unknown. Upstream of *The Angler* are the petrol engined *Em*, built by

Taylor & Bates of Chertsey, with clipper bow and counter stern ('the classiest boat on the waterfront') and *Gerbera*, ex Horsham's but here owned by Hills and licensed to carry thirty passengers. *Gerbera* may originally have been electric and owned under another name by the Thames Valley Launch Co. Further upstream are the Hills rowing boats and beyond is Jacobs yard with *Empress of India* and *Windsor Belle*. Further still is Bart's

Island where the *Windsor Belle* was built.

112 For a detailed history, see *Classic Boat*, 1990. Jenny Bennett, 'The Electric Canoe'.

121 From W.P. Maycock, *A Small Book on Electric Motors*. Isaac Pitman, 1918.

143 For more detail of *Back-To-The-Future*, see 'The Glass Slipper'. *Classic Boat*, August 1990, No. 26.

146 *Classic Boat*, February 1991.

150 Electric Boat Association News, Autumn 1993.

INDEX – BOATS

Numbers in italics refer to illustrations

INDEX – GENERAL